Bringing Ritual to Mind

M000113965

Psychological Foundations of Cultu. ... ...

Bringing Ritual to Mind explores the cognitive and psychological foundations of religious ritual systems. Participants must recall their rituals well
enough to ensure a sense of continuity across performances, and those
rituals must motivate them to transmit and re-perform them. Most religious rituals the world over exploit either high performance frequency
or extraordinary emotional stimulation (but not both) to enhance their
recollection; the availability of literacy has little impact on this. But why
do some rituals exploit the first of these variables while others exploit the
second? McCauley and Lawson advance the ritual form hypothesis, arguing that participants' cognitive representations of ritual form explain
why. Reviewing evidence from cognitive, developmental and social psychology, cultural anthropology, and the history of religions, they utilize
dynamical systems tools to explain the recurrent evolutionary trajectories religions exhibit.

ROBERT N. MCCAULEY is Professor of Philosophy and Director of the
Emory College Center for Teaching and Curriculum at Emory Univer-
sity in Atlanta. He is the author, with Lawson, of *Rethinking Religion*
(Cambridge, 1990). He is also the editor of *The Churchlands and their
Critics* (1996), and has contributed articles to a wide variety of jour-
nals, including *Philosophy of Science, Philosophical Psychology, Synthese,
Consciousness and Cognition, History of Religions, Journal of the American
Academy of Religion,* and *Method and Theory in the Study of Religion.*

E. THOMAS LAWSON is Professor of Comparative Religion at Western
Michigan University, Executive Editor of the *Journal of Cognition and
Culture,* and author, with McCauley, of *Rethinking Religion*. He is the
author of *Religions of Africa: Traditions in Transformation* (1984), and
has contributed chapters to many books, articles to a wide variety of
journals, and a large number of entries to encyclopedias.

Bringing Ritual to Mind

Psychological Foundations of Cultural Forms

Robert N. McCauley

Emory University, Atlanta

and

E. Thomas Lawson

Western Michigan University

PUBLISHED BY THE PRESS SYNDICATE OF THE UNIVERSITY OF CAMBRIDGE
The Pitt Building, Trumpington Street, Cambridge, United Kingdom

CAMBRIDGE UNIVERSITY PRESS
The Edinburgh Building, Cambridge CB2 2RU, UK
40 West 20th Street, New York, NY 10011-4211, USA
477 Williamstown Road, Port Melbourne, VIC 3207, Australia
Ruiz de Alarcón 13, 28014 Madrid, Spain
Dock House, The Waterfront, Cape Town 8001, South Africa

http://www.cambridge.org

© Robert N. McCauley and E. Thomas Lawson 2002

First published 2002

Printed in the United Kingdom at the University Press, Cambridge

Typeface Plantin 10/12 pt   *System* LaTeX 2$_\varepsilon$ [TB]

A catalogue record for this book is available from the British Library

ISBN 0 521 81559 2 hardback
ISBN 0 521 01629 0 paperback

This book is dedicated to
Drindee McCauley and Ruth Lawson
whose insight, courage, love, and support
constantly enrich our lives and give them balance

Contents

List of figures   *page* viii
Preface   ix

1   Cognitive constraints on religious ritual form: a theory
    of participants' competence with religious ritual
    systems   1

2   Ritual and memory: frequency and flashbulbs   38

3   Two hypotheses concerning religious ritual and
    emotional stimulation   89

4   Assessing the two hypotheses   124

5   General profiles of religious ritual systems:
    the emerging cognitive science of religion   179

    Notes   213
    References   221
    Index   228

Figures

1.1 Action representation system   *page* 14
1.2 Principle of Superhuman Agency   27
1.3 Typology of religious ritual forms   28
2.1 Two attractors   43
2.2 The tedium effect   51
3.1 Modes of religiosity   105
3.2 Direction of influence among Whitehouse's thirteen variables   106
3.3 Typology of religious ritual forms   117
4.1 The ritual form hypothesis   138
4.2 Ritual form as a discrete variable   139
4.3 The four relevant kinds of cases for comparing the ritual form and ritual frequency hypotheses   147
4.4 The two hypotheses' predictions about the comparative levels of sensory pageantry for each of the four sorts of cases in figure 4.3   149
4.5 Even-numbered, special patient and special instrument rituals with low performance frequencies   154
4.6 Special agent rituals with high performance frequencies   156
4.7 Kivung rites versus splinter group innovations   161
4.8 Elevated baseline   165
4.9 Special agent version of the ring ceremony   171
5.1 The tedium effect induces perturbations in the stable stage of unbalanced systems   185
5.2 The problem of habituation   186
5.3 A sensory overload ceiling   189
5.4 Constraining ritual innovation   191
5.5 Entering psychologically "dangerous" regions   195
5.6 The characteristic phase portrait of splinter group cycles in Dadul   197
5.7 Bivalent balanced ritual systems   203
5.8 The consequences of excess conceptual control: deflated balanced systems   207

Preface

Slightly more than a decade ago we published a book, *Rethinking Religion: Connecting Cognition and Culture*, in which we launched the cognitive science of religion. For all of the froth that accompanies encounters between the humanities and the cognitive sciences on university campuses, everyone knows that the best work in each area regularly looks to the other for inspiration and correction. Our goal is not to supplant traditional work in religious studies but to supplement it. If our work seems tilted too far toward the scientific, it is only because we aim to redress an imbalance – an imbalance in strategy and approach that favors the particular over the general, the idiosyncratic over the systematic, and the interpretive over the explanatory (as if we could make sense of either item in each pair in isolation from the other). What we are out to do is to help bring an end to the defensive pronouncements of humanists and, especially, of scholars of religion concerning what the sciences can never address productively. Who knows what the sciences can or cannot address productively? Only time and a great deal of hard work will tell.

We should emphasize that this aspiration is not born of any undue confidence about the truth of the proposals we advance. (What we take up are, after all, *empirical* matters.) What should be most striking are the tremendous difficulties connected with even articulating testable theories in these domains, let alone testing them. Instead of disdainful proclamations discouraging such initiatives, scholars of religion should welcome analyses that aim to increase simultaneously theoretical precision and empirical responsibility. Our principal goal in this book is simply to do a little more of that hard work.

We continue our focus on ritual. (For us, one of the most thrilling developments over the past decade has been to learn that others, e.g., Pascal Boyer, 1994 and 2001, are hard at work on supplying cognitive theories about other aspects of religious thought and practice.) Adopting a theoretical strategy prominent in linguistics, in *Rethinking Religion* we presented a theory of participants' religious ritual *competence*, i.e., a theory of their tacit knowledge about their religious ritual systems. We maintain that this competence depends upon perfectly ordinary cognitive machinery that humans possess which is dedicated to the representation of agents and actions generally, not just religious ritual agents and actions. The true heart of the theory resides in two principles (the Principle of Superhuman Agency and the Principle of Superhuman Immediacy) that jointly highlight participants' presumptions about the contributions of culturally postulated superhuman agents to their ritual actions. Briefly, our claim is that the character of those presumptions is the most important factor in participants' overall understanding of their rituals' forms and that religious ritual form is the pivotal variable determining a host of features any religious ritual possesses. We summarize all of the theory's decisive commitments in the second half of chapter 1.

The critical test of any theory's sturdiness is its ability to stand up to the empirical evidence. This is our goal in this book. This is an inherently interdisciplinary undertaking. Many disciplines address human thought and conduct. Relevant evidence, therefore, can arise from numerous quarters. We shall appeal extensively (especially in chapter 2) to experimental research in cognitive psychology. We shall refer at various points to experimental findings from developmental psychology, social psychology, and neuropsychology too. We shall also make abundant use of materials from cultural anthropology and religious studies.

When explicating our theory we shall usually rely on illustrations from religious systems we suspect are likely to be familiar to the largest pluralities of our readers. So, we make numerous incidental references to the ritual practices of the major Western religions – Christianity especially but also occasionally Judaism and Islam. We also make occasional incidental references to rituals with which one or both of us are familiar from religions of Africa and India. One important piece of evidence bearing on one of our theory's claims concerns an ancient Vedic ritual.

Our two focal cases, however, arise out of Melanesia. There are two reasons for this. First, we did not discuss Melanesian materials at all in *Rethinking Religion*. Second, the two ethnographies in question, viz., Fredrik Barth's *Ritual and Knowledge Among the Baktaman of New Guinea* and Harvey Whitehouse's *Inside the Cult*, both concentrate on the connections between ritual, emotion, and memory, which are the central topics we shall address.

More than eight years ago when we first formulated the ideas that fill this book, Pascal Boyer, whom we had met a year or two before, informed us that an anthropologist friend of his in Britain, Harvey Whitehouse, had been working on similar issues. After reading Harvey's early papers, especially "Memorable Religions: Transmission, Codification and Change in Divergent Melanesian Contexts" (Whitehouse, 1992), we began to fear that perhaps we had been scooped. Further reading of his work, however, made it clear to us that our theories differed and often made incompatible predictions. We subsequently met Harvey at a conference at Cambridge University in December 1993. Hearing some of the story that now constitutes his stirring and insightful ethnography, *Inside the Cult*, we were struck by our theory's ability to predict most of the rest of the story, which Harvey corroborated informally in conversation. The appearance of that book in 1995 provided us with the opportunity to consider Harvey's views and evidence at much greater length. Obviously, Harvey's ethnography and his newest synthetic proposals in his second book, *Arguments and Icons*, have been an influence and an inspiration.

At about the same time we received a typescript of a paper from a Cornell University graduate student in experimental psychology, Justin Barrett. Justin had co-authored the paper with Frank Keil, a friend in whose work we had had a longstanding interest. That groundbreaking paper, "Conceptualizing a Non-natural Entity: Anthropomorphism in God Concepts" (Barrett and Keil, 1996), taught us many things, but one of the most important was that there were bona fide experimental *cognitive* psychologists whose *primary* interest was in the cognitive foundations of religion. Ever since, Justin has been relentlessly devising and performing clever experiments – so characteristic of work in his discipline – designed to test various consequences of our, Harvey's, and Pascal's theories, among others. From the outset he has recognized, along with Pascal, the fundamental importance of conducting these experiments with populations in different cultures. He has already undertaken work in North America, Europe, India, and Africa. He is pursuing not just an experimental cognitive psychology of religion but a *cross-cultural* experimental cognitive psychology of religion. In just a few short years the volume, power, and insight of Justin's work has already identified him as a leading contributor to this new field.

Over those same years what has emerged is a nearly continuous discussion in regular email exchanges, punctuated by periodic face-to-face conclaves with Pascal, Harvey, Justin, and others in which we have pondered many of the issues we discuss in this book and a great deal more. We have benefited from these exchanges in countless ways.

Justin has brought to our discussions the tough-mindedness of an experimental scientist, his extensive knowledge of work in experimental psychology (cognitive, social, and developmental), and a wry sense of humor. Justin suggested that we use the figures that we have employed in this book, and he has repeatedly helped us to state with precision the differences and connections between our and Harvey's theories.

Pascal first suggested to us that we write this book. Ever faithful, he has read and reread drafts of every chapter, providing us with dozens of helpful comments. He has made excellent suggestions for streamlining some of our technical terminology. His suggestions were decisive in how we organized the materials at the beginning of chapter 2. He has done everything from aiding us in clarifying our account of cultural transmission to risking influenza in encouraging us in our work on this book.

Other friends, both personal and institutional, have provided us with considerable aid and comfort. We are grateful to the various professional societies where we have presented parts of this book over the years, especially the North American Association for the Study of Religion, the Society for the Scientific Study of Religion, and the International Association for the History of Religions. We also wish to thank the American Academy of Religion for a collaborative research grant that enabled our computers to communicate along the longitudinal axes of the eastern half of the United States. In the academic year of 1998–1999 Emory College and the Massee-Martin/National Endowment for the Humanities fund at Emory University jointly provided Robert McCauley with a year's research leave during which most of this book was written. He wishes to express his profound gratitude for this support.

Earlier versions of parts of chapters 1, 2, and 4 have appeared elsewhere (Lawson and McCauley, forthcoming, McCauley, 1999, and McCauley, 2001).

So many people have influenced our thought that it would be impossible to name each and every one. We are grateful to audiences at Washington University, the University of Turku, the University of Marburg, the University of Bonn, the Free University of Berlin, the University of Vermont, Georgia State University, the University of Waterloo, and the Departments of Psychology and Anthropology at Emory University for their comments and criticisms of various presentations that were connected with this project.

We are exceedingly grateful to more than a score of individuals who have helped us along the way. We wish to thank Adele Abrahamsen, Veiko Anttonen, Larry Barsalou, Fredrik Barth, Bill Bechtel, Robyn Fivush, Marshall Gregory, Stewart Guthrie, Michael Houseman, Mark Johnson, Ziva Kunda, Brian Malley, Luther Martin, Ulric Neisser, Charles Nuckolls, Ilkka Pyysiainen, Mark Risjord, Benson Saler, Brigitte Schoen, Tom Sjoblom, Paulo Sousa, Dan Sperber, Paul Thagard, Christian von Somm, and Eugene Winograd for comments, encouragement, and support at various stages.

Producing a book is no simple task. We are indebted to Ellen McCauley and Mark Risjord for valuable technical suggestions in the creation of many of the figures in this book and to Jamie Martin for further refinements in their designs as well as for their production. We are grateful for a grant from the Quadrangle Fund for Advanced Research at Emory

University to cover the costs of that production. We also wish to express our appreciation to Jessica Kuper and Peter Ducker at Cambridge University Press for their aid and advice and to Carol Fellingham Webb for her copy-editing. Thanks, too, go to David Strand for his assistance with a variety of chores and to Brian Lee for his photograph of the rock art.

Numerous colleagues have commented on parts of this book. We wish to thank Larry Barsalou, Marshall Gregory, David Rubin, Harvey Whitehouse, and Eugene Winograd for their helpful comments on an early version of pages 48–64 and 72–88 of chapter 2. Harvey Whitehouse kindly read and commented on our account of his work in chapter 3, pages 99–123. We are grateful to Brigitte Schoen for forcing us to wrestle with routinized religious activities that – at least pretheoretically – certainly seem like rituals but may not count as such on our theory. She and all the other individuals named above have tried to warn us away from errors. Of course, they bear no responsibility for those that remain.

We are fortunate and grateful to have such fine friends and colleagues. We are also fortunate and grateful to have the unending love and support of our wives, Drindee and Ruth, and of our daughters, Ellen and Sonya and Jennifer, who, even in the face of profound challenges in their own lives, have never faltered in their concern for the success of our projects.

We are lucky men, indeed.

ROBERT N. McCAULEY
E. THOMAS LAWSON

1   Cognitive constraints on religious ritual form: a theory of participants' competence with religious ritual systems

Paradoxes, puzzles, and explanatory problems

Some rituals captivate the imagination. Others provoke boredom.

We are easily moved, often excited, and occasionally even astounded by the sights, sounds, and smells accompanying ritual spectacles. These events stimulate our senses, enliven our emotions, and captivate our minds. The enthronement of popes, the inauguration of presidents, the burial of heroes arrest our attention and embed memories that last a lifetime. Everyone loves sensory pageantry. Some rituals focus the attention, feed the imagination, evoke the remembrance of things past as well as the desires of things to come, and inspire dramatic actions that stand out against their everyday background. Yet the salience of such dramatic spectacles should not obscure the fact that "ritual" often refers to the repetition of small and thoroughly mundane acts. Even though these rituals break with the ordinary world too, they frequently remain thoroughly humdrum. They trigger automatic responses that appear to be completely mindless. If we focus on participants' psychological responses in ritual situations, we cannot fail to notice the different degrees of emotion involved in these two sorts of cases. Some rituals are so emotionally arousing that their effects seem to last forever. In other rituals emotion seems to play little, if any, role.

Compare, for example, the comparatively lavish preparations for weddings and their impact on the participants' emotions with the more modest accouterments and emotional responses connected with routine blessings. The weddings quite regularly involve special music, clothes, foods, and more. By contrast, priests often perform blessings almost as an afterthought.

To draw out this contrast particularly sharply, consider the following comparison between two ritual practices of the Church of England. Any regular member of the Church of England participates in worship services that are structured by the *Book of Common Prayer*. It provides a blueprint for various ritual acts that priests and participants are expected to perform. Some acts apply to everyone whether they are commoners or royalty. But there is nothing like a special royal occasion to highlight the differences between rituals that arouse the emotions and are only infrequently performed and other rituals in the same tradition that are regularly performed and carry little emotional intensity. For example, at the coronation of Elizabeth II, the monarch of the United Kingdom, in Westminster Abbey, not only did all of the ritual participants wear special garments and priceless jewelry, but this very special event was marked by sounding trumpets, singing choirs, chanting priests, cheering crowds, and the participants traveling in horse-drawn carriages (in the age of the automobile).

British coronations are both affairs of state and matters of religion, because the Queen is not only the symbolic head of the government but also the symbolic head of the Church. On this particular political and religious occasion the sensory pageantry in the abbey (and outside for that matter) was overwhelming, the emotional reactions it elicited were considerable. Coronations are infrequent affairs, yet in this same abbey, the scene of this unrivaled splendor, participants perform religious rituals in which they sit and then kneel and then sit again, time after time, as they follow once again the order of service for the day. This stark contrast suggests that it is important that students of religious ritual distinguish the comparatively infrequent ritual situations involving striking levels of sensory stimulation, such as weddings and coronations, from the far more frequent situations of ritual work, which are often quite routine. What puzzles us – what is worthy of scholarly attention – is why ritual systems show such a Janus-face.

With religious rituals, novelty and repetition traffic together in intriguing ways, whether they involve queens or commoners. The fact that ritual phenomena include both activities filled with the sensory pageantry that dazzles and practices that are so repetitious and uninspiring that they verge on the mechanical poses something of a paradox. We want to know why it is that the same system generates phenomena that differ so radically in their emotional effects. Such apparently paradoxical traits encourage us to plumb the depths of religious ritual systems in search of an explanation.

In this book we intend to offer what we hope will be compelling explanations of why some rituals are unique, attention-grabbing events whereas others become such a normal part of daily life that they seem quite commonplace. This paradoxical character of rituals, especially *other* people's rituals, has provided grist for the mills of some of the greatest minds in Western intellectual history.

Some researchers focus on the excitement, others on the boredom. Scholars in the tradition of Van Gennep (1960) have noted that some rituals mark and celebrate unique events that are absolutely pivotal in the lives of the participants. Rites of passage stand out from the mundane ritual background and by their very uniqueness tell both the participants and the observers: "this is special; this happens only once in your life; pay attention." Other researchers have highlighted the habitual and mundane aspects of ritual. Their point is to show how ritual is thoroughly integrated into the affairs of daily life. These scholars focus upon the fact that frequently rituals are so common and ordinary that, because everyone is doing them, no one notices them. They merge with the background. People will count their prayer beads as they engage in commerce and make frequent signs of the cross as they enter and leave buildings (or score touchdowns).

Other puzzles about ritual

Although this contrast will receive most of our attention in this book, it is by no means the only puzzle surrounding ritual we shall address. For example, some religious rituals permit substitutions whereas others do not. A rite of purification may require water, but if no water is available, what then? Substitute sand. Or a sacrifice may require the slaughter of an ox, but an ox is a valuable commodity. A cucumber may be a perfectly appropriate substitute. Why is it that some rituals permit such substitutions and others do not?

Let us take another example. It makes no sense to reverse some rituals' consequences. When faithful Muslims circumambulate the Ka'bah, there is no reversing the blessings they accrue. On the other hand, some rituals can have their consequences reversed. A priest goes through an elaborate ordination ritual. There are pomp and circumstance aplenty. Bishops and sometimes even cardinals participate in the ceremony. Family and friends crowd the aisles of the cathedral. But in contrast to the blessing a Muslim accrues, this ordination can be revoked. Or a person who has been brought into a state of communion by a special ritual of confirmation might be excommunicated. It seems as if sometimes what the gods have done can be undone. Why is this so? And how does it come about?

Rituals generate other contrasts that beg for explanation. For example, some rituals require specially qualified people to bring about their effects, while others do not. Any Yoruba can make an offering at a local shrine but only authorized diviners can carry out divinations. Similarly, anyone can observe some rituals, whereas others remain closed. Consider, for example, the election of a new pope. Only by observing the color of the smoke from the Vatican do observers have any clue as to what is going on among the cardinals.

Competence theories and empirical research

Before proceeding further, we should say a few words about competence theories. Competence theories were first proposed in the study of language. Competence theories in linguistics attribute to the cognitive systems of speaker-listeners of a language a wide array of grammatical principles and processors that generate an even wider array of abstract linguistic structures. The cognitive representations of these general principles and the specific structures they beget underlie speaker-listeners' linguistic competence, i.e., their abilities both to produce and comprehend linguistic strings and to render an assortment of relatively systematic judgments about the syntactic and semantic character of those strings.

These abilities are manifest when language users confront errors. Not only do they readily detect them, they often have robust intuitions about the differences between the various sorts of errors. So, for example:
1 Inquisitive verdant ruminations snooze fiercely.
2 John singed the song before he departed.
3 Harry ringed the bell when the signal was given.
Most native speakers of English recognize both that item (1) differs from items (2) and (3) concerning the character of their abnormalities and, by contrast, that the problems with items (2) and (3) are similar in origin. Such linguistic competence is a form of tacit or intuitive knowledge. Language users do not have conscious awareness of or control over the principles and representations at stake. Once acquired, our cognitive systems for the processing of language seem to work largely automatically.

In *Rethinking Religion* we proposed a theory of religious ritual competence (despite dire warnings about competence theories' sole applicability to linguistic materials). We adopted the competence approach to theorizing about religious ritual because of the striking similarities we noted between speaker-listeners' knowledge of their languages and participants' knowledge of their religious ritual systems. Both languages and religious ritual systems are examples of what we called "symbolic-cultural systems." Symbolic-cultural systems involve symbolic phenomena whose forms are relatively restricted in both their use and their transmission. Linguistic and religious ritual forms are usually not explicitly codified, unlike civil law. Usually very little about these systems is directly taught. They are the kinds of system about which explicit instruction is, at least sometimes, completely absent, and about which, therefore, participants must have some form of intuitive knowledge. That knowledge is revealed by their acquisition of and successful participation in the systems and by their judgments about real and possible uses of the symbols within the systems (Lawson and McCauley, 1990, pp. 2–3).

In our original presentation of the theory of religious ritual competence we looked primarily to religious ritual participants' intuitions about religious rituals as evidence for our claims. With little, if any, explicit instruction, religious ritual participants are able to make judgments about various properties concerning both individual rituals and their ritual systems. These include inferences about religious ritual forms and relationships and about the efficacy of ritual actions.

Our discussions of these matters in *Rethinking Religion* were instructive but informal. Little of the evidence we cited there arose from empirical research about aspects of ritual performance from experimental psychology. In fact, experimental evidence is still hard to come by, though the situation has improved recently. (See Boyer and Ramble, 2001, Barrett, 2000, and Barrett and Lawson, 2001.)

This feature of competence modeling in linguistics (viz., inattention to independent experimental evidence) has attracted substantial criticism over the years, but there is no principled reason why competence theories must remain aloof from a varied range of empirical research. We intend to show how both psychological evidence and detailed ethnographic research can bring performance findings to bear on the shape and fate of competence theories. A competence theory, like any scientific theory, will gain credibility to the extent that it is able to stand up to independent tests with materials it was not originally designed to explain. In addition, competence theories will improve to the extent that they undergo adjustment and revision in the face of recalcitrant findings concerning processing and performance. In fact, it is only when competence theorists prove responsive to research concerning processing and behavior and, when necessary, revise their proposals in its light, that they will be able to use these independent sources of evidence to their advantage. Revisions of competence theories on the basis of performance and processing evidence will not only enhance their empirical accountability but relieve the sense that they are irredeemably idealized as well. We have no doubt that programs of research on competencies with symbolic-cultural systems such as religious ritual systems will benefit from such interaction.

So long as we demand empirical evidence to substantiate our more speculative probings, a theory of religious ritual competence will contribute to our understanding of religious ritual behavior. The critical point is that these sorts of cognitive analyses provide exciting new tools for illuminating dimensions of religion that have, unfortunately, suffered from neglect. Future inquiry into religion should benefit from the fact that cognitive studies have already made significant discoveries about how minds work. What we intend to show is that the resources of cognitive science can make valuable contributions to the scientific study of religion.

A road map for this book

In order to allay such concerns about our own competence theory we shall explore in this book some of our theory's notable implications for the interactions of psychological processing and religious ritual performance. We shall test how well those implications square with both ethnographic details about religious ritual performance and relevant theories and experimental findings from psychology.

In the next section we shall lay out the basic commitments of our theory of religious ritual competence. One of our central theses in this book is that the cognitive variables our theory isolates provide critical insights into the connections between religious ritual and memory dynamics. Two means of enhancing memory that religious rituals routinely enlist are performance frequency and emotional arousal. Presumably, enhanced memory is a relevant consideration in understanding the process of cultural transmission, especially in non-literate societies. Chapter 2 explores these issues and reviews relevant work in psychology and anthropology, showing, in particular, how recent research in cognitive psychology on enhanced memory bears on these questions.

In chapter 3 we examine two cognitive hypotheses for explaining the connections between ritual and memory dynamics. The first is the frequency hypothesis, which holds, in short, that the amount of sensory stimulation (and resulting emotional excitement) a ritual incorporates is inversely proportional to its performance frequency. Harvey Whitehouse offers the most formidable and best defended version of this hypothesis in various papers and in his books *Inside the Cult* (1995) and *Arguments and Icons* (2000). The second is our own ritual form hypothesis, which holds that aspects of the representations of ritual form our theory delineates explain and predict the comparative levels of sensory pageantry religious rituals incorporate. We show that our theory of religious ritual competence, which inspires the ritual form hypothesis, (1) characterizes the forms of religious rituals precisely, (2) specifies principles for distinguishing among these forms, and, therefore, (3) has the resources for dealing with problems that the frequency hypothesis both occasions and cannot, itself, handle. The ritual form hypothesis makes the correct predictions about the connections between performance frequencies and the comparative levels of sensory pageantry and emotional arousal religious rituals incorporate (the principal topic of chapter 4). It also points to further grounds, viz., motivational ones, beyond considerations of memory, for why rituals of different forms have the levels of sensory pageantry that they do. Chapter 3 opens with an extended summary of Whitehouse's ethnography because it supplies many of the materials we shall use to assess the two hypotheses' predictive and explanatory merits.

We devote chapter 4 to a sustained discussion of the comparative predictive and explanatory virtues of the ritual frequency and ritual form hypotheses by examining a wide range of relevant empirical evidence. We are able to compare the two hypotheses so extensively because both are clear (at least compared with most theoretical proposals in the study of religion) and both make straightforward predictions. In many situations the two hypotheses make the same predictions, but in some they do not. It is the latter on which we focus.

In short, both hypotheses do well, but the ritual form hypothesis does considerably better. In *Rethinking Religion* we showed that the Principles of Superhuman Agency and Superhuman Immediacy generate a typology of ritual forms, which organize and thereby, in part, explain a number of features about religious rituals. In chapter 4 we show how the principles that generate that typology of religious ritual forms account for when religious rituals enlist emotional stimulation and when they do not. We also argue that these principles go some way toward explaining *why*. Both hypotheses get at critical cognitive variables, but we shall argue at length that religious ritual form proves the more fundamental of the two, since, among other things, it constitutes what is, perhaps, the principal variable determining rituals' performance frequencies. Therefore, it also constitutes a sounder cognitive foundation for any broader theory of religious modes.

The first half of chapter 5 continues comparing the two hypotheses' explanatory and predictive strengths. In the course of that comparison we sketch a dynamical systems account of the principal cognitive and psychological constraints on the evolution of religious ritual patterns. That account shows how our theory makes sense of some larger historical patterns in the evolution of ritual systems. *Although we focus primarily on the details of Whitehouse's ethnography, our aim is to show how our theory's analysis of this case reveals larger patterns in the evolution of religious ritual systems (and of religious systems generally) that cut across cultures and historical epochs.*

We examine the eruption of ecstatic movements in religions. Sometimes this phenomenon is linked with religious ritual systems abandoning (or at least minimizing) rituals clustered in certain regions of an abstract space of possible ritual arrangements. By explaining why a religion's system of ritual practices will inevitably repopulate this region, our theory anticipates not only one of the most basic patterns in the evolution of religious ritual systems but also one of the factors that apparently enhances *the fitness of a religious ritual system in any cultural setting*. Identifying both stable configurations and characteristic dynamic patterns in the space of possible ritual arrangements enables us to clarify how micro-processes at the psychological level are responsible for sustaining these kinds of religious ritual systems. Our aim is no less than delineating the cognitive architecture of *Homo religiosus* – not merely to understand well-known historic patterns in religious systems better but also to *explain* them.

A theory of religious ritual competence

Theorizing about religious ritual systems from a cognitive viewpoint involves (1) modeling cognitive processes and their products and (2) demonstrating their influence on religious behavior. Particularly important for such an approach to the study of religious ritual is the modeling of participants' *representations* of ritual form. In pursuit of that goal, we presented in *Rethinking Religion* a theory of religious ritual form that involved two crucial commitments.

The theory's first commitment is that the cognitive apparatus for the representation of religious ritual form is the same system deployed for the representation of action in general. The differences between everyday action and religious ritual action turn out to be fairly minor from the standpoint of their cognitive representation. This system for the representation of action includes representations of agents. Whether we focus on an everyday action such as closing a door or a ritual action such as initiating a person into a religious group, our understanding of these forms of behavior as actions *at all* turns critically on recognizing agents.

The theory's second crucial commitment (1990, p. 61) is that the roles of culturally postulated superhuman agents (CPS-agents hereafter) in participants' representations of religious rituals will prove pivotal in accounting for a wide variety of those rituals' properties. On our view religious ritual systems typically involve presumptions about CPS-agents.

Amazingly (by our lights anyway), our claim that a (conceptual) commitment to the existence of CPS-agents is the most important recurrent feature of religion across cultures is controversial. With everything from Theravada Buddhism to Marxism to football in mind, various scholars in theology, religious studies, the humanities, and even the social sciences maintain that presumptions about CPS-agents are not critically important to religious phenomena. On this view cheering at football games or marching at May Day is just as much a religious ritual as is sacrificing pigs to the ancestors. Perhaps this is so. In that case what we have, then, may not be a theory of religious ritual. Instead, it is only a theory about actions that individuals and groups perform within organized communities of people who possess conceptual schemes that include presumptions about those actions' connections with the actions of agents who exhibit various counter-intuitive properties.

If that is not religion (and religious ritual), so be it, but we suspect that this description of our theoretical object covers virtually every case that anyone would be inclined, at least pretheoretically, to include as an instance of religion and very few of the cases they would be inclined to exclude. Overly inclusive views of religion confuse the problematic claim that only meanings matter with the even more problematic claim that all meanings matter. Hence, on these views, virtually anything may count as religion (depending upon the circumstances). Fans of such views should keep in mind, then, that on their view what we are advancing is not a theory of religious ritual. To adherents of these less constrained views of religion, we should repeat that we have only supplied (pardon the redundancy) a theory about actions that individuals and groups perform within organized communities of people who possess conceptual schemes that include presumptions about those actions' connections with the actions of agents who exhibit various counter-intuitive properties.

We do not desire to engage in debates about definitions. In science explanatory theories ground central analytical concepts. Those concepts earn our allegiance because of the achievements of the theories that inspire them. These include their predictive and problem-solving power, explanatory suggestiveness, generality, and empirical accountability. Whatever explanatory value construing "religion" in such a manner exhibits turns on whether or not the theory we have elaborated provides empirically useful insights about religious ritual.

Rituals often occasion an astonishingly wide range of interpretations not only from observers in the field but even from the participants themselves. Their own testimony reveals that the planting of this bush means one thing to the wedded couple, another thing to their neighbors, and a third thing to the ethnographer who questioned them. Even when authorities intent on maintaining the status quo vigilantly police doctrines, the blooming of interpretive schemes remains a wonder to behold.

While the meanings associated with rituals may vary, such variability typically has no effect on the stability of the ritual actions' underlying forms. Although they have brought nearly as many interpretations as the times and places from which they hail, pilgrims to Mecca continue to circumambulate the Ka'bah the same way year after year. Whether in

Rwanda, Rio, or Rome only communicants are eligible to participate in the mass and only priests are eligible to perform it. Not only do other things matter besides meanings, for some explanatory purposes meanings hardly matter at all.

We have just rehearsed the respect in which rituals' details are independent of meanings either participants or scholars assign them. It is important not to confuse these proposed semantic contents of rituals with factual details about their elements. Interested parties may attribute some meaning or other to the fact that an orthodox rabbi must be a male, but that fact is not the same thing as proposals about its significance. Some points of detail may permit considerable variation, such as how high the priest elevates the host, whereas others, like the circumcision of Jewish boys, may not.

We think that religious ritual form and the properties of rituals it explains and predicts are overwhelmingly independent of attributed meanings. There is also a respect in which some very general features of ritual form are independent not only of meanings but even of these specifically cultural details. In other words, these very general features of religious ritual form are independent of both semantic and cultural contents. Clarifying these general features of action is valuable for distinguishing the roles CPS-agents can play in participants' representations of their religious rituals.

The action representation system

Distinguishing ritual form from both semantic and cultural contents will prove useful for many analytical and explanatory purposes. Our cognitive system for the representation of action imposes fundamental, though commonplace, constraints on ritual form. Attention to these constraints enables us to look beyond the variability of religious rituals' details to some of their most general underlying properties. The point, in short, is that religious rituals (despite their often bizarre qualities) are actions too. (Ritual drummers ritually beating ritual drums are still drummers beating drums.) Consequently, this general system for the representation of action is also responsible for participants' representations of their religious rituals' forms.

From a cognitive standpoint, then, postulating special machinery to account for the representation of religious rituals is unnecessary. The requisite cognitive equipment is already available. A wide range of evidence from developmental psychology indicates that human beings readily distinguish agents and actions from other entities and events at an early age. (See, for example, Rochat et al., 1997.) At as early as nine months of age, they seem capable of not merely recognizing agents but attributing goals to them (Rochat and Striano, 1999). This cognitive machinery seems task specific, and it is – with only a few exceptions – ubiquitous among human beings (Baron-Cohen, 1995).

This assortment of resources is what we have collectively referred to as the human "action representation system" (Lawson and McCauley, 1990, pp. 87–95). This action representation system must account for humans' command of the distinctions between agents and other entities and between actions and other events. To summarize, then, we hold that the representation of religious rituals requires no special cognitive apparatus beyond the garden-variety cognitive machinery all normal human beings possess for the representation of agents and their actions.

Cognitive scientists, especially psychologists working on cognitive development, have thought a good deal about how human beings represent and distinguish agents. (See, for example, Leslie, 1995.) Human infants seem particularly sensitive to things in their environments that move irregularly through both space and time. They construe agents as animate entities capable of self-motion who can initiate actions. Presumably, agents do so because they have interests that determine their aims and goals. They are thought to be capable of acting in ways that enable them to achieve those goals, because they seem capable of representing these counterfactual situations to themselves. All of the things that we are tempted to classify as agents seem to have these features in common. Whether agency is properly described as including the ability to entertain attitudes toward these representations is less clear. Even when they cannot see it, dogs seem to *desire* their food when they are hungry, but it is a good deal less obvious just what exactly they might be said to *believe* about it. As humans mature they come to attribute fully *intentional* minds to at least some agents – principally, other human beings. They entertain quite complex representations of such agents. They represent them as capable of entertaining a wide array of attitudes toward their (mental) representations. They also represent them as possessing higher-order mental states whose representational objects are themselves mental representations, and finally, they represent these agents' prodigious representational abilities as pivotal to accounting for their actions. So, for example, humans can readily understand Lucy's flipping the switch in terms of her thinking that Ricky thought that she wished to keep him in the dark.

Agents and their agency are clearly the pivotal concepts for the representation of action, but they are not the whole story. A basic representational framework for characterizing this special sort of event must also capture familiar presumptions about the internal structures and external relations of actions too. Most straightforwardly, actions involve agents who do something often, though not always, to something. We should note here that while cognitive scientists have proposed interesting accounts of our understanding of agency, they have had much less to say about our understanding of actions. We hold that whether a religious ritual action involves waving a wand to ward off witches, building a pyramid to facilitate the flight of a pharaoh to the realm of the gods, or lighting a fire to summon the presence of a spirit, representing such actions will depend upon exploiting a dedicated cognitive system for action representation. Our theory of religious ritual offers some general, preliminary proposals about that system.

In *Rethinking Religion* we introduced a formal system to increase the clarity and precision of our theory's claims about the action representation system and, therefore, about the forms of the religious rituals whose representations it assembles.[1] The precision of formal systems aids in the detection of significant relationships and connections among the phenomena modeled. As a matter of fact, the formal system we employed and the diagrams it generates introduced an exactness to our descriptions that enabled us to see more clearly how rituals' general action structures and the roles attributed to CPS-agents in particular suggest (non-obvious, unfamiliar) principles for predicting a number of those rituals' features. Assuming these principles describe, albeit quite abstractly, capacities that are psychologically real, they also constitute a first pass at an empirically testable hypothesis about the cognitive mechanisms behind participants' abilities to produce judgments about those features.

The formal system employs a set of categories and generative rules for representing action and, thereby, participants' conceptions of religious ritual form. The categories signify the basic components involved in the representation of *any* action. They include participants, acts, and the appropriate qualities, properties, and conditions sufficient to distinguish them. (See, for example, Lawson and McCauley, 1990, p. 120.) The rules describe basic action structures that any normal human being could readily recognize. They generate structural descriptions of people's representations of actions, including their ritual actions. (The diagrams we mentioned in the previous paragraph, which populate many of the pages in *Rethinking Religion*, depict such structural descriptions.) Rituals' structural descriptions portray basic action structures, which:

1 include the roles (agents, acts, instruments, and patients[2]) that distinguish actions (and rituals) from other events and happenings;
2 take – as ritual elements – the various entities and acts, as well as their properties, qualities, and conditions, that can fulfill these formal roles in religious rituals;
3 presume that at least two of these roles must always be filled (viz., that every action has an agent and that the agent must do something);

4 reflect the constraint that although any item filling the role of the agent may also serve as a patient, not all items that serve as patients may also fill the agent role;

5 reveal points of variability in the forms of actions such as whether they involve the use of special instruments as a condition of the act; and

6 accommodate the enabling relationships between actions, such as whether the performance of one act presupposes the performance of another.

Normal human beings have a ready intuitive grasp of all of these matters, the length of this list and the apparent complexity of its items notwithstanding. That appearance of complexity is a function of attempting to describe precisely what is at stake in these intuitions. In fact, most talk about the "cognitive representations of ritual form" does not involve anything out of the ordinary.

A technical sense of "religious ritual"

Actions typically come in one of two sorts. Either they involve agents doing something or they involve agents doing something to something. In other words, some actions do not have patients and some do. In religious contexts only the second sort of action need concern us. Since all religious rituals on our theory involve agents acting upon patients, the structural description of a religious ritual will include three ordered slots for representing a religious ritual's three fundamental roles, viz., its agent, the act involved, and its patient. All of a ritual's details fall within the purviews of one or the other of these three roles. From a formal standpoint accommodating all of the rest of the ritual's details, then, involves nothing more than elaborations on the entries for these three slots. (See figure 1.1.)

Our claim that all religious rituals (as opposed to religious action more broadly construed) are actions in which an agent does something to a patient departs from popular assumptions about rituals. Typically, priests sacrifice goats, ritual participants burn offerings, and pilgrims circle shrines. But in religious contexts people also pray, sing, chant, and kneel. Even though such activities may be *parts* of religious rituals, such activities, in and of themselves, do not qualify as religious rituals in our theory's technical sense. All religious rituals – in our technical sense – are inevitably connected sooner or later with actions in which CPS-agents play a role and which bring about some change in the religious world.

So, for example, initiations are religious rituals on this account. In participants' representations of initiations, CPS-agents are ultimately responsible for the initiate's change in religious status. Sometimes those CPS-agents participate directly. So, frequently, initiations culminate in

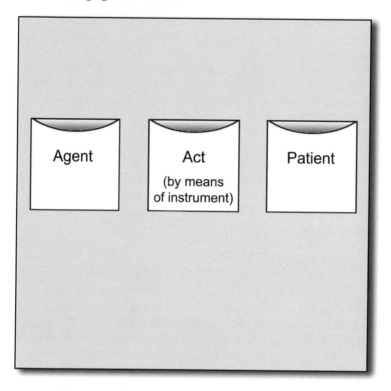

Figure 1.1   Action representation system

the initiate meeting the CPS-agent face to face. Often, though, this link to the actions of CPS-agents is indirect. CPS-agents act through their ritually appointed intermediaries, e.g., an ordained priest.

As noted, it follows on this account that many religious activities are not, typically, religious rituals in our technical sense, even though they may be present in ritual practices and qualify as religious acts. It also follows that even many actions that religious persons repeat in religious ceremonies (such as everyone standing at certain points in a religious service) will not count as rituals either.

We defend these decisions on two principal grounds. The first is what we take to be a telling coincidence. Three relevant but quite different considerations bearing upon distinctions among religious actions coincide. Before we turn to the second ground, we offer a brief account of each of these three considerations.

The first consideration is that, invariably, religious rituals, unlike mere religious acts, bring about changes in the religious world (temporary in some cases, permanent in others) by virtue of the fact that they involve transactions with CPS-agents. Those interactions affect to what or whom anyone can subsequently apply the religious category associated with the act in question. Moreover, the performance of a religious ritual – in the sense our theory specifies – entitles anyone to apply the religious category associated with that ritual exclusively on the basis of the intersubjectively available information, as construed within the framework of the pertinent religious system. So, for example, if the priest baptizes Paul or a rabbi circumcises Joel, then henceforth the terms "baptized" and "circumcised" may be used to describe Paul and Joel respectively, *regardless of the state of mind of Paul or Joel or the priest* when the ritual occurred. (What will matter is only that the priest qualifies as an appropriate ritual agent – which, itself, turns on the priest's own ritual history.) By contrast, this is not true about religious actions that are not rituals in our technical sense. If Paul prays publicly, all we can say is that Paul has appeared to pray publicly. Paul may have been feigning prayer. Only Paul knows for sure. Whereas when a priest baptizes Paul (under the appropriate publicly observable conditions), anyone privy to this event and the relevant parts of the accompanying religious conceptual scheme can know that Paul has been baptized.

The next consideration differentiating religious rituals (in our technical sense) from other religious activities is what we shall call the "insider-outsider criterion." Although mere religious actions are typically open to outsiders, religious rituals typically are not. (Of course, who counts as an "outsider" may change over time.) A non-Catholic is welcome to pray with Catholics but not to take Holy Communion with them. Although anyone can practice yoga, only boys of the Brahmanic caste can be invested with the sacred thread (Penner, 1975). Anyone can chant Zulu war songs; only Zulus can be buried in the *umuzi* (village). With the exception of what we might call "entry-level" rituals (for example, for juniors or new converts), those who are not participants in the religious system are not eligible to participate in that system's rituals in our technical sense of that term.

The distinction between participants in the religious system and participants in a religious ritual is noteworthy. Except, perhaps, relative to entry-level rituals, the latter category's referents constitute a subset of the former category's referents. This distinction, in effect, helps to explicate the notion of "eligibility" for a ritual. Although every member of the family is a participant in the religious system, only the young adult getting married is a participant in that particular religious ritual.

The final consideration is that rituals are invariably connected with other rituals. While participating in anything other than entry-level religious rituals turns unwaveringly on having performed earlier religious rituals, carrying out these other sorts of religious actions does not. So, for example, a Jew must have gone through his bar mitzvah in order to qualify to become a rabbi but that ritual accomplishment is not a necessary condition for him to be eligible to pray. Below we shall develop this idea further in the discussion of ritual embedding.

The second ground for employing our technical sense of the term "religious ritual" simply looks to the success of the resulting research program the theory inspires. The argument, in effect, says that if the overall theory is successful on many fronts, then that fact is relevant to the defense of any of that theory's details. Obviously, that's the case we are out to make. In *Rethinking Religion* we showed that our theory could simultaneously account for an assortment of ritual properties, each of which some others had noted but none of which they had explained – let alone explained in terms of a single, unified theory. Subsequently, other scholars have demonstrated the theory's explanatory power in specific cultural settings (e.g., Abbink, 1995). Now in this book, we show how the theory can explain additional features of religious rituals that we had not even considered before. The argument here, then, is that demonstrating a theory's ability to generate a progressive program of research justifies its technical distinctions, even when they run contrary to widespread, common-sense assumptions. This is not unusual in science. Copernicus' theory rejected the prevailing list of the planets at the time and did not conform to common-sense knowledge about the motionlessness of the earth. The success of his theory redefined what should count as a planet and established that the earth moves. The point of formulating systematic, testable theories in any domain is to get beyond the hodgepodge of suppositions that characterize pretheoretic common sense.

Properties and qualities of ritual elements

People are, of course, agents, but they can also be the patients in some actions, including rituals. This does not mean that the agent ceases being an agent but that he or she is being acted upon rather than engaging in action. So, for example, when Brahman priests invest student initiates with the sacred thread as part of the *upanayana* ritual, even though the initiates are agents ontologically, as participants undergoing this investiture they serve as the patients in these ritual acts. In religious rituals agents with appropriate qualities and properties can do things to other agents who function as the patients of those rituals. We turn, therefore, to these qualities and properties, because a theory that only provided for a general structural description of the relationships among agents, acts, and patients may miss important details. We should be able to represent some ritually salient qualities and properties of the agents, actions, and patients. This requires that we specify, when necessary, what makes the agent eligible to perform the action, what properties a particular act must possess, as well as the qualities of the patients that make them eligible to serve in that role.

The conceptual schemes of particular religious systems will, of course, designate which qualities and properties matter. For example, in one religious tradition it might be necessary for ritual officials to be males, in another that the patient be an unmarried woman who has fasted for three days, and in another that the action be performed at night. Our account of the action representation system can accommodate such cultural variations.

A cognitive representation of a religious ritual will include the formal features that determine participants' judgments about that ritual's status, efficacy, and relationships to other ritual acts. The efficacy of the ordination of a monk in Theravada Buddhism, for example, will have derived from the officiating monks' legitimacy, the appropriate ritual history of the water used in the ritual bath, and the eligibility of the patient. The bathing itself and the previous act of consecrating the water are qualified by the fact that the officiating monks are eligible to carry out such ritual acts. If they are imposters, ritual failure looms. Minimally, it contravenes basic assumptions about the relations between various ritual actions and about those rituals' connections with CPS-agents.

Just as participants possess qualities and properties that may require specification, sometimes conditions on ritual actions do too. Particular ritual acts sometimes require fulfilling particular conditions for their execution; for example, carrying out some task may require particular instruments. Ritual agents often need specific tools in order to do their jobs properly. These tools can be anything the tradition permits – antelope bones for divining, sharp stones for circumcising male children, red ochre for coloring corpses, or nettles for whipping initiates.

Instruments, however, should not be confused with agents. For example, a priest uses incense to sanctify a house or uses rocks of a particular shape to establish a temple site. While these instruments are not the agents, they often specify necessary conditions for the success of the agents' ritual actions. The ritual official may sanctify the house by means of burning incense. What we called the "action condition" in *Rethinking Religion* can specify an element in a ritual, viz., the instrument employed by the agent (the incense) as well as qualities of the instrument the conceptual scheme defines as relevant (in this case, that the incense is burning). A complete representation of a ritual is a representation of an agent with the requisite qualities acting upon an object with the requisite qualities potentially using an instrument with the requisite qualities.

Sometimes such instruments contribute fundamentally to the outcome of the ritual. (The holy water may be fundamental to the blessing of the parishioner.) If so, it is only by virtue of their ritual connections to superhuman agency that they derive their efficacy. (Water that has not been consecrated is just plain old water.)

Enabling actions

In the above cases the requisite qualities of instruments are their own connections with CPS-agents through the performance of earlier rituals. Making sense of a religious ritual typically involves reference to a larger network of ritual actions. The performance of earlier rituals "enables" the performance of the later ones. Because the priest has blessed the water in the font, participants can use it to bless themselves when they enter the vestibule of a church. These earlier rituals that fulfill necessary conditions for the performance of subsequent rituals are what we call "enabling rituals" (or, more generally, "enabling actions"). So, for example, participants can partake of first communion because they were previously baptized. Their baptism enables them to participate in the communion. The validity of their participation in the communion presupposed their successful participation in the divinely sanctioned ritual of baptism.

If there is no direct reference to a CPS-agent in a ritual's immediate structural description, then at least one of its elements must involve presumptions about its connections with one or more (earlier) ritual actions that eventually involve a CPS-agent in one of those rituals' immediate structural descriptions. For example, the action of initiating someone into a cohort of a certain kind requires prior actions performed on the agents involved in the initiation. No uninitiated person can initiate the "newcomer." Ritual practitioners performing the initiation will have to have been initiated themselves. (We shall define ritual "practitioners" as participants who hold some privileged religious status by virtue of which they are able to perform some rituals that other participants, who do not share their status, cannot.) Ultimately, of course, the gods are responsible for the initiating through these connections with the ritual practitioner, i.e., the immediate ritual agents who serve as the gods' intermediaries.

Although it may not always be immediately obvious, ritual actions are systematically connected with one another. The acts involved must follow in a certain order. Some ritual actions presuppose the performance of others. In everyday life, actions of any kind frequently presuppose the successful completion of previous actions, since those earlier actions fulfill necessary requirements for the performance of the action at hand. For example, operating a car presupposes that someone has put gas in the tank. Carrying out a particular religious ritual action typically presupposes the prior performance of another ritual action that enables the current one to be performed.

The classic rites of passage in many religious systems offer the best illustrations. The integration of children into a community precedes their rising to adult status, which, in turn, precedes their marriages. In each case the associated rituals presuppose the successful completion of their predecessors. An example is the sequence of initiation rites among the Zulu. In order for a Zulu male to be eligible for marriage, he has to go through a number of rites of passage starting with the naming ritual and proceeding through the earpiercing ritual, the puberty ritual, and the "grouping up ritual." (See Lawson and McCauley, 1990, pp. 113–121.)

Technically, we can talk about the representation of such a connected set of rituals as "embedded" within the current ritual's structural description. Embedding is a formal notion for representing in their structural descriptions the external relations among rituals that we have described in terms of enabling actions. A diagram of the relationships among these successively performed rituals would start with the *current* ritual (the one under study), which would be depicted at the top of a tree diagram, with all of the logically (and temporally) prior rituals below, connected to it through its ritual elements. So, the *full* structural description of a ritual would include all of these embedded rituals.

A ritual's full structural description contrasts with an *immediate* structural description of its surface features. A full structural description includes that immediate structural description plus the structural descriptions of all of the enabling ritual actions the current ritual presumes as well as accounts of their connections with ritual elements in that current ritual. Recall that in the case of religious ritual, enabling actions are simply (earlier) rituals whose successful completion is necessary for the successful completion of the current ritual. So, for example, weddings are not valid typically, if the priests performing them have not been properly certified ritually by their prior ordination. The priests' ordinations enable them to perform weddings. These ordinations are, therefore, enabling rituals whose structural descriptions must be incorporated (as a property of these priests) into weddings' full structural descriptions.

In the everyday world the exploration of such presuppositions can go on indefinitely either by tracing causal chains (the window broke, because the ladder fell and hit it, because the ground on which it rested was damp, etc.) or by concatenating reasons (John flipped the switch, since he wanted to see the room's contents, since he wanted to ascertain whether he could load them into the truck in the next ten minutes, since, if at all possible, he wanted to complete that job before the police arrived, since he wanted to avoid arrest, etc.). Religious rituals, while engaging the same representational resources, possess a distinctive feature that marks them off not only from everyday actions but also from the other sorts of routine religious actions we mentioned above (such as standing at various points during a worship service). That distinctive feature is that religious rituals (in our technical sense) always presume an end point to such causal or rational explorations. In religious ritual representations things come to an end. Causal chains terminate; reasons find a final ground. In short, the buck stops with the gods. The introduction of actions involving CPS-agents (or agents with special, counter-intuitive qualities) into the conception of an action introduces considerations that need neither further causal explanation nor further rational justification.

Boyer (2001) has argued that human beings possess moral intuitions that arise spontaneously from their natural competence with social situations and for which they have no considered explanations. He suggests that humans' representations of gods seem capable of grounding these moral intuitions, because they include presumptions about the gods' possession of what he calls "strategic information." The gods possess strategic information because humans presume that the gods have, in effect, a "god's eye view" of human social affairs. They can serve as (hypothetical/ mythical) arbiters of moral matters, since they enjoy access to *all* agents' states of mind. (Like Santa, they know if you – and everyone else – have been bad or good, so be good *for goodness sake*.) Of course, not every supernatural entity that religions have proposed possesses this full range of capacities, but at least collectively, not only do they see the big picture, they see – with comparable acuity – all of the relevant intentional details as well.

Religious rituals involve transactions with these strategically informed agents. Armed with this information, the gods – again, at least collectively – have all of the knowledge it takes to *know* what the right thing to do is – morally or ritually. But, of course, knowing the right thing to do is not the same thing as having the power to do it. The gods may meet the necessary epistemic conditions for definitive actions, but why are they also conceived as possessing the *power* to act definitively?

To answer *that* question will require some theoretical extensions of some intriguing psychological findings from other domains. First, human beings tend to ascribe agency far more liberally than the stimuli demand. When we hear unexpected sounds in the basement, we instantly worry about the possibility of intruders. This makes theoretical sense from an evolutionary standpoint. In a world where our ancestors crossed the paths of prey but particularly the paths of predators far more frequently than most of us do now, possession of a hyperactive agent detection device (HADD) would provide obvious advantages (Barrett, 2000). Erring on the side of caution on this front would tend to insure that they were able to serve more lunches without serving as lunch themselves. A HADD will generate lots of false positives, but it will also keep us out of the stew.

This makes good theoretical sense, but is there empirical evidence for this proclivity? Perhaps. Our ape cousins occasionally seem to manifest some similar dispositions. Although Jane Goodall is the first to report this phenomenon in print, it has been widely observed among both chimps and gorillas (Goodall, 1992). In the face of thunder storms, waterfalls, and (in captivity) large, loud trucks, some individuals will commence aggressive displays that are otherwise reserved for intimidating conspecifics. Minimally, they seem to be employing a strategy they typically employ in social settings to deal with perceived problems in other domains.[3]

As we have already noted above, developmental psychologists have provided evidence suggesting that human infants not only deploy the concepts "agent" and "action" but readily apply these concepts in far more settings than is warranted. (See Michotte, 1963, Rochat et al., 1997, and Rochat and Striano, 1999.) Babies differentially attend to a display involving one dot "chasing" another on a computer screen as opposed to another display in which the distances, speeds, and frequencies of change in direction are the same, but where the relations between the two dots do not support such an interpretation.

All of this, then, suggests that human beings may be *naturally* over-prepared to detect agents where they are not, but, as Boyer (2001) notes, *that* is not enough, since most of the time human beings quickly ascertain the false alarm and reset the system. Why do some of these representations *persist* and why do they win such striking cognitive allegiance from human beings? This directs us to a second body of psychological findings.

Research in social psychology over the past few decades provides important resources for answering these questions. Attribution theorists have supplied considerable evidence concerning the human disposition to account for socially significant developments in terms of agents' actions. In fact, human beings regularly overestimate the responsibility of agents for outcomes when situations do not justify it. (See Ross and Nisbett, 1991.) Conspiracy theories abound. Blame is placed even when it is not required. Human beings' preoccupation with agent causality typically results in their underestimating both the influence of variables outside of agents' control and the role of the environment in shaping events around them. It also results in their overestimation of agents' responsibility and the role of personality traits when assessing the causal dynamics of social events. When the chips are down, it just seems easier and more efficient, when making social judgments, for people to credit agents with responsibility for events than it is for them to look for some other sort of cause.[4]

It may, therefore, be particularly easy (and particularly natural) to credit agents with responsibility for socially significant events that are otherwise inexplicable – even if those agents are often invisible and their actions are not obvious, i.e., even if they seem to guide affairs by causal means that are entirely opaque. Boyer (2001) has argued that such assumptions are particularly likely to persist, if the concepts of the agents who are allegedly responsible turn out to be the sorts of concepts that tend, simultaneously, to ambush the attentions of human minds, to lodge permanently in human memories, and to provoke conduct among humans that leads to their subsequent dissemination. In short, Boyer is suggesting that it may be particularly easy and natural to credit agents with responsibility for socially significant events that are otherwise inexplicable not despite but *precisely because* the agents have counter-intuitive properties and they steer events by causal means that are completely mysterious. Boyer has supplied considerable experimental evidence that the concepts of CPS-agents that populate religious conceptual schemes have precisely such cognitive appeal.

To summarize, then, because of our species' long history as both predators and prey, we detect more agency in our environments than conditions warrant. The HADD generates many false positives, most of which human beings debunk straightaway. Some, however, survive, because humans associate them with concepts that, as Boyer argues, possess cognitive appeal. These are invariably concepts of agents, because as the research on attribution reveals, humans are strongly biased to postulate explanations of affairs that rely on agent causality. They are invariably concepts of *powerful* agents, because those concepts do efficient inferential work in the explanation of socially significant matters that are otherwise inexplicable. So, participants presume that CPS-agents possess the power to act definitively *in ritual*, because they are already inclined to credit them with the power to direct matters in life generally.

Religious rituals, then, enjoy representational closure by terminating in the deeds of CPS-agents. The actions of the gods ground religious rituals. From those deeds their normative force arises. Although other human actions pretend to similar normative prestige – from enforcing law to umpiring baseball – none has access to the superhuman considerations that serve as the guarantor of cosmic (as opposed to conventional) authority in religious systems. Despite talk in the humanities and social sciences about civil religion, the religion of art, or the theology of communism, such systems rarely engender such immediate authoritativeness. Our suggestion is that this is because they rarely involve such direct appeals to the specific actions of CPS-agents.

The normative force in question amounts to the assumption that we need discover no further causes, we need give no additional reasons. It should, of course, come as no surprise that, finally, it is what the gods do that matters in religious ritual. Our theory provides descriptions for religious ritual actions, which are, in one respect, exhaustive. For the participants there is no more significant cause to locate, no more crucial reason to propose. The actions of the gods guarantee the comprehensiveness of description, because their actions are causally, rationally, and motivationally sufficient for the ritual actions they inspire. These actions of the gods are the actions our theory defines as *hypothetical* religious rituals. They are actions attributed to the gods to which humans appeal in the course of carrying out their own rituals. So, for example, the authority of popes might turn on Jesus' declaration that St. Peter was the rock on which he would build his church. Participants appeal to such "rituals" as actions enabling their own religious ritual practices.

Agency, CPS-agents, and counter-intuitive properties

On our theory, then, explaining various fundamental features of religious rituals turns on the roles that CPS-agents play in them. In order to understand why this is the case we need to analyze what is involved in the representation of a religious ritual action.

Since all rituals are actions and only agents act, our command of the category of agency (and the inferences that accompany it) is the single most important piece of ordinary cognitive equipment deployed in the representation of religious rituals. The notion "agent" is fundamental in any theory of religious ritual, because it drives our most basic expectations about the form of *any* action. The identification of action turns critically on the identification of agents. The difference between doing and happening rests in the balance. The first involves an agent acting. Turning on a light differs fundamentally from the air-conditioner going on the blink. Similarly, someone doing something differs from something happening to someone. Cutting a log and tripping over a log differ in the way they are represented.

The category of agency constitutes the foundation of social intercourse and of our conceptions of responsibility, personhood, and morality. All of this is, of course, standard fare in philosophical discussion, but it has also captured the imagination of developmental psychologists, who have designed marvelously clever experiments to identify the key role that the concept of agency plays even in the mental lives of young children (Gopnik et al., 1999). These developmental studies show that long before infants acquire and use language they already possess the cognitive resources required for representing such basic ontological distinctions as that between agents and non-agents. These studies indicate that from early infancy human beings represent agents and the actions they perform very differently from the ways they represent other entities and events. Developmental psychologists have discovered that infants know (and therefore are capable of representing) the difference between the agent and patient of an action as well as whether the patient is just an inanimate object or also an agent capable of acting too. This is to say that they distinguish the vital action roles from one another as well as the sorts of entities capable of filling each.

Distinguishing the nurturing mother from the unresponsive bedpost is vital for the infant's well-being. Very young children recognize that agents have goals and desires and that they are generally capable of initiating self-motion (fulfilling those desires to achieve those goals). By roughly the age of four a child grasps the notion that human agents (at least) also have minds and that their understanding of their world depends upon how their minds represent it (Wimmer and Perner, 1983 and Perner et al., 1987). Children recognize agents' intentionality, i.e., they formulate mental representations of other people's mental representations. They come to understand that what people are doing depends upon how they represent their actions to themselves. By roughly school age, children have obtained all of the fundamental presumptions built into what development psychologists call a "theory of mind" – a theory that may undergo further elaboration but whose basic assumptions undergo no substantial change thereafter. (See Wellman, 1990.)

The notable point is that the same presumptions about agents and actions hold for the representation of CPS-agents. Participants' intuitive assumptions about the psychology of agents purchase them vast amounts of knowledge about CPS-agents for free (Boyer, 1996). So, for example, on the basis of knowing that some CPS-agent desires X and believes that doing Y will enable the attainment of X, participants will know that it is likely that the CPS-agent in question will do Y. Or knowing that the ancestors are easily offended, if they are not provided with the best available foods, and that they are likely to cause mischief in the community when they are offended, participants will recognize that they should insure that the ancestors are well fed. Or, again, knowing that the gods have thought carefully about the laws they have instituted for human conduct, participants know that violations of those laws will likely provoke angry responses from the gods.

From the standpoint of the representation of religious ritual, all of this is exceedingly helpful. That is because religious conceptual schemes usually provide ready-made accounts of CPS-agents' conceptions of their ritually relevant actions, i.e., their conceptions of what we have called the "hypothetical rituals." Recall that these are the actions of CPS-agents that get represented in the full structural descriptions of a religious system's rituals.

The "specialness" of religious rituals, then, does not turn on anomalies in their basic action structures or with irregularities in the way that CPS-agents exercise their agency. *Qua* agents, CPS-agents are quite similar to human agents; that is why we can so readily draw inferences about their actions, their goals, their desires, and their other states of mind.

On a few fronts, though, they differ decisively from human agents, and it is those differences that make representations of religious rituals different from representations of ordinary action. CPS-agents exhibit various counter-intuitive properties. Those properties arise from violations of the default assumptions associated with basic categories. So, for example, if something is an agent, then (normally) it is also a physical object and possesses all of the associated physical properties. CPS-agents may differ from normal agents in that they *violate* the constraints this superordinate category, "physical object," imposes. Thus, they may pass through solid objects or be everywhere at once. CPS-agents may violate constraints that other superordinate categories, such as being an organism, impose. So, CPS-agents may be eternal, parentless, or capable of recovering from death (Boyer, 2001).

On our theory, then, very little distinguishes religious rituals from other sorts of actions. A religious system's conceptual scheme provides *special entries* for at least some of the slots in a ritual's structural description. For example, the specific acts carried out in religious rituals (such as sacrifices, blessings, consecrations, and so on) are often unique to religious conceptual schemes. Crucially, only with religious rituals do populations of participants carry out actions that routinely presume enabling actions by CPS-agents with special counter-intuitive properties. (In *Rethinking Religion* we employed the marker "s" in tree diagrams of religious rituals' structural descriptions to designate any of these special properties.) It is these appeals to the actions of CPS-agents that participants regard as so conclusive. What we might loosely call inquiry about the causal or rational foundations of religious rituals will always come to an end when they invoke the enabling actions of CPS-agents. At that point, such inquiry stops. There is no need for proceeding further, let alone the possibility of carrying on such inquiries indefinitely – as is the case with any other sort of action.

It is the roles that CPS-agents play in rituals' representations that are the critical variables that determine many of their important properties. Our theory identifies two principles for organizing this information about the impact of CPS-agents' roles on religious ritual form. They jointly yield a typology of religious ritual forms that systematically organizes the rituals of *any* religious system. It is to these two principles that we now turn.

A cognitive account of various properties of religious rituals

The principles of Superhuman Agency and Superhuman Immediacy categorize the structural descriptions of rituals that participants' action representation systems generate. At a first level of approximation, the Principle of Superhuman Agency (PSA) distinguishes between two kinds of ritual profiles – ones where CPS-agents are ritually connected with the agent of a ritual and ones where they are connected with the ritual elements fulfilling one of the other action roles.

The first kind of ritual profile concerns those religious rituals in which the most direct connection with the gods is through the role of the current ritual's agent. We shall call these "special agent rituals."[5] Special agent rituals connect the initial entry for a CPS-agent with the entity fulfilling the role of the agent in the current ritual. What this amounts to is that one or more previous rituals connect the "buck-stopper," i.e., the initial CPS-agent in the current ritual, to the current ritual's agent. These include such rituals as circumcisions, weddings, and funerals.

The second kind of ritual profile concerns those rituals in which the most direct connection with the gods is through either of the other two roles, i.e., through the patient or through the act itself (by way of a special instrument). These will connect a CPS-agent most directly with the items appearing in the second or third slots in the current ritual's structural description. Most of the rituals in this second group are what we shall call "special patient rituals." These include sacrifices, rituals of penance, and Holy Communion. "Special instrument rituals" also exist. (Many rituals of divination and many blessings are examples of the latter sort.)

The PSA concerns the representation of a superhuman agent's involvement in a ritual (as indicated by the location of its entry in a ritual's structural description). In assessing religious rituals' forms, the PSA focuses attention on the action role(s) of the current ritual that connects most directly with CPS-agents' actions. Participants represent a CPS-agent somewhere in their rituals' full structural descriptions. On our theory the crucial question is *where*. (See figure 1.2.) Whether a ritual is, on the one

Any or all three possibilities for insertion into rituals' structural descriptions

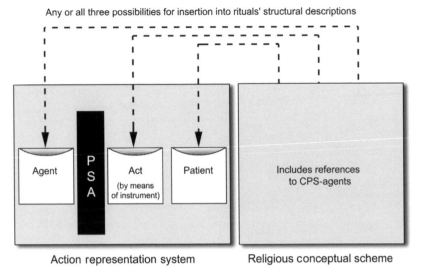

Figure 1.2   Principle of Superhuman Agency (PSA)

hand, a special agent ritual or, on the other, a special patient or special instrument ritual determines participants' judgments about a wide range of ritual properties, including a ritual's repeatability and reversibility. It also bears on whether a ritual can permit substitutions for some of its elements.

Especially since more than one entry for CPS-agents may arise in a religious ritual's full structural description, this account of the PSA demands clarification about which appearance of a CPS-agent in a structural description qualifies as the *initial* one. Determining which connection with CPS-agents in the representation of a religious ritual constitutes the initial entry, i.e., the entry with the "most direct connection" to the ritual at hand, is not too complicated. This is where the Principle of Superhuman Immediacy comes in.

The Principle of Superhuman Immediacy (PSI) states that the number of enabling rituals required to connect some element in the current ritual with an entry for a CPS-agent determines that entry's proximity to the current ritual. Specifically, the initial appearance of a CPS-agent in a ritual's full structural description is the entry whose connection with some element in the current ritual involves the fewest enabling rituals. For example, in a Christian baptism at least the priest (the agent) and the water (the instrument) have ritually mediated connections with God. The priest's connection is more direct, however, since it is mediated by fewer enabling rituals. The water involves at least one additional level of

Action role most directly connected with CPS-agent

		Special agent rituals	Special patient and special instrument rituals
Number of enabling rituals (structural depth)	Level 1	Type 1	Type 2
	Level 2	Type 3	Type 4
	Level 3	Type 5	Type 6
	Level 4	Type 7	Type 8
	Etc.	Further odd-numbered types	Further even-numbered types

Figure 1.3   Typology of religious ritual forms

ritual mediation in order to achieve its special status, which arises, after all, because it was a *priest* who consecrated it. So, according to the PSI, since the priest, who is the *agent* who performs the baptism, has a more direct ritual connection with God than the water with which he carries out this ritual, baptism is a special agent ritual.

These two principles identify the two most important aspects of religious ritual form. They concern

1 what role(s) in the current ritual enabling rituals are connected with (i.e., which determines what we are calling a ritual's "profile"), and

2 how many enabling rituals are required to establish that connection between an element in the current ritual and a CPS-agent (which we shall refer to as a ritual's "depth").

The PSI and PSA work in tandem to delineate a typology of religious ritual actions. (See figure 1.3, which employs the same numbering of types as figure 17 on pp. 128–130 in *Rethinking Religion*.) The most important point about this figure, for our purposes in this book, is simply to distinguish the two kinds of ritual profiles, namely rituals of special agent profiles (which are always rituals of odd-numbered types) and rituals of special instrument and special patient profiles (which are always rituals of even-numbered types).

The principal sources of complexity in rituals' full structural descriptions concern the number and locations of embedded rituals. Recall that embedding is a formal means for representing the enabling rituals the current ritual's performance presupposes. No formal considerations set any principled limits on the possible complexity of the full structural descriptions of rituals that the action representation system can generate, though it seems a safe assumption that such things as memory limitations probably set some practical limitations.

The PSA addresses the action *role* (agent, act, or patient) with which embedded rituals in the current ritual's full structural description are connected via enabling actions. By contrast, the PSI is concerned with the *number* of embedded rituals, i.e., with the number of enabling actions, necessary to connect some element of the current ritual with the actions of CPS-agents. We shall return to these issues in chapter 3 (pp. 113–123), but for the moment, this is quite enough detail to consider some important theoretical morals concerning the connections between:

1 the action representation system and the well-formedness and effectiveness of religious rituals,
2 the PSA's distinction between kinds of ritual profiles and three ritual properties, and
3 the PSI's account of the initial entry for a CPS-agent and (comparative) ritual centrality.

The action representation system and the well-formedness and effectiveness of religious rituals

On one decisive front religious participants represent their rituals differently from the way they represent all of their other actions. All representations of religious rituals somewhere involve connections with the actions of CPS-agents. This is critical to participants' assessments of both their rituals' well-formedness and their efficacy. At least one such connection between some element or other of the current ritual and the action of a CPS-agent is a necessary condition for a ritual's well-formedness. Absent presumptions about such a connection, participants will not judge the ritual in question to be well-formed and, if the ritual is not judged as well-formed, they will judge it as ineffective. Unless eligible agents perform correct actions on eligible patients with the right tools, participants will not judge the ritual effective. Crucially, the eligibility of at least one of the ritual participants or the rightness of a ritual instrument will depend upon enabling actions that establish connections between them and the actions of a CPS-agent. If an imposter performs weddings, the couples are not validly married in the eyes of the church. If someone switches the specially selected bones a Zulu diviner uses, this will explain the diviner's failure to make accurate predictions about the prospective marriage in question.

Considerations of the well-formedness and effectiveness of religious rituals quickly demonstrate the importance of distinguishing between special agent rituals, on the one hand, and special patient rituals, on the other. Well-formedness is only a necessary but not a sufficient condition for the effectiveness of a special patient ritual. So, for example, while the well-formedness of ritual offerings to the ancestors is necessary for these gifts' acceptability, there is no guarantee that the ancestors will accept them (Whitehouse, 1995). Similarly, at least a casual survey suggests that the well-formedness of special agent rituals is considerably more constrained than special patient or special instrument rituals, since the former exhibit much less flexibility concerning ritual substitutions (see below).

The PSA's distinction between kinds of ritual profiles and three ritual properties

The distinction that the PSA introduces between special agent rituals and special patient and special instrument rituals (i.e., between rituals of odd- and even-numbered types in figure 17 of *Rethinking Religion*) has many important consequences. These distinctions between ritual types predict numerous properties of rituals in any religious system. We shall briefly discuss three.

Repeatability   Individual participants need serve as the patients of special agent rituals only once, whereas participants can and typically do perform special instrument and special patient rituals repeatedly. Consider the difference between once-in-a-lifetime initiations and the many sacrifices that ritual participants will perform as part of their religious obligations.

We have already discussed why the buck stops with the gods in representations of religious rituals. Agency is pivotal to the representation of all action. Humans detect more agency in their worlds than subsequent reflection sanctions. Some of those episodes become connected with concepts of agents that have demonstrable cognitive appeal. Boyer (2001) argues that humans accord those agents tremendous knowledge and power in order to make sense of their spontaneous moral intuitions about social relations and to explain myriad social developments about which humans have nary a clue about their underlying causal structures. (When we do not appeal to the gods to explain these situations, we resort to simple-minded anthropomorphic accounts in terms of theory of mind: "America hopes that the European Union thinks that capitalism will succeed where socialism has failed.") The vast knowledge and power these agents possess guarantee the appropriateness and definitiveness of all of their actions.

This explains why some rituals do not require repetition in the lifetime of a ritual participant. In special agent rituals CPS-agents act, at least indirectly, through their ritually entitled middlemen. When the gods do things, they are done once and for all. By contrast, in special patient and special instrument rituals, the gods' closest connections are with the patients or the instruments of the ritual. Whatever ritually mediated connection the agent in such a ritual may enjoy with CPS-agents is comparatively less intimate. Consequently, in these rituals the agents' actions carry no such finality. They are typically done again and again. Initiation into adulthood only happens once per participant, whereas participants will make offerings to the gods over and over and over. That these rituals are repeatable hints that nothing religiously indispensable turns on any one of their performances.

Reversibility Our theory also explains whether a ritual's consequences can be reversed or not. Because the consequences of special patient and special instrument rituals are temporary only, it is unnecessary to have procedures (ritual or otherwise) for their reversal. Only the consequences of special agent rituals can be reversed. Defrocking priests, excommunicating communicants, expelling initiates, and dissolving marriages are all possible, but undoing Holy Communion is not. It establishes a temporary state of grace from which the Christian inevitably falls. Only special agent rituals' consequences are permanent, since in these it is CPS-agents who have acted, either directly or through their intermediaries. These, then, are the only rituals whose consequences might ever need reversing.

Substitutability Because CPS-agents are neither connected with the special patient or special instrument rituals' agents primarily nor serve as the agents themselves, it is not just the effects of those rituals that are fleeting. That special instrument and special patient rituals are repeatable hints that nothing religiously indispensable turns on any *one* of their performances. That virtually every participant repeatedly performs most of these rituals even more strongly indicates that that is so.

Because nothing religiously indispensable turns on any of their particular performances, ritual *substitutions* often arise in these even-numbered rites. Special patient and special instrument rituals are ones that human participants carry out with or on ritual elements that enjoy closer ritually established connections with the gods than they do. Nothing they do carries any lasting effects when their ritual connections with CPS-agents are less direct than are those of either the rituals' instruments or patients. This is just another way to reiterate our theory's claims about the decisive role of CPS-agents (and their ritual connections) in the representation of religious ritual action.

The special ritual connections of instruments or patients do not override the fact that it is the ritually less-well-connected participants who *perform* these rites (i.e., who serve in the role of the ritual agent). These rituals' temporary effects (compared with the effects of odd-numbered, special agent rituals) explain not only why these rituals are repeatable, but also why they often display greater latitude about their instruments, their patients, and even their procedures. For example, a Muslim can use sand for a ritual washing in the desert, where water is a particularly scarce and valuable resource. Often, these rituals also permit substitutions for patients. Participants' consumption of bread and wine for the body and blood of Christ is surely the most familiar example, but the ethnographic literature provides plenty more. Among the Nuer it is particularly auspicious to sacrifice a bull, but since bulls are particularly valuable, a cucumber will do just fine most of the time. Participants may be able to sacrifice bulls when times are particularly good (Evans-Pritchard, 1956 and Firth, 1963). Special patient and special instrument rituals may even display some latitude about the actual procedures involved. Humphrey and Laidlaw (1994) emphasize, for example, that the order of ritual actions in the Puja, its frequent performance notwithstanding, has manifested a good deal of variability over relatively short spans of time.

Research by Barrett and Lawson (2001) shows that subjects find changes in agents more important to their judgments about ritual efficacy than changes in any other aspect of these rituals' structures. However special their properties, the instruments and patients of even-numbered rituals do not guarantee what we have called "super-permanent" effects (Lawson and McCauley, 1990, p. 134, footnote 8). (Super-permanent effects are putative arrangements that exceed even the spatial and temporal limits of participants' lifetimes.) Those instruments and patients are not the agents in these rituals. Whether participants use ritually consecrated instruments or not, the primary consideration influencing subjects' judgments concerns the status of the current ritual's agent – even when that agent's connections with CPS-agents are comparatively less direct than those of the other ritual elements.

Our theory suggests four closely related predictions concerning ritual substitutions. Ritual substitutions will

1 typically involve instruments and patients (as opposed to agents),
2 turn on ritual roles (as opposed to items' inherent ontological statuses),
3 not arise for the agents in special agent rituals (as opposed to special patient rituals), and
4 usually concern the instruments and patients of special patient rituals (as opposed to those of special agent rituals).

All four readily submit to both ethnographic and psychological tests.

The first prediction is completely commensurate with the prominence that our theory accords the *agent* role in the representation of action. The theory predicts that substitutions in religious rituals are, all things being equal, both far more likely and far less problematic when they involve rituals' instruments or patients than when they involve their agents. Again, this turns on the *role* in which those agents serve in these actions not on their intrinsic ontological status as entities capable of serving in that role. After all, some even-numbered, special patient rituals (e.g., Holy Communion) even substitute for CPS-agents – but *only* when they serve as the *patient* of the current ritual, not as its agent.[6] This second prediction is virtually a corollary of the first.

The further prediction that such substitutions for the initial appearances of CPS-agents do not arise in special agent rituals is of a piece with the first two predictions and with the preeminent importance the PSA accords the role of ritual agent. In special agent rituals either the CPS-agent serves as the agent of the ritual or the agent in the ritual accomplishes what he or she does by virtue of the comparative immediacy in the ritual's structural description of his or her ritually mediated relationship with some CPS-agent. In the latter case the gods might be said to certify the ritual action by virtue of their comparative ritual proximity to the current ritual's agent. The point is that in these rituals the CPS-agents are – so to speak – *in* on the action.

Since it is the patients of religious rituals in whom the resulting religious changes are wrought, given the gods' super-permanent accomplishments in odd-numbered, special agent rituals, it stands to reason that, all else being equal, substitutions for the patients of these rituals are also less likely to occur than substitutions for ritual patients in special patient rituals. In special agent rituals CPS-agents bring about super-permanent changes in the ritual patients *once* and for all. If you truly want to go through with it, it is not a good idea to miss your own wedding.

The PSI's account of the initial entry for a CPS-agent and (comparative) ritual centrality

The PSI clarifies which of the (potentially) multiple entries for CPS-agents within a ritual's full structural description is the initial one. The different structural depths of these initial entries from one ritual to the next will determine what we have referred to as those rituals' comparative "centrality" to the overall religious system.

A ritual's centrality to a religious ritual system is inversely proportional to the depth of its initial entry for a CPS-agent, hence the least central rituals are the ones with the greatest depths. The greater a ritual's depth, the more distant are its connections with CPS-agents, and, thus, the less central the ritual is to the religious system.

So, for example, a baptism a Catholic priest performs is valid because he has been ritually certified by the Church, which is connected ritually with the power and authority of Christ. (A variety of different scenarios have been and can be offered to justify that connection.) Since the famous doctrine of transubstantiation establishes that the bread and wine are the very body and blood of Christ, Holy Communion – at least on orthodox Catholic views – is a ritual that requires no appeal to enabling actions in order to locate a CPS-agent.[7] The CPS-agent, Christ, is involved *directly* in the ritual at hand; consequently, a representation of a CPS-agent occurs at the very first level of this ritual's structural description. Hence, Catholic Holy Communion is one of the rituals that occurs at the first level of structural depth in that religious system. By contrast, the baptism's structural description has no CPS-agent at its first level of structure. (It is, after all, the priest who performs the baptism, not Christ himself.) Its structural description requires at least two embeddings of enabling actions (perhaps more – depending upon the preferred scenario) to establish the connection between the agent of that ritual, viz., the priest, and a CPS-agent. Consequently, it falls at no less than the third level of structural depth. It follows that the theory predicts that Holy Communion is a more central ritual to Catholicism than baptism is.

This technical notion of the comparative centrality of religious rituals is valuable, because it both explains and predicts a variety of psychological, social, and even historical aspects of religious ritual systems. It follows, of course, that claims about rituals' comparative centrality are readily testable. The important theoretical point is that multiple independent empirical measures correlate with a religious ritual's centrality.

The most straightforward *cognitive* gauge would simply be to elicit participants' judgments about such matters. This is *not* to say that participants have explicit knowledge about this abstract property of religious rituals or even about particular rituals' (absolute) depths. They do, however, possess a reservoir of tacit knowledge about these matters. Specifically, participants can offer a wide range of judgments about the comparative importance of various rituals. (So, for example, we predicted that the behavior of confirmed Catholics, by and large, will provide indications that they regard Holy Communion as more central to their religious system than baptism.) That still might prove a fairly coarse measure, though, in light of a variety of extraneous variables that could influence participants' explicit judgments (e.g., performance frequency). Consequently, it would be especially valuable to design experiments that tap this intuitive knowledge by means of indirect behavioral measures while controlling for these potentially confounding factors. These might range from such thinly veiled tasks as asking informants to rank their rituals' comparative dispensability to less direct measures testing such things as participants' diverse sensitivities to variations, their default assumptions in reasoning, or their differential recollections of details.

Cognition is not the only source of evidence here, though. Aspects of ritual practice should also provide evidence about rituals' centrality. For example, participants' knowledge about ritual prerequisites generally reflects genuine constraints on ritual practice. A Zulu male really cannot use specially prepared love potions unless he has gone through a series of other rituals beforehand. (See Lawson and McCauley, 1990, pp. 113–121.) Nor can a Hindu perform abbreviated Agnyadhana rituals in his home unless he has previously participated in an initial, full Agnyadhana. An Orthodox Jew's bar mitzvah really is a necessary condition for his becoming a rabbi. These points about ritual practice are so familiar that it is easy to lose sight of their theoretical significance. Because some of these rituals are prerequisites for others, they will prove more central to these various religious systems.

According to the insider–outsider criterion, religious rituals in our theory's technical sense are those religious activities that only participants in the system may participate in. Further restrictions on participation in or, perhaps, observation of religious rituals may also correlate in some way with rituals' centrality. Participants' tolerance for variation in religious rituals is probably another measure. Presumably, that tolerance decreases with rituals' increasing centrality. Ritual practice during periods of religious fragmentation may supply clues about rituals' various degrees of centrality too. The perceived degree of upheaval within a religious system and the probability that diverging religious communities will refuse to identify with one another any longer will surely correlate better with the addition, alteration, or deletion of a comparatively central ritual than with one that is less central.

Conclusion

Various scholars have noted some of these patterns among the properties of religious rituals before. Ours is the only theory, however, that offers a unified account of all of these patterns. It explains and predicts each of them systematically (regardless of the religious system involved). It can do so because, finally, *these properties turn on features of participants' cognitive representations of the forms of their religious ritual actions.* The theory highlights causally important features of those representations that account for participants' (mostly tacit) knowledge about the structures of and relationships among their religious rituals, which in turn explains why actual rituals have many of the properties that they do. It also situates this overall causal framework within the analytical purview of the cognitive sciences.

In this book we will extend this general explanatory strategy to some additional properties of rituals – properties that are even more readily situated within the framework of emerging cognitive science. We shall examine the connections between religious ritual and sensory stimulation, cognitive and emotional arousal, episodic, semantic, and autobiographical memory, and motivation. We end this introductory chapter with three important observations.

First, although we are making predictions about the types of intuitive judgments that informants are likely to make in situations, we are not claiming that such judgments require participants' conscious reflection. In fact, evidence suggests that such judgments are usually not based on conscious knowledge acquired by instruction and honed by reflection.

Second, none of this knowledge about religious rituals depends upon assigning meanings either to the acts participants perform or to the acts performed on them or to the qualities or properties of such acts or to the relationships between the acts. In other words, a great deal of ritual participants' (intuitive) knowledge of their religious ritual system does not depend upon their ability to provide interpretations or meanings for the rituals in which they participate or even for the prior rituals they presume. The dimensions of ritual knowledge that concern us can operate without reference to meaning and often do (Baranowski, 1994 and 1998). A particular ritual participant may not, for example, have a clue about the meaning of apostolic succession or ordination and still know that it takes a priest to get married; another may not have the faintest idea why it is necessary to swallow a bitter herb before going courting but would not dream of approaching his prospective mate unless he had done so (Lawson, 1985).

Sometimes all the ethnographer gets is "we do it because our ancestors did it." Sometimes informants appeal to specialists who possess the requisite knowledge, and sometimes informants are willing to engage in extended semantic commentary. It all depends. The attribution of meaning (let alone particular meanings) either to the ritual as a whole or to any of its parts is not a constant either between or within cultures. In any event, we expect considerable variation about the attribution of meanings.

So, we are not saying that the attribution of meanings does not occur; we are only saying that for many features of religious ritual knowledge and practice meanings simply do not seem to matter much. In some religious systems interpretations may flourish and become resources for sophisticated theological speculation among the intellectual elite. In other religious systems the attribution of meanings remains forever beside the point (Barth, 1975).

Finally, comparing our theory's predictions with findings uncovered in the field permits us to narrow a gap between models of participants' competences with symbolic-cultural systems and participants' actual performance with these systems. This is a gap about which many critics of competence theories (e.g., Clark, 1993) have complained. But our theory does not depend exclusively for its empirical assessment on surveying participants' intuitive judgments about features of their rituals. The theory also makes predictions about ritual practices. In light of its many empirical predictions, we hope our theory will provoke ethnographers into asking new kinds of questions about religious rituals in order to see if the theory will stand up to further tests. It is to such tests that we turn in the remainder of this book.

2 Ritual and memory: frequency and flashbulbs

The cognitive foundations of cultural transmission

We shall explore insights our theory of religious ritual competence provides about aspects of religious ritual performance and their psychological foundations, addressing the complex relationships between religious ritual form, performance frequency, memory, motivation, and emotional arousal as well as the sensory pageantry in rituals that evoke it. In this chapter we focus primarily on questions of memory and its connections with performance frequency and emotional arousal.

These connections are vital to understanding the process of transmitting religious knowledge across generations. It is particularly easy to see why research on human memory may illuminate such matters when considering how non-literate societies transmit religious knowledge. The critical point here is not about the problems of transmitting religious knowledge in the absence of books and printing. It is not even about the problems of transmitting religious knowledge in circumstances in which the huge majority of participants are illiterate. The point is rather about the problems of transmitting religious knowledge when the only *lasting* public representations are iconic items such as skulls, skins, and sculptures, i.e., when the only lasting public representations are non-linguistic. Non-literate cultures bring these issues into high relief, but ultimately, even in literate cultures the transmission of *rituals* often rests not on consulting texts but on participants' memories of their ritual actions.

When non-linguistic public representations play such a central role in the transmission of cultural knowledge, questions about the faithful replication of that knowledge inevitably arise. Are there any regularities in how cultural representations change over time? It is in response to such questions that evolutionary thinking about the sociocultural realm has enjoyed a renaissance over the past two decades. Theories of cultural evolution (e.g., Boyd and Richerson, 1985), sociobiology (e.g., Lumsden and Wilson, 1981), evolutionary psychology (Tooby and Cosmides, 1989 and Plotkin, 1998), and cognitive anthropology (in at least some of its incarnations – e.g., Hirschfeld and Gelman, 1994) are (different) manifestations of this trend. Although evolutionary accounts of cultural phenomena at the psychological level may suffer from some vagueness concerning both the ontological commitments and the mechanisms underlying the processes in question, unlike sociobiology, most have postponed worries about biological determinism and eschewed dismissive conceptions of mental life (Sperber, 1996).

In raising questions about the transmission of cultural knowledge, Dan Sperber (1996) distinguishes between *mental representations* in individuals' heads and *public representations* that are outside of or, at the very least, on the outside of humans' bodies. Sperber argues that the principal problem in the explanation of culture is to account for the distribution of various cultural representations (which may be either mental or public or both). Probably the most popular view about the processes that are responsible for these distributions of ideas is an account of cultural evolution that takes the analogy with biological evolution quite seriously. Richard Dawkins (1982) proposes "memes" as the ideational analogues of genes. Memes are ideas. They spread through populations by their transmission to and replication in minds. Acts of communication transmit these ideas, causing their replication in other minds.

Like genes, memes have consequences for the organisms that carry them. For example, if minds contain the meme for the fourth commandment and regard it as binding, then the people in question are likely to curtail their labor and attend religious services on what they construe as the Sabbath. Possessing memes can have an impact on biological evolution. The conduct memes inspire can affect the reproductive success of organisms. (The transparent illustration here is the fate of the Shakers, who, because of their religious beliefs discouraging procreation, left no offspring and dwindled to extinction as a group.)

Biological evolution, however, is not the whole story with memes. Memes, as it were, have lives of their own. Different memes enjoy greater and lesser frequencies. Proselytizing on behalf of a religious system, for example, may produce converts. Their conversions will affect the probabilities of these converts communicating these ideas to others. Such activities typically increase the frequencies of the relevant representations within a population. Some ideas, though, may be either so difficult to learn or so difficult to remember or so difficult to communicate that they do not become widespread and their frequencies may even decline. Such considerations are the cultural analogues of the forces of natural selection in biological evolution. Just as the processes of natural selection cause some genes to disappear from the gene pool, so too can selection processes in culture cause some memes to disappear from the meme pool. (See Dennett, 1995.)

Both advocates and foes of this analogy between biological and cultural evolution recognize its limits (Wimsatt, 1999). They are universally prompt in noting, for example, that the pace of change is radically different in the two domains. Biological evolution – even as the proponents of punctuated equilibrium[1] construe it – moves at a snail's pace in comparison to the pace at which changes in meme frequencies cause cultural change.

Sperber's epidemiological approach

Sperber regards theories of cultural evolution as examples of a more general class of approaches which he terms "epidemiological." Epidemiology is the study of population-scale macro-phenomena (such as an influenza epidemic) as the collective outcome of processes at the micro-level (such as individual human beings transmitting and succumbing to flu viruses). On this view we should understand tradition and cultural change as the propagation and mutation of cultural representations that provoke in people who possess them "public behaviours that cause others to hold them too" (Sperber, 1996, p. 100).

Sperber objects that theories of cultural evolution of the sort we mentioned above pay little attention to the micro-processes at the psychological level affecting the distributions of mental representations. Broadly, he argues that the nature of the human cognitive system differentially encourages the acquisition (i.e., learning) or recollection of some cultural representations as opposed to others and, therefore, that these cognitive considerations constitute selection pressures on cultural representations and, indirectly, on the cultural forms for which they are responsible.

Sperber's commitment to epidemiological analysis in combination with his scruples about the metaphysical extravagances inherent in cultural anthropologists' assumptions about such putative cultural items as marriages and myths[2] requires both that he discuss such cultural forms in terms of *cultural* representations and that he characterize them as simply those representations that are comparatively widespread. Sperber insists that explaining cultural forms should consist exclusively in accounting for *why* such representations (both public and mental) are, in fact, widespread.

Although Sperber eschews a specifically evolutionary orientation in favor of a more general epidemiological one, both sorts of studies address, first, the comparative *distributions* within a population of items possessing some particular cluster of features or other and, second, the *causal processes* that produce these distributions. In biological evolution natural selection is the most prominent (although not the only) sort of causal process influencing the distributions of organisms and their genes. By contrast, epidemiological theories about the distributions of cultural representations highlight causal processes that may prove nearly as varied as the items whose distributions those theories address. In the study of cultural transmission it is chains of cause and effect relations between mental and public representations that determine those cultural representations' distributions. Since those causal chains, no doubt, constitute sets of events of the most diverse sorts, Sperber calls not so much for explanations of the resulting distributions directly, but rather for the delineation of the underlying variables that influence those causal chains. Sperber argues that most of these micro-processes are cognitive and, therefore, that a theoretical account of cultural change cannot neglect the findings of cognitive psychology.

Basically, theories of cultural evolution assume that minds *replicate* memes. Sperber (1996, pp. 108 and 118) contends that attention to work in cognitive psychology on communication and memory suggests that *the replication of mental representations is the rare limiting case rather than the norm.* Sperber emphasizes (1996, p. 31) that "recall is not storage in reverse, and comprehension is not expression in reverse. Memory and communication transform information." The transmission of culture does not turn on precisely replicating mental representations. It could not. Most acts of communication result in the transformation of ideas.[3] Moreover, our memories are notoriously fallible. Mutation occurs far more often in cultural transmission than it does in biological evolution. (Consequently, biological evolution moves at a snail's pace relative not only to the pace at which changes in meme frequencies cause cultural change but also to the pace at which changes in memes themselves cause cultural change.) By attending to pertinent findings in cognitive psychology the epidemiologist of cultural representations gives "an account of the type of causal factors that have favoured transmission in certain circumstances and transformation in certain directions" (1996, p. 28). It is the second of these two topics that especially concerns us here.

Sperber rightly emphasizes findings in cognitive psychology that indicate that communication is not as uncomplicated and that memory is rarely as reliable as we are wont to presume. The transmission of culture virtually always involves the transformation of culture on Sperber's view. The critical point, though, is that these transformations are not utterly random: "[r]esemblance among cultural items is to be explained to some important extent by the fact that transformations tend to be biased in the direction of attractor positions in the space of possibilities" (1996, p. 108).

On Sperber's view the cognitive foundations of the processes of cultural transmission make some sorts of cultural representations more likely to persist than others. Similarities between cultural representations turn primarily on these evolutionary vectors – which the character of human cognition shapes. Over many cycles of transmission divergences from these attractor positions will certainly arise; however, because of these cognitive constraints, subsequent transformations in further cycles of transmission will typically steer cultural representations towards one of the attractors again.

Dynamical properties of religious ritual systems: two attractors

Considering the psychological foundations of cultural forms within such a framework reorients research on a topic like religious ritual. Now the central questions concern how cognitive factors contribute to rituals' persistence and transmission. Religious rituals seem particularly appropriate objects for such analyses, since they are so often both provocative and public in all of the right ways. They seem paradigmatic cases of "public behaviours that cause others to hold them [as mental representations] too" (Sperber, 1996, p. 100).

We shall argue that if religious rituals evolve, then they will usually come to approximate one or the other of two sorts of arrangements. They will evolve either (1) in the direction of rituals that involve low amounts of sensory stimulation, resulting in low levels of emotional arousal, that are repeated and have comparatively high performance frequencies[4] or else (2) in the direction of rituals that incorporate higher levels of sensory stimulation and emotional arousal and are non-repeated, i.e., rituals in which each participant serves in the role of their patient only once. (See figure 2.1.) The crucial point is that the theoretical principles that we described in chapter 1 delineate two major kinds of ritual profiles – special patient and special instrument rituals on the one hand and special agent rituals on the other (i.e., even- as opposed to odd-numbered types in figure 1.3), which correspond in their details, respectively, with these two sorts of arrangements. Consequently, the theory offers vital intelligence about the cognitive factors responsible for shaping the evolving distributions of religious rituals.

Let us briefly summarize our overall take on these matters here in anticipation of the arguments and analyses that follow. Our theory makes a number of distinctions concerning the forms of religious rituals. The cognitive considerations motivating the most prominent of those distinctions, viz., that between special agent rituals and special patient and special instrument rituals, are integrally connected with these two attractor

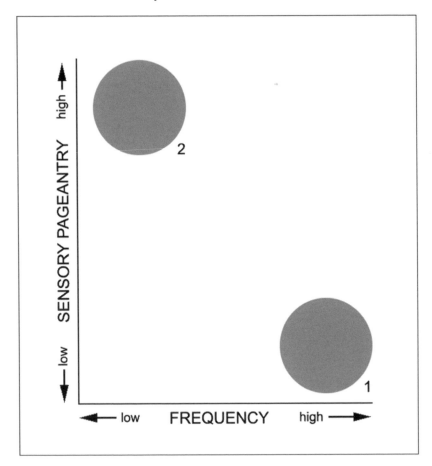

Figure 2.1 Two attractors

positions. Our theory of religious ritual competence identifies the underlying "micro-processes at the [cognitive] psychological level" that decide
to which of these two sorts of arrangements, i.e., to which of these two
attractor positions, religious rituals gravitate (in order to increase the
probabilities of their continued transmission). We are arguing that participants' representations of how CPS-agents are implicated in their religious rituals, ultimately, determine whether or not religious rituals are
repeatable[5] as well as the mnemonic dynamics those rituals enlist. Consequently, those representations also determine the rituals' performance
frequencies and their levels of sensory pageantry (and resulting emotional
punch). Because they determine which rituals cultivate extraordinary

emotional states, these representations of how the gods are connected with various rituals also explain *why* some rituals are well suited to motivate participants to transmit their religious systems to others.

The key connections are as follows. *Within* any particular religious system,[6] the rituals that gravitate toward the first of these attractors, i.e., toward less sensory stimulation and less emotional arousal, though higher performance frequencies, are the special patient and special instrument rituals. According to our theory of religious ritual competence, with these even-numbered types of rituals the CPS-agents do not bear the responsibility for doing what needs to be done, since their *principal* or most immediate connection with the current ritual's elements is not with that ritual's agent. By contrast, all of the rituals that evolve toward comparatively high levels of sensory stimulation and emotional arousal are special agent rituals, in which it is the ritual agent, among all of the ritual's elements, who has the most direct ritual connection with a CPS-agent. This is to say that in these special agent rituals – according to our theory – the gods are ultimately responsible for what happens.

Why do some types of cultural representations constitute attractor positions in the space of possibilities? Sperber comments: "To say that there is an attractor is not to give a causal explanation; it is to put in a certain light what is to be causally explained: namely a distribution of items and its evolution, and to suggest the kind of causal explanation to be sought: namely, the identification of genuine causal factors that bias micro-transformations" (1996, p. 112). In this chapter we undertake that task.

We concur with Sperber's generally negative assessments concerning both the directness of communication and the fidelity of memory. The *replication* of mental representations *is* the rare limiting case in the vast majority of cultural transmissions. None the less, we shall argue that religious rituals usually evolve toward one or the other of these two attractor positions, and both boost the probabilities of *accurate* memory. Ironically, although the evolution of religious rituals usually involves their transformation across generations in the direction of one or the other of these two attractors in the space of possibilities, it leads them to either of two comparatively stable arrangements in which their subsequent transformations are both less likely and less likely to prove severe. In short, the cognitive analysis we shall offer suggests that one of the main "attractive forces" of these two attractor positions is that each, in its own way, constitutes an arrangement that enhances the probabilities of accurate memory for many features of the cultural representations in question.

Sperber's analyses emphasize the *variability* that arises among cultural representations in the course of their transmission, which, we agree, is surely the predominant pattern. Sperber only alludes indirectly to the wide range of factors that provoke such variability, when he stresses that even comparatively clear communication need not presuppose the replication of mental representations. (See Sperber and Wilson, 1986.) Still, a comprehensive epidemiological approach to the distribution of cultural representations must also explore cognitive factors that can *increase* the probabilities of comparatively more faithful transmission – resulting in greater *stability* among those representations across cycles of transmission.

Cultural transmission, after all, involves at least three processes:
1 the *generation* of representations,
2 the *retention* of those representations, and
3 the *communication* of those representations.
Sperber's work focuses primarily on the third process and emphasizes the challenges it poses to the stability of cultural representations. Fredrik Barth, whose views we shall discuss later in this chapter, draws conclusions about the first process on the basis of his reflections about the second, and, although he highlights the variation among the cultural materials that he studies, finally, he emphasizes the contributions of various social conditions to the stability of cultural representations. We, by contrast, shall look at the second process and, in the next chapter, at one factor affecting the third, emphasizing some considerations that may increase the comparative stability of cultural representations in the course of their transmission. *All* of these projects deserve a place in an epidemiological account of the distributions of cultural representations.

We should emphasize from the outset that we are *not* maintaining that cultural transmission in the contexts we discuss results in the utterly faithful replication of religious rituals from one generation to the next. We are simply calling attention to considerations that may increase the comparative faithfulness of the transmission of religious rituals when they approach either of the two attractor positions. Arriving at an attractor position will typically result in less substantial variation and greater stability among cultural representations. We are only arguing that in the case of religious ritual enhanced mnemonic accuracy is one of the reasons why this just might occur.

We shall explore results from experimental psychology that suggest that, at least under the two sorts of circumstances these two attractor positions represent, memory tends to be not only more accurate than usual but often startlingly so. We suspect that this is not by chance. The two sorts of circumstances towards which religious rituals migrate constitute attractors, because, in part, they embody cognitive dynamics that promote substantially improved mnemonic accuracy. What we will be exploring are precisely the "causal factors that bias micro-transformations" in the evolution of religious rituals in these directions.

Literacy might seem to pose a fundamental challenge to the prominence we accord such psychological considerations. The invention of a system of public representations that encodes language, i.e., the invention of writing and reading, may be the single most important development in human evolution that has influenced the causally salient micro-processes at the psychological level implicated in cultural transmission. All else being equal, the probabilities of both the transmission and the *faithful* transmission of *written* information may seem considerably higher – by virtue of its being written – than are the corresponding transmission probabilities for information which only occurs as mental representations and momentary public representations (such as utterances and ritual performances) or as more lasting public representations of a non-linguistic sort.

Still, even if that is true and even if literacy were widespread, an empirically adequate theory of cultural transmission must address the problems that non-literate cultures pose for at least three reasons. First, although increasingly rare, non-literate cultures still exist (despite the rest of the world's best efforts at eradicating them) and provide some of the data to be explained. Second, many forms of cultural knowledge, including religious knowledge, first arose in non-literate settings. Any satisfactory account of their origins and early evolution, then, must address transmission in such cultural environs. Third, as we shall argue below, these psychological variables shape religious ritual and its transmission *in literate settings as well*. Even where literacy exists its impact does not override that of these psychological factors.

Studying cultural transmission in non-literate settings is interesting for another reason. Cultures that do not possess literacy will help to isolate the most basic psychological variables – whatever they prove to be – impinging on the transmission of cultural knowledge. Non-literate cultures constitute the nearest thing available to (naturally occurring) test cases for theories about the pertinent psychological processes.

Chapter overview

The transmission of cultural knowledge (not just religious knowledge) depends substantially on human memory. Presumably, this is uncontroversial with respect to non-literate cultures. Thus, examination of current memory research and especially research on memory in natural contexts may well contribute to our understanding of cultural transmission. In this chapter we shall examine two sorts of ritual arrangements that correspond to the two attractors we identified above and that seem to abet the accuracy of human memory for actions.

In the next section we briefly examine the first attractor. That attractor focuses on repeated rituals with low levels of sensory pageantry that rely on performance frequency to insure their faithful recollection and transmission. We shall briefly survey psychological research on memory for routines and materials with which we are thoroughly familiar by virtue of frequent exposure or rehearsal. Our treatment is concise, because the effects are uncontroversial. At the end of the section we also develop a brief for taking special interest in secret, infrequently performed, non-repeated religious rituals in small, non-literate cultures.

On pages 56–64 we examine experimental studies pertinent to our second attractor position. There we review some especially suggestive findings from the past decade or so concerning outstanding recall for some extraordinary episodes that occurred outside psychologists' laboratories and independently of any experimentalists' manipulations. The classic illustration is the memories of older Americans for where they were when they heard John Kennedy had been shot. People reliably regard these so-called "flashbulb memories" (Brown and Kulick, 1982) as uncommonly vivid. They also usually reflect uncommon confidence in their accuracy.

Before exploring in the final section the implications of this research for religious ritual systems, we introduce on pages 64–72 the special problems for cultural transmission and memory that the Baktaman system of initiations presents. This case is nearly a perfect illustration of a system that faces the dilemma of relying on human memory for the transmission of cultural knowledge while simultaneously erecting tall barriers to accurate recollection. We devote the remainder of this section to reviewing Fredrik Barth's commentaries on how the Baktaman and other Mountain Ok groups in central New Guinea handle this dilemma.

The final section of the chapter aims to substantiate three claims. The first is that religious rituals in non-literate cultures often approximate the kinds of circumstances and manipulate many of the variables that the experimental literature indicates *do* make for accurate flashbulb memories. In short, some religious rituals seem to migrate to our second attractor position. One way to cut straight to the heart of the argument of this and the next three chapters is to point out that these rituals are *always* special agent rituals, i.e., non-repeated rituals of odd-numbered types.

Our second claim is that emotional arousal can help to enhance the accuracy of our memories for such episodes, but our third is that the mere consolidation of narratives – in the course of what may be numerous "retellings" of "our" stories to others – may not be necessary to explain every naturally occurring case of extraordinarily accurate recall. In the course of this discussion we shall advocate what we call the "cognitive alarm hypothesis."

In the final section we offer a brief meditation on ritual innovation among the Baktaman and an argument that mnemonic accuracy cannot be irrelevant to cultural transmission. We then end with an analytical summary of the materials in this chapter with an eye toward their implications for religious ritual patterns.

We should stress that we regard this consideration of psychological and ethnographic materials as a two-way street. Familiarity with psychological findings concerning human memory will aid our understanding of religious ritual materials; however, the religious ritual materials we examine also provide a unique backdrop for assessing hypotheses about memory that have arisen in experimental psychology. The persistence and continuity of some non-literate, "traditional religions" for hundreds – perhaps even thousands – of years (at least until they faced such destabilizing forces as missionaries, colonialism, industrialization, world wars, and television) should begin to clarify why the study of the transmission of such religious knowledge might prove suggestive for research on memory. Putting this claim even more sharply, the transmission of secret, infrequently performed, non-repeated religious rituals of extensive duration in non-literate societies seems to pose as formidable a challenge for long-term memory as social life is ever likely to present. Understanding that process, therefore, may offer insight into some variables that contribute to effective long-term recall. To put all of this a bit more tendentiously, we are, in effect, suggesting that the religious systems of some of the most isolated, technologically undeveloped cultures in the world have, perhaps for millennia, regularly exploited many important variables that only recently systematic, scientific research has discovered enhance recall.

Frequency effects and memory for cultural materials: psychological findings

The first attractor position we identified above relies overwhelmingly on the frequent performance of rituals to insure their comparatively faithful recollection. A broad range of experimental findings in cognitive psychology indicate that the frequent performance of religious rituals should enhance the probabilities of their subsequent recollection (all other things being equal). Both frequent exposure to rituals and frequent rehearsal and performance of rituals will increase the probabilities that they will be reliably remembered. Although most participants in most religious systems usually only have to *recognize* rituals, a subset of those participants, whom we shall call the "practitioners" of religious rituals (e.g., priests), must meet a more difficult standard. These individuals, who must actually perform the rituals again, must be able not merely to recognize them but to *recall* them as well.

Psychologists have produced a mound of experimental evidence indicating that greater amounts of cognitive processing with particular items will improve memory for those items. Whether through repeated exposure or active rehearsal, "in general, the more processing information receives, the better it is remembered" (Barsalou, 1992, p. 118). Classic experimental papers have documented these effects. Endel Tulving (1962) has shown that the more often subjects are exposed to a stimulus, the better they remember it. Dewey Rundus (1971) has shown that the probability of recall for items increases linearly with the number of times the subject has rehearsed the items earlier.

These are circumstances, tried and true, that religious ritual systems have regularly exploited. High performance frequencies solidify memory for many religious rituals – a critical contributing condition for their persistence as cultural forms. Participants perform some religious rituals repeatedly – sometimes even daily – so that such rituals become as familiar as any other daily routine.

Psychologists construe the cognitive foundations of memory for such actions in terms of *scripts*. Arguably, a ritual is a *prototype* of a scripted action. A script is a cognitive representation for "a predetermined, stereotyped sequence of actions that defines a well-known situation" (Schank and Abelson, 1977, p. 41). The script gives shape to recollections for such actions, since it is "a knowledge structure in long-term memory that specifies the conditions and actions for achieving a goal" (Barsalou, 1992, p. 76). Although participants may be unable to distinguish particular past performances, the attributes those performances share constitute the framework of the thoroughly familiar routine that the script represents. The scripts, rather than representations of individual episodes, are the resulting knowledge structures that inform recollection.

When participants perform rituals routinely, their actions become part of a script. That means, among other things, that they become habitual and automatic. Their memory for carrying out these action sequences is largely procedural (rather than declarative). Participants may have a much richer sense of *how* to proceed than they have for *what* they are doing (Barth, 1975, chapter 25, and Rubin, 1995). Even if participants are largely incapable of formulating this knowledge propositionally about how to proceed, they still know how to do what must be done. Their knowledge is *implicit*. (See Roediger, 1990 and Reber, 1993.)

The relative stability of many religious rituals results, at least in part, from the accurate memory that results from their frequent performance.

Frequently encountered instances of the same form leave less room for distortion in memory. Even if each new performance of a ritual presents an opportunity to introduce variation, when memory for that ritual is robust, new performances may, in fact, tend to forestall variation. That process does not completely explain ritual stability, though, since, in part, it presumes it. At least two other considerations also contribute to the stability of religious rituals.

One of these considerations is the peculiar character of their publicity. Religious rituals regularly require activity that is both collective and co-ordinated. Such coordination presupposes participants' abilities to an-ticipate one another's actions. Since the success of religious rituals often depends upon the cooperation of numerous participants, this imposes constraints on their performance.

A second consideration concerns the special sort of cultural represen-tations associated with religious rituals. Reducing variation is a mark of religious ritual action (Staal, 1979). Typically, (substantial) variation is not tolerated in religious ritual, *because* the relevant CPS-agents forbid it. Many *religious* representations and those concerning CPS-agents, in particular, possess practical and epistemic authority that is renowned for being automatic and overwhelming. If the gods *dictate* actions of a specific form, participants usually comply.

Both the frequency and the stability of many religious rituals facili-tate their retention. What makes for good recollection, though, may not make for good communication. Frequent repetition may produce reliable memory, on the one hand, but, on the other, the frequent repetition of a cultural representation may diminish the attention people give that mate-rial. Familiarity with cultural representations may not breed contempt so much as it eventually just breeds indifference. Harvey Whitehouse (2000) construes such indifference as one mark of what he calls the "tedium effect," which results from doing the same old thing time after time after time. Figure 2.2 exhibits the region within the space of possible ritual arrangements that the tedium effect threatens.

Sperber claims that the constant repetition of cultural representations tends to diminish their cognitive relevance, i.e., their ability to provoke comparatively large numbers of inferences without much cognitive effort. "The repetition of representations having the same tenor may decrease their relevance and bring individuals either to lose interest in them or reinterpret them" (1996, p. 116). He holds that if a frequently repeated cultural representation persists, then our goal should be to explain why it retains its cognitive relevance. Sperber suggests that rituals may retain their relevance because of their effects. Rituals often reorder relationships, resulting in new social arrangements.

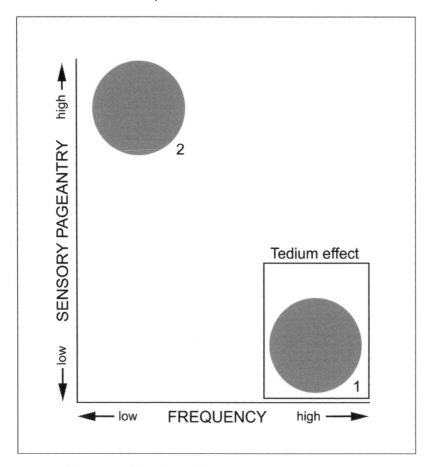

Figure 2.2   The tedium effect

Explicitly connected with an entire constellation of cultural representations (which collectively make up what we have called a "religious
system"), religious rituals as cultural forms are not merely self-
perpetuating. Sacrifices to the ancestors, for example, do not only model
subsequent performances of that ritual. They also invoke a host of *assumptions about the ancestors* (among other things). Performing the sacrifices
increases the probabilities of transmitting each of the associated cultural
representations. Distinguishing between actions and beliefs is perfectly
reasonable, but in cultural evolution these two types of cultural representations often prove intimately intertwined. To the extent that ritual
performances serve as cues for additional religious representations, their

retention is also a prominent catalyst in the propagation of religious systems generally.

As many scholars have contended (e.g., Goody, 1987), however, literacy seems to render most of these concerns about memory for religious materials superfluous, because, for example, literacy enables a religious community to standardize many (though not all!) aspects of rituals and other religious materials in books, manuals, and sacred texts. This largely eliminates any need either for elevated levels of recall or for any other extraordinary devices for reaching a consensus about such matters within a religious community. Various new technologies and institutional forms reliably accompany the development of literacy. Formal education is among the most important. Such cultural arrangements can greatly affect the knowledge a culture possesses and the cognitive styles it fosters (Scribner and Cole, 1981).

Literacy may also change our standards for what counts as satisfactory recall. Ian Hunter (1985) argues that extended verbatim recall for a text of fifty words or more occurs *only* in literate cultures. This claim is not uncontroversial. Whitehouse (personal communication) maintains that evidence exists of more substantial verbatim recall of linguistic materials in non-literate societies than Hunter allows for. (See chapter 3.) Still, most of the time humans are notoriously weak at remembering extended passages word for word without the aid of an independent, authoritative text (or other form of inscription) to guide them.

David Rubin (1995) cautions against imposing unrealistic expectations – grounded on transactions in *literate* cultures – on memory and transmission in oral traditions. He notes that although the singers of epics within existing oral traditions (embedded in larger literate cultures) may claim the ability to sing familiar epics verbatim, even comparisons of multiple performances by the same singer fail to sustain those assertions. Claims to remember cultural materials of any substantial length "word for word" typically depend upon possessing literacy (or tape recorders). Without such aids it is difficult to see how extended cultural performances could be evaluated so exactingly.

The accomplishments of the singers Rubin studied (following Parry, 1971 and Lord, 1991) *are* impressive, though. Through extensive exposure the singers of epics and ballads have developed not only a solid familiarity with the contents of specific pieces but a tacit mastery of their respective genres' constraints as well. Rubin shows how multiple constraints on the forms of such materials render them quite regular on many fronts and jointly impose substantial restrictions on the range of viable variation. Considerable minor variation in representations can arise without violating participants' perceptions that they are dealing with yet another token of the same cultural type. It is a combination of *current values and perceived variation*, as much as actual variation, that matters. The critical issue is not just whether representations have, in fact, undergone change, but also whether participants notice that change and whether those changes matter to them. The relevant community may acknowledge a wide range of versions as tokens of the same type. (If particular rituals are types, then particular performances of those rituals are tokens of those types.)

Although the various constraints each genre imposes on its materials restrict their modification, by no means do they rule it out altogether. Thus, Rubin's discussion provides many of the critical details that stand behind Sperber's general claim that: "In an oral tradition, all cultural representations are easily remembered ones; hard-to-remember representations are forgotten, or transformed into more easily remembered ones, before reaching a cultural level of distribution" (1996, p. 74).

Our conceptions of both the conditions of transmission and the resulting processes of recall should not rely upon the model of these processes exhibited in parlor games. There the model has been to restrict the transfer of some piece of information "from one person to the next with no individual seeing more than one version ... In oral traditions, it would be unusual for this pattern to occur. Many versions of the same piece are heard, often from different people" (Rubin, 1995, p. 133). The interpersonal connections, according to Rubin, are multifarious – like those between the nodes in a net rather than like the sequential links in a chain. Frequently, participants have multiple experiences with (what they regard as) the same cultural materials. Nor are performers typically restricted to a single performance.

Often multiple versions of some cultural product circulate, all of which fall within the scope of admissible variation. *Communities* of participants collectively uphold these practices. They sanction instruction, consultation, rehearsal, and performance as well as tacit negotiation of the range of acceptable variants. These practices of the engaged community are at least as responsible for the retention and transmission of such materials as any prodigious mnemonic accomplishments of individual cultural experts. (We shall return to these issues in the final section.)

Rubin's study concentrates on oral traditions embedded within literate cultures (e.g., ballad singing in North Carolina). He holds that these oral traditions seem to enjoy lives of their own, comparatively insulated from the impact of literacy on both the practitioners and the larger culture.[7] This insulation bears on production. For example, Rubin (1995, pp. 282–284) reports that when asked to compose a new ballad about a train wreck, three of eight North Carolina ballad singers commenced singing their compositions *immediately* after reading the newspaper account of the incident. This insulation also bears on the assessment of performances. Although, when tested from six to twelve months later, these singers showed recognition memory well above chance for their own stanzas, not one could recall even a single stanza from the ballad he had composed. The point is that such limitations in no way impugn these subjects' status as expert ballad singers. The cultural systems undergirding such practices enlist social and cognitive dynamics that largely operate independently of the influences of literacy.

A useful strategy both for glimpsing these forces in isolation and for learning what other cognitive devices assist in the propagation of religious systems is to study the transmission of such materials in the absence of literacy and any other cognitive prostheses involving symbolic codes. This is to study the transmission of religious systems in settings that more closely approximate the emergence of such systems in prehistory.

Rubin is less helpful here. His comments about the connections between literacy and religion reflect the prevailing biases of most contemporary scholarship on that topic, inadvertently favoring the few (text-based) "world religions" over the thousands of religious systems that have existed in completely non-literate settings in human history. Rubin suggests (1995, p. 320) that it is quite difficult to imagine "religion without writing," yet religion as a cultural form predates the invention of writing and to this day some religious systems prevail exclusively in non-literate cultures. (See Donald, 1991, Lawson and McCauley, 1993, Mithen, 1996, and McCauley, 2000.) How do small communities of non-literate hunter-gatherers or practitioners of primitive forms of agriculture without sophisticated technology or permanent settlements remember and transmit religious rituals that are lengthy and elaborate?

That question's import is especially striking once we contemplate that under such conditions life is often notoriously nasty, brutish, and short. The first two adjectives may no longer be politically correct, but the third is uncontroversial. The evidence about peoples at the dawn of human history as well as about traditional societies even in the twentieth century indicates that average life spans are very short. Barth, for example, notes (1975, pp. 25 and 270–273) that the Baktaman of New Guinea are "essentially limited to two living generations." (In 1968 only six of eighty-two persons below puberty had a living grandparent, and thirty-nine had lost one or both parents.) Such societies do not have the benefit of a large cohort of elderly cultural experts. Barth (1975, p. 260) reports that another Mountain Ok group, the Augobmin, lost all of the members of their most senior generation in a very short time and, consequently, lost the final three stages of male initiation in their religious system as well. The fragility of cultural knowledge in these settings is palpable. (See too Barth, 1987, p. 48.)

In such circumstances the frequent performance of rituals will usually suffice to insure accurate memory for the rites in question. The first attractor involves repeated rituals with high performance frequencies and comparatively low levels of sensory pageantry. Participants develop scripts for these rituals. Scripts can specify an extensive series of connected actions. Once they possess such scripts, participants usually perform these sequences of actions automatically, without much conscious reflection. Although their repeated performances may not be perfect copies, participants' retention levels are often quite remarkable, even by the standards of technologically sophisticated, literate cultures. Transmitting these rituals seems to rely on little else.

Still, frequency effects cannot explain participants' memories for *all* religious rituals, because some occur quite rarely either in the life of the community or, at least, in the lives of individual participants. The classic rites of passage are the most obvious examples of the latter sort (though they are not the only ones). Most religious systems initiate individual participants only once, hence these rites of passage are examples of (odd-numbered) "non-repeated" (special agent) rituals. Still, in many religious systems participants can *observe* such non-repeated rituals even when they are not directly involved in them themselves. So, frequency may influence memory for these rituals too, at least when they are publicly accessible. In some religious systems, though, three further circumstances – either separately or in combination – pose additional barriers to explaining recollection for all such rituals exclusively on the basis of frequency.

First, in many religious systems these rituals are *not* widely accessible. In these systems most participants experience these rituals only once, viz., on the one occasion when they go through them themselves. Second, often not only is each participant's experience private, but demands for *secrecy* discourage after-the-fact disclosures. Many religious systems surround all or parts of these non-repeated rituals in secrecy. Third, in some religious systems all of the members of some group (usually an age cohort) undergo such rituals at the same time. Depending upon the range of ages included, this can make for *extremely infrequent performance* of these rituals (so that their accessibility hardly matters). Barth (1975, p. 45) estimates, for example, that approximately ten years on average separates successive performances of any of the various degrees of male initiation among the Baktaman.

How are these special agent rituals, at least some of which are quite rarely performed and shrouded in secrecy, retained and transmitted – especially in non-literate societies? These are rituals that are guaranteed to cluster around our second attractor position.

Flashbulb memory and enhanced recall for actions

Other areas of memory research will help account for the transmission of non-repeated special agent rituals performed either infrequently or secretly or both (especially in the preliterate past or in contemporary non-literate cultures). The critical criteria for relevant studies will be minimal reliance on frequency effects, no reliance on literacy, and evidence of comparatively impressive long-term recall for actions, especially, but for persons and places as well. (It is hard to imagine a theory of *ritual* in which persons and their actions are not the pivotal analytical considerations.)

The following discussion explores some recent investigations of so-called "flashbulb memory," ending with a summary and short discussion of the extraordinary findings recently reported by Ulric Neisser and his colleagues. What is of interest about that study are the variables that seem to make for virtually ceiling-level effects – concerning accuracy and confidence in particular – for subjects' recall for actions, settings, and persons. "Ceiling-level effects" are results in which subjects' performances meet the very highest standards tested. After a year and a half *all* of the subjects in this landmark study (Neisser et al., 1996) had *completely accurate* memories for the events in question. Moreover, they *knew* that they did.

Flashbulb memory

Prototypical flashbulb memories concern our recall for the *circumstances* in which we learned of some significant event that, usually, was unexpected[8] – rather than our recall for that event itself, which we may *not* have experienced *even indirectly* (by way of some electronic medium) (Colegrove, 1899/1982). For example, few Americans born before 1935 are unclear about the circumstances in which they heard that Pearl Harbor had been bombed. Similarly, along with the next generation, they can usually recite with confidence how they heard about President Kennedy's assassination. These experiences are what Steen Larsen (1988) called "reception events," which concern how we learned of the personally or socially significant event in question. Since most people are not present and do not experience these momentous events directly, their flashbulb memory is not for the focal event but rather for how they found out about that event. Their flashbulb memory is for the details of the typically commonplace circumstances under which they learned about the extraordinary event rather than for the details of the extraordinary event itself.

This is not to say that many people do not have comparably impressive recall for details about the focal event too. Many Americans born before 1955 know that Mrs. Kennedy wore a pink suit on the day of the assassination and that she appeared to begin to crawl out of the back of the convertible moments after her husband was shot. The difference, though, is that many Americans born *after* 1955 know those details too, whereas they have no special recollection at all for how they heard about the assassination, since they acquired that information as items of general knowledge. Of course, this distinction between memory of the extraordinary event itself and memory for the associated reception event is less neat in the age of television in which large portions of the population are able to view some of the culturally significant events in question *indirectly*. Tens of thousands of Americans, for example, were not told that Lee Harvey Oswald had been shot. They saw it on television as it was happening. Recent research has revealed interference effects of television viewing in putative flashbulb memories (Neisser and Harsch, 1992).

Roger Brown and James Kulik, who first proposed the flashbulb metaphor, characterize these memories as ones in which "almost everyone testifies that his recall of his circumstances is not an inference from a regular routine. It has a primary, 'live' quality that is almost perceptual. Indeed, it is very like a photograph that indiscriminately preserves the scene in which each of us found himself . . ." (1982, p. 24). Since flashbulb memories usually concern recollections connected with events that are isolated, unexpected, and arousing, they seem to arise independently of "such well-established determinants of memory as primacy or recency or repetition" (Brown and Kulik, 1982, p. 25). Brown and Kulik speculate that a special neural mechanism may automatically register all available information connected with the context when learning suddenly of a "significant novelty" that is emotionally arousing. They refer to it as the "Now Print" mechanism (following Livingston, 1967a and 1967b).

Brown and Kulik note that the flashbulb metaphor variously suggests brevity, surprise, and indiscriminate illumination (of the circumstances at learning). On the face of it, the first two suggestions seem to make sense. It does not take much time to deliver the vital details about the focal events, and, all things being equal, brief episodes seem easier to remember than longer ones. Prolonged episodes not only introduce more material, but almost inevitably more material becomes more complex material as well.

Similarly, surprise seems no surprise. In his study of Swedes' memories for how they heard about the assassination of Olof Palme, Sven-Åke
Christianson (1989) found that his subjects' initial assessments of how
surprising they found the news proved a significant variable in predicting their overall recall a year later. Surprise, however, does not appear to
be a necessary condition for flashbulb memories. Eugene Winograd and
William Killinger (1983) found that many subjects had flashbulb memories for their reception events for the death of a close relative after an
extended illness, which, however emotionally charged, was, ultimately,
not very surprising – at least not by the time it occurred.

As to the third of those suggestions, even Brown and Kulik emphasize
that the illumination is not *altogether* indiscriminate. Some details surrounding such reception events seem to stand out while others seem less
memorable. The former include such details as our actions (and what
was going on generally) just before learning the news, the place where we
learned it, and at least some of the persons present and what they were
doing. (Not coincidentally, these seem important items when thinking
about memory for rituals.) The less memorable details include that indefinitely large class of apparently peripheral matters such as which pair
of shoes we were wearing or what was hanging on the walls or the color of
the car in front of us. This is broadly consistent with the Easterbrook
hypothesis, which holds that all forms of arousal tend to narrow the
scope of our attention. Narrowing of attention inevitably results in subjects according considerable prominence to some details while completely
neglecting others (Heuer and Reisberg, 1997).

In Christianson's study (1989) of memories for learning of the Palme
assassination, subjects recalled central details of their reception events
reasonably well after one year. Their recall proved much poorer, though,
for a wide range of peripheral information. Christianson holds that what
his subjects have remembered is the standard components or gist of a narrative account of the reception event. Following Neisser's (1982, p. 47)
earlier proposal that narrative structure "does more than explain the cano-
nical form of flashbulb memories; it accounts for their very existence,"
Christianson also suggests that the rehearsal and conventions associated
with the formation of stable narratives – rather than any special neural
mechanisms – are primarily responsible for the form of flashbulb memories, for the consistency of subjects' reports over time, and, therefore, for
a good deal of their (apparent) accuracy as well.

Christianson's study does not provide compelling evidence about accuracy, though, because he did not collect his initial data until six weeks
after Palme was killed. It seems reasonable to suppose that those six weeks
provided ample time for subjects to have told their stories repeatedly

and, in the process, to have consolidated their narratives according to the conventions to which Christianson, Neisser, and others have pointed. (Rubin [1992] suggests that what we are calling "narrative consolidation" may occur in as little time as a week.) The accuracy of Christianson's sub-jects about the gists of their narratives one year later may have resulted from nothing more than their simply telling an already familiar story with an utterly conventional form one more time rather than accurately recall-ing their reception event for the Palme assassination. The fact that most of Christianson's subjects told the same general stories approximately fifty-eight weeks after this event as they told six weeks after it is interest-ing, but it does not show that those initial six-week-old stories were, in fact, accurate accounts of how they learned that Olof Palme had been assassinated.

Comparatively speaking, though, Christianson's study is exemplary on this front. The salient problem with most studies of flashbulb memory (including Brown and Kulik's) until the last decade has been the failure of researchers to determine the accuracy of their subjects' responses. In light of both the detail and the profound vividness and confidence regularly associated with flashbulb memories, this concern might seem needlessly scrupulous. But various studies of eyewitness memory have indicated that neither subjects' confidence about their recollections nor their precision reliably predicts their accuracy (Wells and Murray, 1984). The critical questions for now are, first, whether flashbulb memories are accurate and, second, whether similar dissociations between confidence and accuracy can arise even for flashbulb memories.

Questions of accuracy

Neisser (1982, p. 45) supplied a personal anecdote that suggested that flashbulb memories are not always accurate. He had recalled that he heard of the bombing at Pearl Harbor while he was listening to a baseball game on the radio. (The problem, of course, is that baseball games are not broadcast in December.[9]) It was the explosion of the space shuttle *Challenger*, though, that gave Neisser and Nicole Harsch an opportunity to ascertain experimentally whether such anecdotes were rare exceptions or genuine indicators that our confidence in such memories may often be unfounded.

Within twenty-four hours of the *Challenger* accident Neisser and Harsch (1992) obtained reports from subjects about the circumstances under which they learned of the explosion. They then tested subjects' recall two-and-a-half years later and then again about six months after that. (On neither of these two occasions did subjects know in advance that they would be asked to recall this material.) Their findings when they tested the memories of their subjects after two-and-a-half years were intriguing. Most important, many of Neisser and Harsch's confident subjects, who otherwise gave every evidence of possessing an accurate flashbulb memory in this situation, were *completely wrong* in their recollections about all of the tested items from their initial report. This group included three of their thirteen maximally confident subjects, who – with respect to the relative accuracy of their responses – said that they were "absolutely certain." The visual vividness of subjects' recollections predicted their accuracy no more reliably than their levels of confidence did. Although some subjects reported highly vivid, visual imagery associated with their memories, they too were, sometimes, completely wrong.

Neisser and Harsch were so surprised by these findings that (as noted above) they decided to interview their subjects again approximately six months later, i.e., roughly three years after the explosion of the *Challenger*. They wanted to see if, among other things, their first test or the intervening six months affected subjects' recollections and to discover what cues, if any, might suffice to aid the recall of those confident subjects who were, in fact, mistaken about the accuracy of their memories.

Neisser and Harsch suggest that each of their tests of their subjects (at two-and-a-half years and at three years, respectively) generated a finding that impugns "the simplest form of the emotional strengthening hypothesis" (1992, p. 30). The first finding (from their tests at two-and-a-half years) was the absence of any significant connections between emotion and recall. Although the initial questionnaire did not ask for precise measures of subjects' emotional states, it had elicited detailed statements about subjects' emotions. No coding scheme that Neisser and Harsch devised for subjects' responses yielded any grounds for regarding emotion as a predictor of subjects' accuracy. The second and even more telling finding in the interviews six months later was that, of the subjects who were mistaken, all traces of their original memories, which they had recorded the day after the *Challenger* exploded, "seemed to have disappeared entirely" (1992, p. 30). Neisser and Harsch could find *no* cues that could elicit the correct memories in their subjects. They even let subjects peruse their original written responses to the questionnaires! Apparently, a couple of these subjects were *so* confident about the accuracy of their current (inaccurate) "recollections" that, in order to discredit their responses to the initial questionnaire, they argued that people sometimes misreport events at first!

Besides appearing to raise problems for theories of flashbulb memory that look to emotional arousal as a decisive variable, Neisser and Harsch's findings also offer some support for Neisser's earlier conjectures about the central role of constructing a narrative. Although many of their subjects seemed utterly incapable of accurately recalling their original accounts of the events in question, the stories subjects told at two-and-a-half years did prove strikingly consistent with the stories they gave in their interviews six months later.

Neisser and Harsch's study provides abundant evidence for the fallibility of at least some flashbulb memories.[10] Many of their subjects totally missed the mark yet claimed to be highly confident about the accuracy of vivid memories concerning their reception of what at least some of them took to be emotionally stimulating news about a socially significant event. Understandably impressed by these findings, Neisser and Harsch conclude that "[f]lashbulb memories . . . may be appreciably less reliable than other cases of vivid and confident recall" (1992, p. 30).

This conclusion is undoubtedly true about *some* of their subjects' flashbulb memories but not about all of them. Some of Neisser and Harsch's subjects, who were also "absolutely certain" about the accuracy of their recollections, had every right to be so confident, since they accurately recalled all of the items on which they were tested. To the extent this study could measure it, their flashbulb memories proved completely accurate. The question remained, though, whether some events can produce accurate flashbulb memories *across an entire population* in the way that John Kennedy's assassination is popularly thought to have done. Neisser and his colleagues found evidence that the 1989 Loma Prieta earthquake did for those who experienced it.

Neisser and colleagues (1996) in both Georgia and California studied subjects' memories concerning the 1989 Loma Prieta earthquake. This was a study of memory for *reception events* for the subjects in Georgia; however, for the Californians, the study, in part, concerned memory for an event that subjects had *experienced* first-hand. Subjects in this experiment filled out questionnaires from as little as twenty-four hours to as much as three weeks after the quake (because of logistical difficulties).

The experimenters tested subjects approximately eighteen months later, focusing in particular on three items for which they had data that apply to both direct experiences and reception events, viz., place, others present, and activity just before the target event. The experimenters compared Californians' memories of their experiences during the earthquake both with their memories for how they learned about the collapse of the Oakland Bay Bridge and with Georgians' memories of how they learned about the earthquake. The Georgians' memories proved least accurate. The Californians' memories for their experiences were most accurate, and the Californians' memories for how they heard about the Bay Bridge were in between. All of the differences were significant.

The crucial finding in this study, though, concerns the *character* of the Californians' memories for their *first-hand experiences* of the earthquake. The accuracy of their responses for the three target items as well as their confidence in that accuracy were at the highest possible levels. *None* of the Californians made the substantial errors that some subjects made about their reception events in the *Challenger* study or that some of the Georgians made in this study. Moreover, *all* of the Californians were quite confident that they had not made such errors. The study seems to demonstrate that some events *can* produce both startlingly accurate memories for actions, settings, and persons and justifiably confident assessments of their accuracy by those doing the remembering.

Neisser et al. (1996, p. 340) emphasize one obvious difference between the ceiling-level accuracy of the Californians' memories in this study and the mixed results concerning the accuracy of subjects' memories in other experiments on flashbulb memory. The Californians were recalling not a reception event but an event that they themselves had *experienced*. Not only were these memories more accurate than the Georgians' memories of their reception events, but they were even more accurate than the Californians' (overwhelmingly accurate) memories of their own reception events concerning the news of the Bay Bridge. "Being personally involved in an event is evidently more memorable than just hearing the news of one" (p. 346). Directly experiencing an isolated and unexpected event of significance seems to confer substantial mnemonic advantages over just receiving news of one. All else being equal, *"participants"* in such events are significantly more likely to remember accurately and to be confident about that accuracy than mere "observers" are.

Neisser et al. (1996, p. 338) note that "most life events and experiences involve 'participation'"; however, it is not so clear that most of the events (viz., reception events) that generate flashbulb memories (even the inaccurate ones) are ones that involve the participation of the rememberer. So, Neisser et al. (1996, p. 338) then ask "[w]hat was so special about participating in an earthquake?" Presumably, it is *participation in momentous events*, not earthquakes per se, that is special. Earthquakes typically earn this designation by virtue of their comparative calamitousness. This, however, is something most people only learn about after the fact. Most of the subjects who experienced the Loma Prieta earthquake were neither profoundly concerned about their own safety at the time nor immediately aware of its headline-grabbing destructiveness. This suggests that the subjects' spectacular memory performance did not turn on any special Now Print mechanism. Thus, Neisser et al. (1996) opt for the processes underlying narrative consolidation as the pivotal variables influencing subjects' enhanced memory here, though they remain uncommitted about the most salient aspect of that process. They point out that it could be the simple process of shaping our own *distinctive* story about how we were involved in this significant event. On the other hand, it could be the result of *rehearsal*, since these are precisely the sorts of stories we tend to share repeatedly. (Even Brown and Kulik found a high positive correlation between subjects' ratings of an event's "consequentiality" and their reports of rehearsals – see Brewer, 1992, pp. 281–282.) Or it could be both.

The one thing that Neisser and his colleagues stress is that emotional arousal did not seem to play any special role. They provide at least two reasons. First, most of their California subjects did not report great arousal at the moment they felt the quake. Earthquakes are common in California, and most of the subjects did not perceive any imminent danger to themselves. Second, the California subjects' various reports of their emotional arousal (during and immediately after the quake and upon learning about the Bay Bridge) did *not* correlate with the accuracy of their memories.

That the processes undergirding the consolidation of narratives rather than emotional arousal are the principal variables funding the California subjects' extraordinary performance makes sense.[11] As Neisser et al. (1996, pp. 348 and 352) emphasize, most of their subjects did not find the experience of the earthquake itself greatly arousing. Experiencing a non-arousing event would not seem to contribute to extraordinary recall. Moreover, the news of the earthquake's more serious effects accumulated bit by bit over a few hours (at least). Again, *by the subjects' own reports*, no single consequence (not even learning the news about the Bay Bridge) produced startling arousal levels. (The means of the two California groups' ratings of their level of affect upon learning of the Bay Bridge collapse were 5.28 and 5.29 on a 7-point scale.) Presumably, it would be learning of the earthquake's momentous consequences (concerning the Nimitz freeway, the Bay Bridge, the damage throughout the region, etc.) that would convince people of its significance and, thus, provide an incentive for subjects to remember where they were at the time and to share that information with others as *participants* in this culturally significant event. Gradually coming to realize – probably over many hours for most subjects – that they were participating in a (literally) earth-shattering event surely does produce a "benchmark" in subjects' life stories – as Neisser (1982) maintained – even if it does not produce any specific moments of exceptional emotional arousal.

A hypothesis that looks to the processes behind narrative consolidation does make better sense of the earthquake findings than does any hypothesis that focuses primarily, let alone exclusively, on emotional arousal. In light of other studies, though, it is not clear that a narrative consolidation hypothesis alone will suffice to explain all examples of accurate flashbulb memories. After all, in Christianson's study (1989) recall one year later for what were, presumably, *well*-consolidated, six-week-old narratives did *not* yield the sorts of ceiling-level effects for accuracy that the Loma Prieta earthquake produced (whether the original six-week-old narratives were themselves accurate or not). (See Neisser et al., 1996, p. 340.) Still, if the critical variable underlying narrative consolidation is rehearsal, perhaps destructive earthquakes in California simply provoke significantly more retellings (or rethinkings), at least among the public, than assassinations in Sweden (or explosions of manned spacecraft in the USA) do. This, of course, is a matter about which these various studies provide little useful evidence. (See Neisser et al., 1996, p. 354.)

Neisser and his colleagues (1996, p. 352) are clear that their findings do not thwart all emotional arousal theories of flashbulb memory. Because so few of their subjects' initial experiences of the earthquake proved emotionally arousing, their data only bear on the very strong versions of such a theory that maintain that substantial and immediate emotional arousal is a necessary condition for accurate flashbulb memories. The possibility remains, of course, that either substantial levels of emotional arousal or simply elevated levels of emotional arousal for an extended period of time in conjunction with other variables (such as subjects' direct participation in what they take to be a momentous event) may still play an important role in flashbulb experiences that yield comparatively accurate memories. Before we explore this possibility in the final section of this chapter, however, we will, in the next section, examine a proposal from cultural anthropology that addresses the transmission of religious ritual under circumstances that profoundly challenge the capacities of human memory.

Social constraints on the generation of cultural representations

One of the few anthropologists who has paid careful attention to the role of memory in his research on cultural transmission is Fredrik Barth in his classic study (1975) of the ritual and knowledge of the Baktaman of central New Guinea. We shall argue in the next section that the seven degrees of Baktaman male initiation demonstrate how performances of religious rituals exploit many of the variables that experimental psychologists have shown make for more accurate memories of specific episodes.[12] Before we pursue that line of argument, though, we shall first examine

Barth's own discussion of the transmission of ritual materials among the Baktaman.

The fragility of knowledge among the Mountain Ok: analogic coding

The Baktaman are one of many Mountain Ok groups who reside in the central highlands of New Guinea. They numbered 183 (with six deaths and three births) at the time of Barth's fieldwork in 1968. (Barth returned to the region for three months in 1981–1982.) All of the evidence indicates that prior to 1968 the Baktaman had only two fleeting contacts, in 1927 and 1964, with anyone outside related Ok groups occupying the lands within a few dozen miles or so of their own territory. Barth describes the Baktaman as "persons entirely unacquainted with Man in any other form than themselves" (1975, p. 6).

Prior to "colonial pacification" in 1964, relations among these Ok groups were rocky. Although these groups are close enough to intermarry, to recognize clan relations across groups, and to invite one another to observe religious rituals, suspicions of sorcery and comparable offenses led to frequent wars and raids. Barth's research indicates that one-third of Baktaman deaths over the previous two decades had resulted from such violence.

The system of male initiation among the Baktaman fulfills all of the conditions for an ideal test case outlined on pages 55–56 above. In addition, this system introduces a few additional barriers to ready transmission that we have not yet discussed. The Baktaman are a *small, nonliterate, isolated* group of hunters and subsistence farmers. They move within their region every few years as their gardens exhaust the nearby land. Males go through seven degrees of (non-repeated) initiation in their lives. (A cohort of men – most of whom were in their thirties – had yet to undergo the seventh degree initiation when Barth arrived.) Because entire age cohorts undergo these rituals together, they occur quite *infrequently* – approximately once every ten years.

All Ok have additional opportunities to observe what are, at least, roughly comparable initiations among their neighbors. Barth estimates that seniors have four or five such opportunities between performances in their own group. This is roughly once every two to two-and-a-half years (Barth, 1987, p. 25). However, since the number of neighboring groups is small, since unhappy relations sometimes preclude invitations, since the invitations involve only parts of the performances, since these other groups perform these rites no more frequently than the Baktaman do, and since other groups' rites differ from those of the Baktaman on various fronts, these opportunities are less valuable aids to memory than they might initially appear. In addition, Barth reports that at least once within memory the resulting visit from such an invitation provided the hosts with an opportunity to ambush and slaughter their guests! With such possibilities in mind, observers might be somewhat distracted.

The rituals are *long*, ranging from a few days to a few weeks. Perhaps posing another barrier to easy recollection, earlier initiation rituals in the series are sometimes *deceptive*. Later rituals often reveal how earlier rituals were misleading on one point or another. On at least one count, the deception is double layered (across three degrees of initiation).

All of the rituals include parts kept *secret* from non-initiates, i.e., from females and junior males.[13] Baktaman expectations about secrecy are extraordinary. Senior males threaten initiates with death if they violate ritual secrecy. Not only are initiates prohibited from discussing these secrets with non-initiates; most of the time they are also prohibited from discussing them among themselves. Incredibly, they even seem to exhibit "a wariness and vagueness in *thinking* about them" (1975, p. 221). As far as Barth could tell, initiates respected the prohibitions on overt behaviors, at least. (One cult leader was so concerned with secrecy that he hid his clan's sacred relics in the forest, and when he died unexpectedly, these articles were lost.)

Barth maintains that secrecy is inimical to ready transmission of the religious system's symbols in another way. The impact of these demands for secrecy is so substantial that it undermines any hope of forging widespread logical coherence among Baktaman beliefs. Barth argues at length that what he calls "analogic coding" grounds whatever order inheres in the cultural knowledge of the Baktaman (1975, pp. 207–231). "The medium is one of metaphor, as in the manipulation of sacred concrete objects and ritual acts to generate statements about fertility, dependence, etc." (Barth, 1987, p. 75).

What exactly is analogic coding? First of all, it is *not* what Barth refers to as "digital coding." Presumably, digital coding is where non-linguistic public representations are organized into systems manifesting properties something like a genuine code, with rules of correspondence and *univocal* connections between items. The Baktaman rites do exhibit some compositional relations, since the Baktaman reuse a few symbolic objects and activities as components in larger symbolic configurations. However, whatever productivity they exhibit is not based on any systematicity[14] nor on any "logical closure" nor on some "limited set of alternatives" (Barth, 1975, p. 208; also see p. 229). Each setting in which the Baktaman reuse a ritual object involves what are otherwise undisclosed symbolic nuances. But as often as not they invite largely new interpretations that introduce new values for various cultural items: "the sacred symbols of the Mountain Ok are not only multivocal, but also deeply multivalent" (Barth, 1987, p. 76).

Each symbol turns on "a very simple non-verbal metaphor sketchily exploited" yielding "complex harmonies." Barth (1987, p. 68) states that these non-verbal metaphors "somehow 'feel' compelling and right, but they are based on fortuitous analogies." Apparently, the underlying "metaphors" are "non-verbal," because the symbols are non-linguistic concrete objects (i.e., lasting, non-linguistic, public representations) and because the Baktaman are either unwilling to articulate these symbolic relations or incapable of doing so or both.[15]

Barth explicates these metaphors and idioms in terms of general resonances among the concrete symbols that figure in Baktaman myth and ritual from one symbolic context to the next. He identifies broad *themes*[16] – relations with the ancestors, fertility, security and welfare, etc. – with which various concrete symbols are associated in particular Baktaman rites. He maintains that it is these underlying thematic connections among concrete symbols across different contexts that constitute the knowledge Baktaman initiations present. He states "it is the themes of the rituals, not their sources of metaphor, that are explicated and ordered in the rites" (1975, p. 211).

Barth (1987, p. 76) suggests that participants in such a tradition possess this core knowledge *intuitively*. The anthropologist cannot reduce such knowledge to unambiguous propositional form, but this does not entail that either its contents or its effects are utterly random. "I am pleading for the recognition of positive achievements deriving from the potentialities of particular communicative forms . . . The medium in which the knowledge is cast allows other and rich forms of understanding, and directs its practitioners in large part to use them" (Barth, 1987, p. 76). Barth is fairly clear about those other forms of understanding analogic coding facilitates. He states (1987, p. 79) that these initiations transform "a group of young persons into men" who possess "a general area of common sensibilities and intuitions" and "a range of understandings sufficient so its members can be moved by the same symbols and thoughts." The initiations instill in the initiate distinctive cognitive dispositions and sensibilities concerning self, cohort, society, and Nature.

Barth (1975, p. 229) insists that "an analogic code must . . . be understood in the context of its praxis," noting that secrecy and the complete absence of exegesis and texts are the pivotal features of Baktaman praxis that have shaped this code's form and the transmission of Baktaman culture. He underscores that the Baktaman not only have no writing, in 1968 they did not even seem aware of its possibility. The tools the Baktaman have invented for retaining knowledge are meager.

The total corpus of Baktaman knowledge is stored in 183 Baktaman minds, aided only by a modest assemblage of cryptic concrete symbols (the meanings of which depend on the associations built up around them in the consciousness of a few seniors) and by limited, suspicious communication with the members of a few surrounding communities. (1975, p. 255)

The inevitable vagueness surrounding the use of symbols in such an analogic code requires that an analysis of transmission highlights neither "the sayable" nor "[the] said" but only what is "received," "reactivated," and "constantly re-created," i.e., those metaphors and idioms that "catch on and are re-used" (Barth, 1975, p. 229). This process is not utterly unconstrained, though. Barth apparently holds that these metaphors and idioms manifest enough stability and involve enough precision to justify talk of "those who know the code" (1987, p. 21).

To explain the persistence of these metaphors and idioms that Baktaman males confront for the first time in their initiations, Barth appeals to frequency effects. He argues that "the . . . corpus of Baktaman knowledge . . . will only persist to the extent that its parts are *frequently* re-created as messages and thereby transmitted" (1975, p. 255, emphasis added; also see p. 101). It is through "the repetition of the knowledge they [i.e., the initiations] contain in numerous other temple performances that men become adepts in handling the sacred symbols" (1975, p. 258). Baktaman men regularly encounter these symbols by participating in their routine *repeated* (special patient and special instrument) rituals. There those multivocal concrete symbols reintroduce – though none too precisely – the general themes that underlie the analogic code and that stand at the center of those infrequently performed *non-repeated* (special agent) initiations. The preservation of these metaphors and idioms by which Baktaman knowledge is communicated turns primarily on their employment in repeated communications (however vague) about the themes underlying Baktaman ritual praxis. Indeed, these metaphors and idioms in large part *constitute* Baktaman knowledge. (See Barth, 1975, p. 229 and 1987, p. 76.)

We should, however, emphasize two things about Barth's appeals to frequency effects:

1 they do *not* concern the *initiations'* performance frequencies but the frequency with which Baktaman men confront – in their repeated rituals – many of the symbolic materials those non-repeated initiations feature, and

2 both Barth and his informants (1987, pp. 26–27) deny that any cues
or constraints, which the frequently confronted metaphors and idioms
occasion, suffice to account for the similarities between two consecutive
performances of initiations within any community.

Barth explicitly concedes that the Ok do *not infer* the forms and details of
their initiations from their knowledge of either the persisting metaphors
and idioms, the sacred, concrete symbols, the repeated rituals in which
they are deployed, or the underlying themes they address. Barth describes Baktaman ritual knowledge as "constantly communicated about,"
for example, in the repeated rituals, "yet poorly shared and precariously
transmitted" presumably because of the inevitable vagueness associated
with analogic coding and because of the long delays separating consecutive performances of each initiation (1975, p. 222).

Barth and his informants agree that it is the attempts by the seniors
responsible for staging these initiations to *recall* past performances that
are the primary influence on the shape of the next one (1987, p. 26). In
Cosmologies in the Making (1987), Barth concentrates specifically on this
process of recall and transmission of cultural knowledge in the various
Ok groups, including the Baktaman.

Although he characterizes his specific approach as "generative" there,
his project also fits into a more general framework, which Barth endorses,
that can also be fairly described as "epidemiological." Barth (1987,
pp. 83–84) finds the factors responsible for producing *divergences* in
individuals' experiences and thoughts far more interesting than depicting
"collective representations" (about which Barth expresses skepticism).
He (1987, p. 28) too insists that "every person's mind is full of representations of cultural objects, which are handled by mental processes and in
due course give shape to the person's acts." For Barth, like Sperber, the
principal task is to delineate the causal variables that shape the distributions of cultural representations. He states:

My focus is on...this aggregate tradition of knowledge: the (variety of) ideas
it contains, and how they are expressed; the pattern of their distribution, within
communities and between communities; the processes of (re)production...and
how they may explain its content and pattern of distribution; thus, the processes
of *creativity*, transmission, and change. (1987, p. 1, emphasis added; see too p. 74)

Barth's project is *generative* in orientation, because he focuses on the
creative processes that underwrite these (re)productions of cultural materials and the forces that constrain them. Although recall may inform it,
the overall process in question is just as much one of *producing* an initiation as it is one of *re*producing a copy of an earlier performance of that
initiation again.

Barth argues that the first step in pursuing such inquiries is to carry out the comparative study of variation. Such comparative inquiry will supply materials for hypotheses both about the interconnections between various cultural forms and about their implications for "systematic covariation in varying contexts" (1987, p. 11). These hypotheses should arise, so to speak, from the bottom up. Barth warns against premature attempts to establish correlations across cultures, since this will – at a much-too-early stage in these inquiries – forestall researchers' efforts to develop better informed hypotheses. Barth holds that the pursuit of such hypotheses should arise well along in the process of describing the cultures in question and that the formation and assessment of those hypotheses should only occur while attending to the distinctive praxis and context of each culture.

Social influences on the (re)production of Ok rituals

Barth (1987, p. 84) advocates the study of "a living tradition of knowledge – not . . . a set of abstract ideas enshrined in collective representations." Thus, he aims to discover "*within* a tradition of knowledge, the patterns of variation and thereby the underlying *processes* of thought, innovation, and stimulus at work within it" (1987, pp. 19–20). Barth holds that the "basic problem is to find the most fertile way to conceptualize the locus and mechanism of incremental change," i.e., to identify "the *mechanisms* involved in such creativity" (1987, p. 27). All of this may look very much like Sperber's concern with specifying the micro-processes at the psychological level that affect the distributions of cultural representations, but Barth locates the principal mechanism of incremental change at a different level of analysis. His chief concern is with the influence of Ok *social arrangements* on ritual experts' activities and mental states. Barth confines his psychological comments to but a few speculative observations (1987, pp. 30–31, 38, and 73).

Barth (1987, p. 78) highlights four salient aspects of Ok social organization:

1 the small, mutually suspicious Ok communities,
2 the distinctions between genders and various degrees of initiation across each of these communities,
3 the single ritual experts on whom ultimate responsibility for directing various initiations falls (1987, pp. 28–29), and
4 the secrecy surrounding the initiations and their highly infrequent performance.

Although Barth thinks that all of these social arrangements influence the generative (re)production of Ok initiations, it is ritual experts' recall of past performances and constitution of new ones that are the central issues both for Barth and for us.

The prevailing affirmation throughout Ok communities is that the ancestors specified the details of male initiations. It seems impossible that without written records – perhaps even with them! – ritual experts could remember every relevant detail of a performance that lasted for days or even weeks and occurred ten years before. Among anthropologists who have studied the Mountain Ok, it is uncontroversial that they do not. During his initial fieldwork among the Baktaman, Barth (1975, pp. 239–40) detects nine examples of possible ritual innovations for which he has some evidence. Barth is not at all sure, though, about how aware Ok ritual experts are of the amount of innovation – beyond overt borrowing from another Ok group – each new performance involves. At least some of the time, it is clear that Ok ritual experts can improvise or guess. (See Barth, 1987, pp. 29 and 31.) Barth notes that the conditions of transmission in these cases *require* that they do so.

A pivotal question is how much latitude ritual experts have when they face these periodic opportunities for cultural innovation. Barth (1987, pp. 55, 79, and 86) generally seems to see most of the centripetal forces in this process arising from Ok social arrangements. By contrast, what centrifugal forces arise come from what Barth takes to be less constrained aspects of the psychology of creativity, which Ok demands for secrecy only exacerbate. He says, for example, that his model envisions "an interplay of (largely divergent) processes of individual creativity and modification and (largely convergent) cross-influence and borrowing" (1987, p. 80; see too pp. 55, 79, and 86).

In addition to the comparatively conservative effects of borrowing, Barth identifies other social conditions, which, he believes, impose restrictions on the ritual experts' freedom. Perhaps the most important is simply the expectations of various segments of the audiences to whom they must play and with whom they may consult in advance of the performance. The relevant audience segments include other experienced senior males and other ritual experts, who have their own recollections and conceptions about how things should go. Barth (1987, p. 29) suggests that decorum and collegiality usually insure that the resulting performances are "canalized but not controlled by the sanctions of each respective audience."

Barth (1987, pp. 62–64) also proposes that such variables as cohort size, the optional character of some higher degrees of initiation among some Ok groups, and the number of community-endorsed ritual experts on hand can incline presiding ritual experts to explore some symbolic environs rather than others. Ok social arrangements and praxis also indirectly influence the direction of ritual experts' creativity, since they dictate the system of analogic coding as the principal medium of cultural communication. (See Barth, 1987, p. 75.) These and other social arrangements among the Ok inspire Barth (1987, p. 86) to "urge that we . . . recognize the penetration of society deep into the privacy and psyche of the individual . . . Thereby we may also avoid mystifying creativity and that which is created . . ."

Barth's account of the social considerations that limit variation in cultural creativity among the Ok is both plausible and intriguing. It supplies valuable insights about the restrictive influences of social arrangements on the process of cultural innovation. Because of such social constraints and borrowing among the Ok, Barth insists that their ritual systems are "genetically and historically connected," their considerable variation notwithstanding (Barth, 1987, p. 8). His examination of the social bases of checks on the *generation* of new materials in cultural transmission provides an important supplement to Sperber's emphasis on the psychological constraints on *communication* and *memory*.

In the next section, we will briefly sketch how various prominent variables considered in the psychological studies we reviewed earlier play out in the transmission of Baktaman initiations. While discussing the Baktaman system of male initiation, we will make a case for the following three claims:

1 that these rituals manipulate many of the psychological variables pertaining to flashbulb memory that researchers have noted,
2 that even if it does not contribute directly to the recollection of the rituals' details, (manufactured) emotional arousal has a role to play in memory for these rituals, because it helps to mark them as socially significant events worthy of careful attention and faithful recollection, and
3 that neither the rehearsal nor the uniqueness of participants' stories associated with narrative consolidation appears sufficient to explain memory for these rituals.

Memory for ritual among the Baktaman

Although the conditions of cultural transmission among the Ok yield "a movable, impressionable and everchanging inheritance, only approximately shared in the group" (Barth, 1987, p. 79), Barth devotes most of his discussion to clarifying social forces that contribute to increased stability in Ok initiations. Like Barth and unlike Sperber, we too are identifying forces that tend to constrain variation in the transmission of religious rituals. On the other hand, like Sperber and unlike Barth, the forces on which we are concentrating are *psychological* rather than social.

Factors contributing to ritual stability

Whitehouse (1992) advances a proposal in Barth's behalf for making *cognitive* sense of the notion of analogic coding as a key to whatever *memory* exists for Baktaman initiations. Whitehouse emphasizes that the Baktaman manipulate concrete, non-linguistic symbols in their rites rather than memorize linguistic formulae. (The *rare* formulaic utterances that occur in Baktaman initiations are extremely simple statements that never involve more than a few words and are usually sung. See, for example, Barth, 1987, pp. 5 and 47.) Whitehouse's proposal, like the one we will present, also looks to the considerable sensory pageantry that characterizes Baktaman initiations. Baktaman initiations stimulate all of an initiate's senses. Barth remarks often on the wide range of sensory cues associated with Baktaman rituals and symbols. Whitehouse argues that both the concrete symbols and the sensory cues provide ample materials for subsequent mental imagery. Extensive experimental research has revealed the ability of mental images to organize memories, to distinguish specific episodes, and to serve as mnemonic cues – especially for spatially and dynamically related materials (Paivio, 1986 and Rubin, 1995). Whitehouse's proposal makes perfect sense cognitively. (See too Barth 1987, pp. 29–30.)

In the absence of a fuller cognitive account of how frequent encounters with the prevailing metaphors and idioms in repeated rituals will suffice to explain the retention and transmission of such an extensive, secret, and elaborate set of initiations (for which Barth himself provides evidence of their non-negligible stability), it does not seem inappropriate to suggest, as Whitehouse does, that other cognitive dynamics may be involved beyond those that Barth considers (all too briefly). The psychological research on flashbulb memory we reviewed earlier points to additional variables that may influence the retrieval, reconstruction, and transmission of Baktaman initiations. The second attractor position we have identified in the space of religious ritual arrangements (where rituals are performed infrequently but contain high levels of sensory pageantry) exploits mnemonic dynamics quite different from the first (where frequently performed rituals contain low levels of sensory pageantry). This second attractor closely approximates the sorts of conditions that seem to make for accurate flashbulb memories.

Besides the social considerations to which Barth points, he provides two additional forms of evidence that pertain to the relative stability of

Ok initiations during the time period in question. By reviewing the place
of other mnemonically significant variables in Baktaman rituals and by
examining the role of accuracy in forging a sense of community and
continuity, we will, in effect, supply two additional forms of indirect
evidence.

The first sort of evidence arising from Barth's account concerns the
coincidences among various informants' reports, which were collected
independently of one another. Barth's Baktaman informants independently provided him with what were surprisingly similar accounts of the
initiation rituals about which he inquired. Moreover, thirteen years later
during his second stay in the central highlands of New Guinea, Barth
reports on an Enkaiakmin informant at Bolovip who not only readily described one of their ten-day-long initiation rituals, but who made various
comparative comments about differences from and similarities to the corresponding rituals among neighboring Ok groups. Barth notes that this
informant's comments about Baktaman practices squared with his own
knowledge of the Baktaman ritual in question that he acquired more than
a decade before.

What we shall call the "*partial* compositionality" of Baktaman initiations simultaneously provides both a second sort of (indirect) evidence
from Barth's writings for some measure of stability among these rites as
well as a possible (partial) explanation for such stability. Baktaman initiations exhibit compositionality to the extent that familiar repeated, special
patient rituals, such as sacrifices, occur as *parts* of these non-repeated,
special agent initiations (not unlike the role of the repeated communion
ritual in the non-repeated first communion or confirmation rituals in
Christianity). In both the fourth and fifth degree initiations, frequently
performed, repeated rituals that are well known to the seniors serve as
central components. They surely help to anchor memories for each initiation as a whole.

Still, the contribution of this compositionality either as evidence for
or as explanation of ritual stability is limited. This is why we describe it
as "*partial.*" When familiar repeated rituals surface in the other five initiations, they amount to but a few among *scores* of separate actions that
collectively constitute the initiation. They are occasional episodes in initiations that sometimes go on for days and even weeks. That familiar rites
play a so-much-more-limited role in these other five initiations suggests
that this partial compositionality cannot carry too much of the mnemonic
burden. So, since neither the partial compositionality of Baktaman initiations nor (as Barth and his informants seem to agree) opportunities to
observe corresponding rituals among neighboring groups will suffice to
explain even the limited evidence of stability among Ok rites that Barth

supplies, it is not implausible to suggest that other variables may carry some of the weight.

All religious systems enlist cultural mechanisms – the most popular of which is literacy – to aid in their transmission. We have good reason to expect that – in cultural settings like that of the Baktaman, where many of these cultural mechanisms, and literacy in particular, have yet to be invented – persisting religious systems will evolve so as to, first, exploit *naturally* available mnemonic aids and, second, develop alternative *cultural* mechanisms that capitalize on just the variables experimental research is finding are relevant to enhancing accurate memory. What follows is a quick inventory of how the system of Baktaman initiations fulfills these expectations.

Neisser and his colleagues suspected that *experiencing* the Loma Prieta earthquake *first-hand* and, thereby, having a sense of *participating* in what proved to be *a socially important event* were critical variables in their subjects' astonishing performance. (The latter consideration is essentially the variable Brown and Kulik dubbed "consequentiality.") Their California subjects were not remembering when they heard the news; they were remembering when they experienced the news (even when they didn't! – see Neisser et al., 1996, p. 354). Baktaman initiations almost certainly instill within initiates as much *a sense of having participated in a significant event in the history of their community* as experiencing an earthquake that eventually proves to be moderately destructive does in our own.

Individual involvement is an inherent feature of initiations. Initiates do not sit idly by observing what goes on. At least in Baktaman initiations the initiates are constantly forced to do one thing or another, and they have plenty of things done to them. Here too initiates do not remember when they heard about a notable event. Instead, they remember *participating* in it.

Two further Baktaman practices promote among initiates a sense of their participation in these significant events. By *initiating entire age cohorts at once*, the Baktaman insure that although participation is individual, it is not isolated. Throughout their lives, initiates interact daily with age-mates with whom they have shared their most culturally significant moments and who share their most culturally significant secrets. Baktaman practice also requires that the *most recently initiated cohort help the cult leader conduct the next performance* of the initiation (for the next age cohort). This clarifies an operative expectation – at least once initiates pick up on the pattern – that they strive to remember what they have learned and what they have undergone, since they must help out the next time around. It also helps to insure that the knowledge remains *distributed* throughout the various cohorts of initiates (Barth, 1987, p. 77). Like the practice of using altar boys, the Baktaman opt for the most recently acquainted individuals (though, recall that the gap between two performances averages ten years) instead of the most experienced individuals to serve as ritual assistants.

The Baktaman ritual system employs many means for impressing initiates with the social and cultural significance of these initiations. Besides both secrecy and its enforcement, the duration and scope of the initiations also mark their social consequence. For example, according to three independent informants, seventh degree initiation takes a couple of weeks, including a period of eight days when the entire population abandons the village! Barth notes that such measures suggest to the initiates that the fate of their whole community is directly connected with their own ritual accomplishments. From the Baktaman perspective, these initiations are the most culturally significant benchmarks in a male's life. Undoubtedly, the primary means in the rituals themselves for impressing participants with the importance of their initiations, though, is the *emotional arousal* they induce.

Whether emotional arousal contributes directly to enhanced recall for the details of an event is not our immediate concern here.[17] The salient points are that it can serve to *flag an event as one worth remembering* and that doing so need not initiate some special Now Print mechanism to contribute to the recollection of details. Neither possessing nor rehearsing flashbulb memories for reception events makes any sense, if subjects have not also remembered that those events involve the "reception" of news about some initially provocative event deemed personally or socially significant. (Presumably, they will remember why it was deemed significant as well. See Brewer, 1992, p. 299.) Only what subjects perceive or rapidly come to perceive as significant events occasion flashbulb memories.

Whitehouse (1992 and 1996b) seems a good deal more enamored than we are with Brown and Kulik's emotion-driven Now Print hypothesis. More recently, he (2000, pp. 8–9 and 120–122) cites a proposal of Wright and Gaskell (1992) about a cognitive processing loop that constitutes a single mechanism for explaining both flashbulb, standard episodic, and semantic memories. They construe all three of these mnemonic accomplishments within the framework of schema theory. In short, the more times any input demands attentive cognitive processing, the more likely it is to stand out as an episodic memory. (If the mind can immediately fit some input into a schema, then it is an instance of one of the categories that populate our existing semantic memory.) Those inputs that repeatedly resist schematization will stand out as the truly unique sorts of events that – in the extreme – resemble the conditions of flashbulb memories. Because we are unable to readily schematize such events, they can stir the emotions, which often accompany them anyway, even more. Without the guidance of an organizing schema, the mind seizes upon "indiscriminate details" of the events in question (Whitehouse, 2000, p. 120).

Tulving (1983) is responsible for the traditional distinction between *episodic* and *semantic* memory. Flashbulb memories are a special sort of episodic memory, typically characterized by elevated levels of vividness, confidence, and, as we have seen, sometimes even accuracy. Episodic memories concern recollections of specific events in a person's life. Memories for such specific episodes constitute the core of a person's sense of his or her unique life history. Semantic memory, by contrast, is the general knowledge of the world that many people share. Many Americans know, for example, that automobiles produce air pollution, but for most the ability to recall such knowledge does not turn on the recollection of a specific episode from the past, either when they heard this claim for the first time or when they experienced a particularly grievous example that led them to this inference. Beyond these common-sense grounds for this distinction, Tulving surveyed a long list of experimentally established dissociations between episodic and semantic memory (Tulving, 1983).

Numerous empirical questions remain about whether Wright and Gaskell's unified model can accommodate these dissociative findings, let alone the diversity of findings concerning flashbulb memories that continue to mount. One obvious basis for hesitation is the fact that not all particularly vivid episodic memories involve the sort of cognitive disorientation that would accompany the failure to activate a schema. For example, in the case of earthquakes, life-long Californians are quite clear about what is going on. They just did not expect an earthquake to happen then and there.

The cognitive alarm hypothesis and Baktaman initiations

Our aim, then, is not to endorse Brown and Kulik's proposal but rather to sketch an alternative. The detail, vividness, confidence, and, perhaps, even accuracy associated with flashbulb memories may completely depend on perfectly ordinary mnemonic means. Nevertheless, sudden, substantial, emotional arousal is a kind of general alarm for the cognitive system, an especially efficient means for signaling events and materials meriting our attention. Emotional arousal may have nothing directly to do with supplying the details in memory but only with occasioning increased cognitive alertness (which is *not* the same thing as engaging some *unique* mnemonic mechanism).

Antonio Damasio (1994 and 1999) has advanced proposals about some of the possible neural underpinnings for such a system. Generally,

Damasio has suggested that much memory depends upon the coordination of information about cognitive and bodily states, including the complex biochemical patterns that underlie the wide array of our emotions. He argues that this integration results from the operation of subcortical structures. These structures exchange information with the central nervous system, the autonomic nervous system (which monitors and controls many of the body's automatic operations such as the beating of the heart), and the neocortex (which is the seat of our higher cognitive functions). On his view our memories and our cognitive proceedings generally are intimately intertwined with reports concerning our bodily and emotional states.

More specifically, Damasio has suggested that the amygdala (one of the many subcortical structures tucked underneath the brain) is the crucial site for the integration of this information. He has found that patients with damage to their amygdalas, although basically normal in their ability to draw inferences and to manipulate propositional knowledge, are, none the less, severely impaired on at least one related front. They seem to lack a form of judgment. They are, in effect, incapable of making prudent decisions – indeed, virtually oblivious to the need to make them – because they seem no longer able to assess the comparative importance of the states of affairs that the propositions they wield describe. They are unable to *appreciate* the implications of situations, even though they seem to comprehend them. They seem to have all of the necessary cognitive information but they lack the somatic and emotional cues necessary to deal with it appropriately.

Research (reported in Heuer and Reisberg, 1997) suggests that the effects of beta-blockers may offer further clues about the underlying mechanisms. When experimental subjects have received beta-blockers, emotional stimuli fail to produce the forms of memory facilitation found for normal subjects. These substances decrease the effects of norepinephrine. Norepinephrine increases glucose in the blood, and glucose is the fuel that powers metabolic functioning. So, it looks as though emotional stimulation turns up the heat, so to speak. In normal subjects it increases the amount of glucose available in the blood, which is a necessary condition for increased cognitive (and mnemonic) activity.

Our cognitive alarm hypothesis, then, holds that when current circumstances are the cause of our emotional arousal, we will increase the attention and cognitive resources we devote to them, which, in turn, will increase the probability of their subsequent recollection. But that sort of memory consolidation may only arise if that initial, heightened alertness receives ongoing vindication in subsequent experience concerning our sense of the event's significance. (We not only have no flashbulb memories for the false positives, we usually have no recollection of them at all!) The experimental literature we have reviewed clearly indicates that profound emotional markers at the moment are not necessary for flashbulb memories. They may not even be sufficient. Nothing we have said, so far, suggests that the hypothesized mnemonic impact of emotional arousal can persist completely independently of other relevant processes. Emotional arousal may achieve nothing more than apprising us that current events are (or, at least, may be) ones worth remembering (even if they are not!) and increasing the availability of the fuel that is necessary for initiating the consolidation of memories. Still, three points deserve some discussion here.

First, the ongoing vindication in subsequent experience of that initial, increased alertness may come in any of a number of forms. More specifically, it may range from explicit, conscious judgments about the importance of an event's consequences to unconscious effects of the sort of *prolonged* emotional stimulation (see below) that many of the Baktaman initiations provide or even the far less extreme levels of arousal that the unfolding news about the Loma Prieta earthquake's consequences surely induced over the first twenty-four hours following that event.

Humans usually react emotionally when they perceive present events to be particularly important for their lives. Taking advantage of that association, Baktaman initiations (and hundreds of other religious rituals around the world) manipulate participants so that they feel considerable emotion during these rituals. This stimulation of initiates' emotions shapes their perceptions of the relative importance of these rites, helping to mark them as culturally significant events that merit their complete attention currently and their faithful recollection in the future. Barth states that "*major discomforts characteristically follow immediately after the revelation of major secrets*, and are consistent with their forbidden and esoteric character" (1975, p. 54, emphasis added).

The Baktaman use two standard means for stimulating initiates' emotions. The first is *surprise*, which they typically produce in one of two ways. First, Baktaman initiations begin unexpectedly. Many commence with senior men awakening initiates in the middle of the night and driving them into the forest. The Baktaman have a second technique for producing surprise at least the first few times they use it in any particular initiation. Throughout the most grisly ordeals connected with these rituals, they routinely reassure initiates that the current agony will be the last. On dozens of occasions in these rituals, these claims prove false.

Talk of grisly ordeals suggests the second and most important means for arousing initiates' emotions. Once the initiations begin, seniors subject the initiates to a wide array of *sensory pageantry* – both positive and negative sensory stimulation. Some initiations end with communal meals and celebrations, but usually before initiates reach those stages of these rituals, they will have often undergone extreme deprivation and excruciating torture. Consider some of the more gruesome details from the third degree initiation:

> Each novice is held and has his elbows pounded with sacred black stones . . . The novices are also assured that this is the only hardship they will suffer.
> As soon as this is completed, however, the seniors grab bunches of nettles and whip the novices over the face and chest . . . They are then presented with the leaf package of the dog's black gut contents and cooked penis. They are forced to eat the black mixture and at least lick and suck the penis . . . they are encouraged by the assurance that this is the very last trial they must endure.
> . . . The novices are made to crawl on their hands and knees between the legs of the line of men; each man they pass under whips them with the burning nettles over back, legs, and particularly the genitalia . . . the novices are then assured that this completes their tortures . . .
> They are . . . made to sit around the two fires . . . crowding them closer as the flames grow hotter . . . This starts a four-day ordeal: blistered and burned by the fires they are now kept continuously awake . . . they are allowed no water . . . At irregular intervals they are again forced into the fires and burned. (Barth, 1975, pp. 64–65)

Hardships and torture (and associated deceptions and surprises) that are both protracted and substantial invariably accompany the communication of each piece of previously forbidden knowledge.

The measures for stimulating initiates' emotions that the Baktaman have built into their rituals may enhance memory in another way. Rubin (1995) emphasizes that a genre's formal constraints can substantially reduce the range of possibilities at any particular point in a text. Analogously, the temporal coincidence of distinctive stimuli in multiple sensory modalities may also restrict the set of possible events that could have occurred. Simultaneously experiencing a specific constellation of stimuli across our various sensory modalities may serve to "triangulate" (*at least*) on some very small set of possible events and corresponding actions (to be remembered). In short, the sensory experiences in question may jointly define a *distinctive* action profile.[18]

Second, whether the mnemonic mechanisms and processes in question are "perfectly ordinary" ones or not, other experimental evidence suggests that emotional arousal does facilitate recall under some circumstances. Laboratory studies suggest that subjects' recollection for both central and peripheral information about emotionally arousing stimuli can exceed that for neutral stimuli (Heuer and Reisberg, 1990 and Reisberg, 1995). Moreover, at least one study of flashbulb memory (Bohannon and Symons, 1992) found that subjects' reports of their initial emotional arousal predicted both the amount of information they generated and the consistency of their stories over time. Emotional arousal may be one of some number of conditions that are jointly sufficient to produce such effects. (See Brewer, 1992, especially pp. 303–304.)

Studies of post-traumatic stress disorder might seem to indicate not, since it seems to introduce considerable mnemonic disruption (Heuer and Reisberg, 1997). It is unlikely, though, that post-traumatic stress disorder is the proper comparison case here. The positive regard of initiated adults, the participation of entire age cohorts, and the profound cultural importance accorded these initiations generally cast these ordeals in a considerably different and, ultimately, more positive light than the events that elicit traumatic stress disorders. Undergoing these initiations is a universally recognized *achievement* among the Baktaman. They do not generate persisting fear or shame but rather a culturally approved sense of accomplishment.

Finally, it is not at all clear that appeals to *narrative consolidation* will suffice to explain whatever mnemonic achievements fund the transmission of Baktaman initiations. Neisser and his colleagues considered two possibilities here. First, narrative consolidation may yield confidence, consistency, and perhaps – with *participants* in culturally significant events like destructive earthquakes or Baktaman initiations – even accuracy in memory because of the emerging *distinctiveness* of each person's story. But this seems unlikely in the case of the Baktaman, since everyone's story in any particular age cohort is essentially the same. Indeed, it is critical that this is so.

Neisser and his colleagues also consider the possibility that the mnemonic impact of narrative consolidation ultimately turns on *rehearsal*, i.e., the many retellings that go into the formulation of a standardized version of each distinctive story. But this proposal looks no more plausible in the Baktaman context than the first. The reason is that many features of Baktaman culture, including taboos, hyper-secretiveness, a fear of sorcery, and "a more diffuse wariness and reluctance to speak about . . . occult forces" (1975, pp. 258–259), militate against initiates rehearsing narratives about their initiation experiences. We have already noted Barth's observation that initiated Baktaman seemed reluctant even to think about such matters most of the time. Initiates make up a "*mute* fellowship of privileged participation" (Barth, 1975, p. 221, emphasis added). Barth asserts that "in their initiations and temple organizations the Baktaman have constructed a communicative apparatus which they themselves approach with such reluctance and trepidation as to endanger the very knowledge it contains" (1975, p. 260).

During the short time between the seniors' decision to perform an initiation and the performance itself, of course, some conversation about ritual details occurs. Although such review may not invite full-blown rehearsals of initiates' narratives, it certainly encourages them to run through these events again mentally (even if this is many years after the fact).

Barth reports on at least one sort of circumstance where less inhibited discussion of the initiation rituals among the seniors is, apparently, acceptable, viz., when the decision to perform an initiation occurs during a power struggle over cult leadership. Such struggles can result from dissatisfaction with either the conscientiousness or the effectiveness of the current leadership or from sheer individual assertiveness by the pretender(s). Upon completion of the seventh degree initiation, men are eligible to take over cult leadership. Not only is succession to these posts open, but rivals can unseat current cult leaders. In the face of rivals' criticisms cult leaders may decide to consult with other seniors about their memories for ritual details and in the process try to garner their support.

Either the triumph of dissidents or a cult leader's flexibility in response to such dissent can result in innovations. For example, in the single instance of such conflict that Barth observed, the cult leader compromised. He agreed to changes in the performance of the sixth degree initiation that the dissidents had advocated on the basis of their knowledge of how neighboring groups to the west performed a similar ritual.

Two points deserve attention. First, this episode notwithstanding, Barth *repeatedly underscores* how formidable the cultural barriers are to discussions of myth, ritual, and cosmology. Most of the time Baktaman hyper-secrecy and associated taboos seem to preclude the rehearsal that makes for the easy consolidation of stable narratives. We are *not* claiming that these cultural factors preclude the formation of narratives, but only that whatever stability initiates' narratives possess does not look as though it results from their (overt) rehearsal. These are precisely the sorts of considerations that lead Barth to place so much emphasis on social constraints and analogic coding in his account of the transmission of Baktaman ritual knowledge. Whether the factors Barth cites will suffice to explain as much retention of Baktaman initiation rituals as occurs, we cannot say (since, among other things, no one really knows just how much retention that is). However, that religious systems in such settings will evolve to take advantage of other aids to memory seems a reasonable proposal and that the Baktaman system of male initiation manipulates many of the variables that researchers on flashbulb memory have found make for accuracy seems clear.

Second, *all* of those participating in the particular episode that Barth observed regarded these changes as *innovations*, i.e., everyone agreed that these adjustments were new and that they did not accord with what they *remembered* about previous performances. The resulting compromise, of course, shows that perfect fidelity to past practice is not an unwavering ideal for the Baktaman, but, more important, it also suggests that *a collective conception not only about the accuracy of recollection but about the importance of that accuracy sustains such conversations* – Barth's comments about Baktaman failures to acknowledge ritual innovation to the contrary notwithstanding (1975, p. 240).

Collectively, participants must retain enough knowledge of these rituals to preserve a sense of both continuity and community. The functionally relevant measure of continuity is participants' sense that what they are doing presently is the same sort of ritual action that they or their forebears did before and (though not necessarily with the Baktaman) that their compatriots might be doing contemporaneously somewhere else. From such temporal factors as timing and sequence to such structural factors as the identities and properties of agents, various features of actions condition participants' judgments about the similarities and differences of religious ritual performances (Lawson and McCauley, 1990, especially chapter 5).

In pluralistic societies concurrence both about the criteria for particular rituals and about the facts concerning particular performances of those rituals is diagnostic in identifying religious communities. Rituals, after all, are not incidental to religious systems. Their performance is integral both to situating individuals within the larger religious community and to sustaining that community.

The rivalry for cult leadership on which Barth reports shows unequivocally that innovations may be introduced into Baktaman initiations. But the two factions participating in the discussion (and the resistance of the more conservative seniors especially), the universal recognition that the proposed changes constituted innovations, and the general acceptance of the eventual compromise all suggest that the participants possessed overlapping conceptions of what would count as a sixth degree initiation and that those conceptions informed this dispute throughout. (Otherwise, it is not very clear how the conversation could have even occurred.)

Whitehouse argues that whether people accurately recall such events is not what matters, but, instead, whether they "are inclined to think that they ought to be able to remember, and often claim to be able to do so" (1995, p. 206). Whatever participants' criteria for identifying particular rituals, the issue is not whether the current performance, in fact, matches its predecessors on all counts but simply whether enough of the current participants are satisfied that it does. Apparently, what matters is whether a ritual produces conviction about mnemonic accuracy – as opposed to the thing itself.

At least some of the time, though, such achievements do seem to turn on the accuracy of participants' memories. That is not to imply that accurate memory is the only means for accomplishing such an end. Reaching consensus about such matters may rely, in part, on any number of devices from uncompromising coercion to rigid codification. The history of the great world religions, alone, provides countless instances when religious authorities have readily resorted to ruthless methods for imposing consensus about matters of ritual and belief. Still, plenty of less extreme forms of social negotiation are available for resolving these problems. As we have seen from Barth's discussion, these are forms of negotiation in which the question of mnemonic accuracy may prove only slightly more likely to arise in the explanation of their operations. Arguably, these more subtle forms of social coercion are all the more effective precisely because they so often go undetected. As we noted, the Baktaman seniors' overt discussions and negotiations about the sixth degree initiation that Barth witnessed notwithstanding, he maintains that Baktaman cultural change is largely unacknowledged (1975, p. 240).

Without fierce coercion, though, and often even with it, memory is vital to these determinations and accuracy a prominent, if not preeminent, value. Ritual failures, if not great dangers, regularly accompany inattentiveness to the gods' decrees.

Whitehouse reports on a situation of collective recollection of long unused, cultural knowledge among the Mali Baining of New Britain Island. We shall take up the events in question in greater detail in chapter 3, but one point is very simple. Whitehouse (1995, pp. 123–124) stresses that "considerable emphasis was placed on accurate recall and the faithful reproduction in minute detail of ancestral techniques of costume production and performance ... Whether or not the details ... were faithful reproductions of past performances, they were explicitly described as such by participants." Recall is often the psychological process that is critical to the resuscitation of cultural materials – especially, it seems, in nonliterate societies. We recognize with Whitehouse that neither seeking nor valuing accuracy in recall guarantees it. We recognize that rituals often undergo substantial transformations in the course of their transmission, but it is hard to imagine that such goals and values have *no* impact on the accuracy of recall for cultural knowledge.

Our claim here is not merely about desires for and perceptions of accurate memory at the object level but about genuine accuracy as an explanatory mechanism at the theoretical level. Collective recollection is *not*, after all, utterly unconstrained. Absent irresistibly powerful forms of overt or covert intimidation about such matters within a culture, some standards must restrict these negotiations or, otherwise, the problem of explaining the community's collective sense of continuity in these proceedings looms ominously.[19] *Our emphasis in this discussion has not been on the achievement of perfect accuracy in these settings but on the contributions of psychological mechanisms – that make for more faithful recall – to this communal sense of continuity in the transmission of cultural materials.*

An analytical summary: preparing to move from memory dynamics to ritual patterns

We have explored the role of human memory in the transmission of religious rituals in non-literate societies. Religion and its rituals were born before the invention of literacy.[20] Without *systems* of public, external symbols for recording information, non-literate communities have to rely overwhelmingly on human memory for the retention and transmission of cultural knowledge. Religious expressions either evolved in directions that rendered them sufficiently memorable or they were – quite literally – forgotten.

Non-literate cultures bring all of these issues into sharper focus, but most of the time they are no less relevant in literate settings – especially when memory for ritual is the topic. Even in literate settings memory for ritual rarely turns on memory for texts. Participants usually do not consult ritual manuals when they exist, and even if they did, no manual could ever be comprehensive.

If religious systems, in fact, evolve in the direction of greater memorability, at least in the absence of special cultural tools for the faithful preservation of such representations, then the relevance of these matters to the transmission of religious ritual should be clear. Except for some comparatively new religions, most religious systems, including all of the great world religions, emerged among populations that were mostly illiterate (even if there was a literate elite). Thus, it should come as no surprise that religious systems and ritual systems, in particular, have evolved so as to exploit variables that facilitate memory. No doubt, the invention of literacy ameliorates these variables' influence on the shape of religious materials. However, contrary to the champions of literacy's impact on cultural forms (e.g., Goody, 1987), we shall argue that the availability of such cultural tools neither eliminates that influence nor even surmounts it.

For a host of reasons – having to do with everything from the prominence many religious systems accord oral traditions to the prominence many scholars of religion accord myth – research in this area has focused mostly on memory for verbal materials rather than on memory for actions. Religious rituals usually include verbal components and ritual practitioners sometimes do what they do primarily with words. "I now pronounce you husband and wife" (Ray, 1973). At least some of the time, though, rituals involve no utterances at all or the utterances they do contain have only a minor role – certainly from a mnemonic standpoint. Barth, for example, maintains that ritualized verbal pronouncements in Baktaman initiations are infrequent, simple, and short (1975, chapter 25).

In the past two decades, especially, experimental psychologists have made considerable progress in clarifying the variables that contribute to extraordinary recall for events that arise in the normal course of life. It should come as no surprise that religious rituals evolve in directions that tend to exploit such variables. We have suggested that this is usually achieved in one or the other of two ways that correspond to the two attractors we identified in the space of possible ritual arrangements.

Probably, the most obvious of these variables is frequency. If people experience events of the same type frequently, they tend to remember that *type* of event well, though not necessarily the details of any of the particular instances of that type. Their discursive knowledge of these matters is stored in semantic memory, i.e., our store of general knowledge about the world the recollection of which does not turn on the retrieval of information about specific episodes from our lives. When Jains carry out the Puja ritual – in which they attend to the *daily* needs of the god – they become adept at its performance. Although they are completely fluent with the ritual's details, it is quite possible that they do not remember even one of their previous performances *distinctively*. (Of course, both what participants must remember and how they need to access this information is a function of their various roles in rituals. We shall return to these matters in chapter 3.)

Very nearly all religious rituals are performed over and over again and certainly all rituals in which human participants take part are. The sole exceptions are what we have called "hypothetical rituals," which are religious actions that a religious ritual system presumes, perhaps even describes, but which no human participant ever actually performs. Examples from Christianity might include the transfiguration of Christ, the representation of the Church as his bride, and the appearance of the stigmata on the bodies of potential saints. Such hypothetical rituals are not confined to Christianity, though. The Buddha's achievement of enlightenment, the command in the cave to Muhammad to recite, and Isaiah Shembe's fourth confrontation with God's lightning all qualify too, since in each case their presumption establishes these individuals as conduits to supernatural authority sufficient to legitimate subsequent ritual actions.

(See Lawson, 1985, and Lawson and McCauley, 1990, p. 113.) Still, with some religious rituals some or all of the participants may change from one performance to the next, and some rituals occur quite infrequently. (Investitures of particularly long-lived religious leaders who serve for life come to mind.) So, as we have noted, considerations of frequency cannot explain memory for and, hence, transmission of *all* religious rituals. Barth's study of Baktaman initiations examines the right kind of case. Those infrequent initiations and the accompanying circumstances and cultural practices of the Baktaman pose exacting challenges to long-term memory.

We argued that psychological research on extraordinary recall for specific episodes (in episodic memory) will help illuminate the second attractor position to which so many religious rituals migrate. Thus, we examined some of the salient variables that have emerged in the study of flashbulb memory and their possible relevance to Baktaman initiations (and to comparable circumstances in other cultures). Some religious rituals capitalize on many of the prominent variables that contribute to extraordinary memory. However, the crucial point for our purposes in the next chapter is that they do so *selectively*.

Consider, for example, the emotional arousal characteristic of the second attractor position. We advanced the cognitive alarm hypothesis, which holds that emotionally arousing circumstances will facilitate accurate memory for pertinent features of the associated materials, at least if subsequent experience continues to vindicate the heightened attention devoted to them that the emotional arousal elicits. But as we noted in chapter 1, although many religious rituals are profoundly emotional experiences, not all rituals stimulate participants' emotions. In fact, some rituals are dull. Whereas some rituals incite substantial emotional excitement, others are performed so mechanically that they seem completely bereft of emotional power. Religious rituals vary widely on this dimension.

The general question is, what are the variables that determine or, at least, predict when rituals incorporate the various mnemonic variables that they do? What are the conditions that dictate which mnemonic variables any particular ritual exploits? For example, participants perform some rituals far more frequently than others. Or, to pick up on the variable at hand, why are some rituals so emotionally stimulating, while others are so utterly routine? Casting these issues in terms of our framework here, why do many rituals gravitate toward the first attractor, while many others gravitate toward the second? And why do a few fail to gravitate toward either?

Harvey Whitehouse offers the most developed theory to date concerning these matters. We shall devote considerable attention to his views, since not only is his theory the best theory available up to now, it is also a theory that is broadly *cognitive* in orientation.

Whitehouse agrees with us that at least part of the reason *why* some rituals are so emotionally provocative is in order to promote their memorability. In various works (1989, 1992, 1995, 1996a, 2000), Whitehouse describes his fieldwork experience among the Mali Baining of the East New Britain Province of New Britain Island. The inhabitants of Dadul, the village where he undertook the first half of his fieldwork, are participants in a cargo cult known as the Pomio Kivung. The highly repetitive ritual system of the Pomio Kivung consists of various ritual acts none of which participants perform any less often than once every five weeks and the *most elaborate* of which they perform daily. Among the many theoretically interesting features of the Pomio Kivung ritual system is that participants' knowledge of their rituals arises almost exclusively on the basis of the *frequency* with which they perform them.

As Whitehouse (1992) emphasizes, the Pomio Kivung ritual system stands in stark contrast to that of the Baktaman. Where the Kivung system relies almost completely on the frequency of ritual performances to insure their memorability, the Baktaman initiations occur so infrequently that their retention and transmission must depend upon very different factors. While the Baktaman initiations usually involve considerable stimulation of the initiates' emotions, Whitehouse repeatedly highlights how monotonous and uninspiring Kivung rituals are. We shall begin chapter 3 by summarizing Whitehouse's discussion of the mainstream Pomio Kivung movement, the eruption of a splinter group that he witnessed, and the ritual systems of each.

3   Two hypotheses concerning religious ritual
     and emotional stimulation

Whitehouse's ethnography

In October of 1987 Harvey Whitehouse entered the village of Dadul in the Eastern Province of New Britain Island in Papua New Guinea to begin his fieldwork among the Mali Baining. Unbeknownst to him then, his arrival was one of the catalysts for a series of events that made not only for considerable excitement in the area over the next eighteen months but also for an ethnography (Whitehouse, 1995) that is as theoretically fertile as it is dramatic. Inevitably, the short summary which follows will capture little, if any, of the drama, but it will point to some of these materials' theoretically suggestive aspects.

New Britain Island lies off the eastern coast of Papua New Guinea. The Mali are one of five subgroups of the Baining people, who occupy the rural regions of the Gazelle Peninsula, which constitutes the northern half of the island's Eastern Province. A different ethnic group, the Tolai, occupies the more developed northeastern corner of the Gazelle Peninsula. A third ethnic group, the Pomio, inhabit most of the southern half of the province. Comparatively speaking, the Tolai, unlike the Baining and the Pomio, have prospered from contacts with the industrialized world.

From the late nineteenth century until the end of World War I the area was under German administration. Exclusive of the traumatic Japanese occupation during World War II, from 1919 until independence in 1975, Australia administered the region. Other than government officials, the principal European influences were Christian missionaries, who – by the 1930s and with the cooperation of the Tolai – had both converted the various peoples of the Eastern Province and, for the most part, successfully suppressed their traditional religious systems (Whitehouse, 1995, p. 40). Broadly similar to the religious systems of hundreds of other groups in this region of the world (including the Baktaman), traditional Mali Baining religion focused on sacred relics of the ancestors, a temple for their storage, and – connected with their possession – a system of infrequently performed initiations as well as a broader collection of rituals, which senior males supervised.

Dadul, where Whitehouse spent the first half of his period of field-work, had arisen as the result of Methodist missionaries' attempts to establish permanent settlements centered around churches. Its residents abandoned Dadul during World War II. It was not resettled until the 1960s, when most of the Baining people in the nearby village of Sunam moved there to avoid domination by and, ultimately, even contact with Tolai immigrants. From the outset it was opposition to Tolai culture and influence that motivated this resettlement of Dadul (Whitehouse, 1989).

The Pomio Kivung

By the mid-1970s nearly everyone in Dadul had joined the Pomio Kivung, which was simultaneously a millenarian cargo cult and a political move-ment seeking autonomy, if not outright independence, from both the cen-tralized national authority and Tolai influence. The Kivung had arisen among the Pomio about fifteen years previously. Pomio Kivung doc-trine holds that adherence to the Ten Laws (a modified version of the Decalogue) and the faithful performance of an extensive set of rituals, including the payment of fines for the purpose of gaining absolution, are essential to the moral and spiritual improvement that is necessary to hasten the return of the ancestors. The most important of these ritu-als aims at placating the ancestors, who make up the so-called "Village Government." Headed by God, the Village Government includes those ancestors whom God has forgiven and perfected.

The spiritual leaders of the Pomio Kivung have been its founder, Koriam, his principal assistant, Bernard, and Koriam's successor, Kolman. Followers have regarded all three as already members of the Village Gov-ernment and, hence, as divinities. All three have resided on earth phys-ically (specifically in the Pomio region of the province), but their souls have dwelt with the ancestors all along.

Achieving sufficient collective purification is the decisive condition for inducing the return of the ancestors and inaugurating the "Period of the Companies." The Period of the Companies will be an era of unprece-dented prosperity, which will result from the transfer of knowledge and an industrial infrastructure for the production of technological wonders and material wealth like that of the Western world. The Period of the Com-panies is, however, also a time of temptation during which the Village Government will be able to ascertain whether individuals will indulge themselves in a time of plenty or whether they will use their newly achieved power and prosperity responsibly, supporting the Kivung movement, performing Kivung rituals, and continuing to seek absolution through the payment of fines.

The Period of the Companies will be a time of temptation, presumably, because things will not, in fact, be as they seem. The ancestors will not return with the bodies they had on earth. Instead, Koriam claimed, the ancestors will come as white-skinned, "foreign investors" and "Western scientists and industrialists" (Whitehouse, 1995, p. 43). When the Period of the Companies ends faithful Kivung members will enter an eternal paradise on earth, known as the "Period of the Government," while those who succumbed to temptation and lived immoral, decadent, luxurious lives will be dispatched to hell. The Period of the Government will signal an end to conflict, suffering, labor, death, and reproduction. Participants in this paradise will shed their dark skins, disclosing their unblemished white skins underneath.

The Kivung seeks a paradise on earth, but its means are not religious only. The Pomio Kivung movement also peacefully pursues political goals, including the general welfare and political autonomy of its membership. Koriam and Alois Koki, Kolman's principal assistant, have held seats in the national assembly and have defended Kivung interests. Various Kivung supervisors, who serve as intermediaries between the central Kivung leadership and the various local congregations, hold offices in provincial and local governments. Kivung members presume that the utterances of the Kivung leaders serving in official government capacities frequently carry a double meaning. They address current political matters, but their comments may have a deeper religious significance as well.

Besides a detailed eschatology, Kivung ideology also includes an elaborate program for moral and spiritual purification. As noted above, it stresses conformity to the Ten Laws and ongoing participation in numerous rituals aimed at the members' improvement and at enticing the ancestors – primarily through daily food offerings – into interacting positively with the community and eventually returning.

The coherence of Kivung beliefs has always been a concern of its leaders. The movement has displayed a lasting concern with the logical integration of its beliefs, doctrines, and practices. Proselytization does not rely on the cultivation of secrecy and mystery but rather on the persuasiveness of a logically integrated program addressing personal, communal, and cosmic issues. As a consequence of (1) its political goals in this world, (2) this concern for rigorous systematization of beliefs, and (3) the virtual absence of literacy among its members, a comparatively centralized and stratified system of authority has emerged within the Pomio Kivung. Its apotheosized leaders pronounce on religious matters, and the cadre of supervisors carry this information to various Kivung communities, while simultaneously monitoring and guiding the orthodoxy of local congregations. Meanwhile, local leaders (all of whom are male) periodically visit the seat of central Kivung authority in the Pomio region of the province for consultation and instruction. These measures all help to preserve and standardize Kivung belief and practice.

Among the local leaders are "orators" (Whitehouse, 1995, p. 48), who preside at, among others, the nine most notable meetings of the entire Kivung community that occur each week. Their principal responsibility is to address the assembled believers, especially after the daily Cemetery Temple rituals and at community meetings that occur simultaneously with the twice-weekly rituals at Bernard's Temple. They deliver speeches after the Cemetery Temple rituals that report on and interpret the testimony of the "witness" that day (Whitehouse, 1995, p. 70). The witness's job is to sit in a cubicle in the temple for about an hour carefully listening to determine whether or not the ancestors have come to partake of the food offerings that that day's team of cooks has prepared. The presumption is not that they consume the food itself, but rather that they savor "the respect, goodwill, generosity, deep faith, and devotion which the living supposedly put into its preparation and presentation" (Whitehouse, 1995, p. 67). Generally, the ancestors' presence reflects positively on the moral status of the community, while their absence reflects negatively.

The orators also speak twice weekly at community meetings that occur during the ritual proffering of food to the ancestors in Bernard's Temple. On these days their jobs include speaking on the basic tenets of Kivung faith, pointing out recent transgressions, resolving disputes, and at the end giving an essentially standardized, fifteen-minute sermon on one of the Ten Laws, so that across any five-week period they have preached on all ten.

This only begins to hint, though, at the amount of time, energy, and resources Kivung rituals consume. Attending just these nine meetings requires about nine hours per week from every member of the *entire community*. This, however, would be a huge *underestimate* of the amount of time that members spend either preparing for or participating in Kivung rituals. Whitehouse (1995, p. 78) counts the nine temple rituals among "the most elaborate and time-consuming activities within Kivung communities." He estimates that food preparation for these rituals alone consumes twelve person hours per day. On a *daily* basis they also involve the maintenance and preparation of the temples, the delivery of the food, the witnesses' monitorings, and the cleaning up. And these are not the only Kivung rituals. The entire community must also participate in fortnightly rituals in each of the two sacred gardens as well as a monthly ritual for collective absolution. Married Kivung members also perform a weekly Family Temple ritual to present food offerings to their deceased kin in their homes, while widows and widowers must do so twice a week.

Unlike that of the Baktaman, the Kivung system aims to instill in participants a familiarity with and some understanding of a large body of propositional materials. Its centralized and carefully delineated religious authority, its logically integrated body of doctrines, and, in particular, its unending cycles of ritual performance help to achieve this aim, even in the face of the complete absence of texts (and members' pervasive illiteracy). Koriam demanded that Kivung communities meet in this nearly perpetual fashion in order to insure uniformity of belief and practice throughout the movement. To help in this effort he also dispatched his patrolling supervisors to insure standardization and to discourage variation.

Frequency is, of course, the crucial mnemonic variable the Kivung system exploits. The Kivung ritual system is a quintessential illustration of a ritual system situated at the first attractor, relying exclusively on performance frequency to insure recollection of rituals. Both the frequency with which members perform rituals and the frequency with which the orators confront Kivung believers with lengthy, largely canned speeches about the basic tenets of the faith insure that participants master Kivung cosmology, principles, and practices. Whitehouse comments that

the continuity of kivung religion . . . is not threatened by memory failure. The very frequent repetition of all the sacred rituals of the kivung is sufficient to ensure a high degree of standardization . . . the effect is to "drum home" every detail of the religion to the community at large. The explicit goal is to create a single, unified system of ideas within each individual. (1992, p. 784)

Whitehouse also repeatedly underscores just how boring and monotonous all of this repetition of ritual and doctrine is, the developed rhetorical skills of the local orators notwithstanding:

the characteristic activities of Pomio Kivung members are not intrinsically very exciting . . . Temple rituals are performed somewhat mechanically, like other uninspiring chores, and seem to be neither intellectually challenging nor emotionally arousing . . . it is not productive of the kind of high excitement that is stereotypically associated with Melanesian "cargo cults." (1995, pp. 86–87)

Apparently, during the daily routine of rituals glassy-eyed Kivung devotees in Dadul not infrequently yawned and even nodded off. This is all the more telling since Whitehouse arrived amidst a period of notable religious upheaval.

The splinter group

About two months before Whitehouse and his wife arrived, a young man named Tanotka was possessed by a prominent local ancestor, Wutka. According to the only witness, Baninge, who is Tanotka's matrilineal, parallel cousin, i.e., Tanotka's "brother" in the Mali Baining kinship system, during this possession Wutka delivered startling news through Tanotka. The force of Wutka's messages was (1) that in addition to Koriam's revelations, the Kivung had parallel origins in the region of Dadul and Maranagi, (2) that these two villages were now poised to usher in the return of the ancestors, and (3) that Tanotka would be a pivotal figure for bringing this miracle about.

Over the subsequent months interest in Tanotka and his revelations grew. Three developments, in particular, stand out. First, within two months of Tanotka's initial possession, two members of the Village Government appeared in Dadul requesting permission to live there for a while. These ancestors seemed dedicated to keeping the entire village of Dadul under constant scrutiny. Consistent with Baninge's interpretation of Wutka's pronouncement that Dadul and Maranagi were on the threshold of bringing in the new era, these white-skinned people followed Dadul residents around, watched what they did (even when what they were doing was thoroughly commonplace), and asked them all sorts of questions about a wide range of topics. Using the conventional euphemisms for referring to the ancestors, the orators cautioned the people to answer all of these visitors' questions honestly and fully. Regular attempts to explain the character of anthropological research did little to persuade Dadul's residents to abandon their suspicions about the true identities of Whitehouse and his wife. Instead, they only clarified the cover story these two ancestors were employing.

The second startling development was that the witnesses, beginning with Baninge's father at the Cemetery Temple in Maranagi, began to hear the ancestors' voices as they endorsed Tanotka's revelations and his status. Because one of the Dadul witnesses did not hear these voices during his vigils, it was soon agreed that "the witness only needed to hear the voices 'in his head' rather than 'through his ears'" (Whitehouse, 1995, p. 98). With the possibility of such important daily communication from the ancestors, the duration of the witnesses' vigils was approximately doubled – to two-and-a-quarter hours each day. During the subsequent four months the ancestors spoke to the witnesses over eighty times. The ancestors' utterances regularly proved to be responses to queries that the orators permitted Baninge to submit with the presentation of the daily offerings in the temples. The ancestors' willingness to reply to these queries only enhanced the credibility and prestige of Tanotka and Baninge.

Indirectly, Baninge pressured the orators on his own behalf. By carefully manipulating the contents of his queries to the ancestors, he was fortunate enough to elicit consistently convenient replies from the ancestors as reported by the witnesses. Wutka, for example, was alleged to have said, "I am pleased with Baninge; when will the orators stand by the side of Baninge? It is true that the orators tell everybody to obey the Ten Laws but who will stand by the side of Baninge?" (Whitehouse, 1995, p. 101). For the first few weeks the orators had persisted in delivering their stock speeches at the regular community meetings. Under such pressure, though, they quickly abandoned their cautious distancing of themselves from Tanotka and Baninge and generally acceded to their authority. Witnesses soon reported the ancestors' pronouncements that Tanotka and Baninge's spirits were already part of the Village Government. Like the leaders of the mainstream Kivung movement, they were, in effect, ancestors on earth (Whitehouse, 1995, p. 101).

For our purposes, though, it is the third of these developments that is of greatest interest. Shortly after Tanotka and Baninge's apotheoses, *new rituals* connected with the Dadul-Maranagi splinter group were introduced. In the orthodox Kivung system the necessary conditions for provoking the onset of the Period of the Companies always included not just the purification of individual Kivung members but the overt demonstration of the entire community's commitment to moral and spiritual improvement through the collective performance of Kivung rituals. Initially, Baninge supplemented these Kivung rituals, but eventually the splinter group's new rituals completely overshadowed the standard Kivung rites.

We shall argue in the course of this chapter and the next that these events exhibited numerous theoretically significant features. Some of those features were manifest from the outset. The first ritual innovation linked with the splinter group arose in connection with a special occasion. The witnesses had reported the ancestors' repeated complaints about the sorry state of the Cemetery Temple and its leaky roof, in particular. With the ancestors' testimony and the support of the first orator, Baninge convinced the community to build a new Cemetery Temple and to celebrate the event in an unprecedented fashion.

At the recommendation of Baninge and Tanotka this temple dedication included resuscitating practices and figures from *traditional* Mali Baining religion. An *awan*, a traditional dance, supplemented a night of singing, dancing, and feasting. Only a few senior men had ever actually observed these traditional religious activities and that had been decades ago. Their recollections contained gaps and inconsistencies. However, knowledge of the system – if only by description – was still available, and given their essentially deified status, Tanotka and Baninge had no trouble providing authoritative instructions about how to fill in the gaps and resolve the discrepancies.

The standard dancers in an *awan* are the *awanga*, but this *awan* also included the *ilotka* among the dancing celebrants. Both the *awanga* and the *ilotka* are traditional masked figures whose bright headdresses and enormous costumes make them appear larger than life. Including the *ilotka* is interesting. So far as Whitehouse could ascertain, they were not traditionally part of the *awan*. Instead, they are salient figures in the second sort of traditional Mali Baining dances, the *mendas*, which are elemental in the traditional system of initiation.

In conformity with patterns characteristic of Mali Baining religious traditions, Baninge slipped away on the night of the temple dedication and had a dream in which Wutka pronounced, in effect, that Tanotka would take over *soon* from Kolman as the pivotal figure who would usher in the new age. Mindful of etiquette and custom, Baninge shrewdly manipulated events behind the scenes so that various senior men agreed to hold a new celebration of this revelation. This was the first event in which the entire community exhibited its loyalty to Tanotka and the new ideas that emerged from the events that began with his possession. That very day a lengthy report from a witness indicated the ancestors' endorsement of the contents of Baninge's dream, affirming Tanotka's authority and vital importance. At the festivities (just five nights after the temple dedication), "emergent ideas now resounded and danced in the night air, endorsed by the ancestors and celebrated by the living" (Whitehouse, 1995, p. 107).

Whitehouse regularly emphasizes how this and further novel rituals that would occur over the subsequent months were the overt manifestation of the entire religious community's gradual surrender of responsibility to the leadership of Tanotka and Baninge. In order to assuage local concerns about authority, a delegation including Tanotka, Baninge, and the first orator visited Kolman and – in what may seem like an incredible development – received, if not his approval, then at least an affirmation of his willingness to tolerate Tanotka and Baninge's movement. Allegedly, Kolman's tolerance was a function of what he perceived as a competition among various aspiring prophets in the region. His confidence in the truth of the old adage that "time will tell" apparently informed his tolerance of this and other such movements.

Four days after the celebration of Baninge's first dream, the residents of Dadul performed a third ritual (modeled on the monthly Kivung ritual for collective absolution) in response to a dream of Tanotka's. And so events continued for nearly six more months. Eventually, Tanotka removed himself to Maranagi, in part to direct things there. In the mean-time Baninge became increasingly assertive in Dadul. Dreams, visions, pronouncements, and reports prompted both increasing the performance rate of Kivung rituals (e.g., the twice-weekly meetings coordinated with the ritual offerings in Bernard's Temple now occurred on a daily basis) and creating new rituals aimed at bringing about reunification with the ancestors.

Quickly, these new rituals surpassed the orthodox Kivung rites in importance. Many of the new rituals were variations on a ring ceremony that one of Baninge's dreams inspired (Whitehouse, 1995, p. 110). According to Whitehouse the ring represented an enclosure under the protection of the Village Government into which Tanotka and Baninge were leading the splinter group members (but no one else) – on the assumption that they had now collectively achieved considerable favor in the eyes of the ancestors. In the ritual Tanotka (and later Baninge) stood at the center of a ring, and as signs of their loyalty and faithfulness each member entered the ring to shake his hand and give him money. Whitehouse (1995, p. 113) holds that their presence in the ring symbolized the splinter group's reception as God's chosen people. If this ritual's cosmic promise failed to capture members' interest, two other features of the ring ceremony were sure to get their attention, at least initially. On the instructions of their new leaders, members performed the ritual at dawn and they wore traditional genital coverings only, which rapidly became the preferred attire for all activities, including the standard Kivung rituals.

None the less, since after three months the miracle had not occurred, it appeared that the splinter group members were unable to secure their position in the ring. With enthusiasm flagging, Baninge announced a mass exodus of the Dadul membership to Maranagi in order both to break all ties with the world of non-believers and to join forces there with Tanotka and his followers for the performance of the final ritual necessary for inaugurating the Period of the Companies. At Baninge's instruction, the Dadul splinter group members took additional steps to renounce the outside world. They stopped confessing to the Catholic priest, who visited fortnightly. They also wrote insulting letters to the principal of a nearby school, to an official of the provincial government, to a Kivung orator in a neighboring village, and to people in Sunam. As a further sign of their faith that a cosmic transformation was imminent, they also ceased to work in the village's gardens and, just before undertaking the migration to Maranagi, they held a huge feast, for which members killed *all* of the pigs in Dadul.

The Dadul residents' arrival in Maranagi marked the beginning of approximately five weeks of even more emotionally provocative rituals.

These rituals would take place in a *traditional* Baining roundhouse that the men of Maranagi had constructed according to Tanotka's orders. A large feast and (unsuccessful) "preparation ceremony," which began with the standard ring ceremony, marked the opening of the roundhouse (Whitehouse, 1995, p. 137). These were followed in comparatively quick succession by a membership ritual (after Baninge invited some influential outsiders into the splinter group), a mass marriage in which Baninge paired off all eligible members of the splinter group with one another, and a long series of all-night vigils also based on the ring ceremony. Each of these rituals involved a wide array of sensory pageantry, including some combination of near-nudity, feasting, singing, and dancing (either by participants or by *awanga* and *ilotka*). The initial preparation ceremony and the final weeks of vigils introduced acute physical suffering to this list.

Especially over the course of the nightly vigils awaiting the ancestors' return, the people faced increasingly severe distress. Usually after huge feasts, they crowded into the roundhouse for these rituals. Overcrowding produced stifling heat and made even the smallest movements difficult. These conditions produced considerable discomfort. On the evening before the first vigil that Baninge and Tanotka had predicted would actually foment the miracle, the people took the unusual measure of eating the pork fat that they used for cooking, since their physical transformation would occur before they would suffer any ill-effects. Instead, widespread nausea and vomiting marked the vigil. Some argued, after the fact, that the unappealing scene that resulted was why the ancestors had failed to return that night as predicted.

Although the vigil on the very next night did not introduce the Period of the Companies, it enlarged participants' excitement for the next four nights especially. During that vigil an ancestor's apparent possession of an eighteen-year-old female, Lagawop, transfixed the splinter group members. Her possession dominated the next two nights' vigils as had her description (after the temple rituals on the second day) of her communications with her deceased grandparents. On the third night in the midst of her possession, members of Baninge's family insisted that it was Satan who possessed her and not her grandfather. After some of them attacked her physically, she announced in her possessed state that it was, indeed, Satan who was controlling her. Activities over the next day and the fourth night's vigil focused on her exorcism.

For our purposes what was of theoretical interest about her possession, though, was the character of her pronouncements on the first night, in particular. Although as a female she had held no positions within the local Kivung ecclesiastical hierarchy and as an eighteen-year-old she had had limited experience of the adult world, her statements demonstrated her thorough grasp of the entire body of Kivung doctrine, which she expounded upon at length in her possessed state. "Lagawop was able to repeat extensive logical strings of kivung ideology for literally hours at a time in the manner of an experienced orator" (Whitehouse, 1992, p. 785). Her performance eliminates any doubts about the ability of at least some participants to master a complex religious system on the basis of frequent exposure alone.

After more weeks of feasting and vigils, food became less plentiful. For some hunger began replacing nausea as their primary somatic state during the vigils. Baninge led a group back to Dadul to retrieve the last food from their gardens; however, they found that people from neighboring villages had stolen most of what remained. While Baninge's expedition was in Dadul, a message arrived from Tanotka indicating that they had successfully expelled Satan from Maranagi and now, finally, the ancestors' return was at hand. The Dadul residents returned to Maranagi, because, as Whitehouse (1995, p. 149) notes, they "were frightened to risk exclusion from the miracle now that they had invested so many resources in the pursuit of it." Moreover, remaining in Dadul was no longer such an inviting option. They had alienated the people in most of the neighboring villages. They had slaughtered all of their pigs and neglected their gardens for weeks. Neighbors had stolen the food that had remained. "The houses were dilapidated, and the bush was advancing into the clearing" (Whitehouse, 1995, p. 149).

The final nightly vigils were especially agonizing physically. In addition to the nudity, the singing, the dancing, and the overcrowding (and all of its consequences), now the people were also hungry and faced new prohibitions on relieving themselves and on sleeping during the vigils (Whitehouse, 1996a, p. 188).

Although it took a number of months for the splinter group to emerge as a movement distinct from the mainstream Kivung system, it ended abruptly. When a government health inspector had seen conditions in both Dadul and Maranagi, he commanded the residents of Dadul to return home to clean up their village and resume productive activity. Along with similar admonitions to the people of Maranagi, he ordered the destruction of the roundhouse as a public health hazard. The members of both groups complied on pain of prosecution.

Sensory pageantry, codification, and the ritual frequency hypothesis

Whitehouse offers a proposal for explaining the contrasting patterns between the ritual practices of the orthodox Pomio Kivung and the

Dadul-Maranagi splinter group. He suggests that the *frequency* of ritual performance is the critical variable that determines just how much emotional stimulation any ritual involves. Whitehouse (1992) advances a version of what we shall call the *ritual frequency hypothesis* to answer the general questions we have raised concerning the memory dynamics religious rituals enlist.

In Whitehouse's hands the ritual frequency hypothesis fits into a larger theory about modes of religiosity that he lays out in various papers (1992, 1996a, and 1996b), in the final chapter of his first book (1995), and at length in his second (2000). Whitehouse situates the frequency hypothesis within a more extensive pattern of correlations dealing not just with ritual, memory, and emotion but with ideological factors and social and political arrangements as well. Whitehouse appeals to this larger theory of religious modes to make sense of the differences between the Kivung movement and the splinter group he witnesses. In this section we shall describe the frequency hypothesis and briefly sketch Whitehouse's overall position with particular attention to his account of the connections between ritual and cognitive variables.

As noted above, we and Whitehouse agree that processes of cultural transmission have rendered mnemonic considerations some of the most important reasons *why* some religious rituals incorporate more emotionally arousing features than others. What we most clearly differ about, though, is *which* religious rituals assume this garb. This is to say that we disagree about the conditions under which rituals are likely to include high levels of emotional arousal. In the next section we will return to some of the topics we examined in chapter 1, in order to show how our theory of religious ritual competence and the account of the cognitive representation of religious rituals it contains inspire an alternative hypothesis that identifies what we think is an even more fundamental cognitive variable explaining why rituals move towards one of the attractor positions or the other. There we will argue that it is participants' mostly tacit knowledge of *ritual forms* that is the critical cognitive variable that largely determines not only rituals' performance frequencies but also such things as how much emotional firepower a religious ritual possesses.

Our theory of religious ritual competence supplies the means for characterizing the forms of rituals precisely, and it includes principles that distinguish between these forms. We shall show how the typology of religious ritual forms accounts for when religious rituals enlist emotional stimulation and when they do not. The PSA and PSI not only provide a basis for predicting when religious rituals are emotionally arousing and when they are not, but also go some way toward further explaining *why*, thus enriching our understanding of cultural transmission in this domain.

This will be the point where the apparently minor differences with White-house that we noted in chapter 2 about how elevated levels of emotion influence the consolidation of some episodic memories will really begin to matter.

Exciting times

On at least one dimension the new rituals the splinter group introduced contrasted conspicuously with orthodox Kivung practices. Recall that Kivung rituals are repetitive, monotonous, and dull. They do not excite emotion. They routinize religious practice and instill an elaborate set of logically integrated doctrines. By contrast, the splinter group's rites involved a great deal of sensory pageantry – both positive and negative. As a result, participants were anything but bored! Splinter group members reliably found the feasting, singing, and dancing – let alone the nudity – emotionally exciting. The vigils in the roundhouse during the last few weeks were no less emotionally provocative, though the experiences they engendered were not uniformly pleasant. With the overcrowding, the heat, the nausea, the sleep deprivation, and the other physical discomforts, misery was probably the dominant emotion near the end. Even this, though, was suffering to bring about a greater good. The splinter group construed it – *night after night* – as the *final* purification necessary to induce the ancestors' return with the dawn of the next day (Whitehouse, 1996a, p. 188).

In this respect the splinter group's rituals resembled the Baktaman initiations more than the standard Kivung rituals. It seems uncontroversial that both the amount and the diversity of sensory stimulation in splinter group rituals and Baktaman initiations substantially exceed that in any of the Kivung rites. That claim requires a sidebar.

By this comment we do not mean to suggest that the amount of sensory stimulation connected with any ritual is easy to quantify or compare, especially across modalities. The difficulties are *enormous*. For example, is the intensity of light more or less visually stimulating than the diversity of color? Or, worse yet, does the gustatory stimulation of eating pork fat exceed the auditory stimulation of singing?

Acknowledging both the enormity and the complexity of the difficulties involved, we shall make various intuitive judgments about these matters as we compare the competing hypotheses. For at least two reasons, though, intuition may not be so bad here. First, for most of our purposes we need not place too high a premium on precision, since the judgments in question are all *comparative*. The critical question that will arise will not be precisely how much sensory pageantry any ritual involves but simply whether one ritual involves more or less sensory pageantry than another. Making *accurate* comparative judgments often requires very little *precise* knowledge. For example, when looking at a map of the United States we do not need to know their precise areas in order to judge that Montana is larger than North Carolina. For most of the relevant judgments the differences in the rituals' levels of sensory pageantry are so substantial that they present no problems. That the splinter group's nightly vigils were more emotionally inspiring than the Kivung temple rituals is not controversial.

That leads to our second reason why intuitive judgments will suffice in the comparison of our theory with Whitehouse's. However daunting the justification of such judgments may prove, that is not what is at issue. What is is the content of those judgments, and Whitehouse and we *concur* about the comparative levels of sensory pageantry in the Baktaman, Kivung, and splinter group rituals. There is no disagreement about what the facts are here concerning the relevant comparisons. End of sidebar.

Stimulating ritual participants' senses is the most straightforward, sure-fire means available for arousing their emotions. The intuition (again acknowledging myriad complications just off stage – see, for example, Tucker et al., 1990) is that the resulting levels of emotional excitement are often at least roughly proportional to the levels of sensory stimulation. These emotional responses are virtually always involuntary, and with particularly intense sensory stimulation, they are often difficult to control.

Some religious rituals are renowned for their sensory pageantry. Rituals employ countless means of arousing participants' emotions. Consider everything from the feasting, dancing, and singing of the Dadul-Maranagi splinter group to the pageantry of a royal wedding or the investiture of a pope. No sensory modality has been forgotten. Religious rituals are replete with the smells of burning incense and the tastes of special foods, the sounds of chant and the sights of ornate attire, the kinesthetic sensations of the dancer and the haptic sensations of the fully immersed. As we noted in the previous chapter, some rituals have included far more gripping ways of provoking haptic sensations, in particular. The Baktaman and hundreds of other groups worldwide, whose initiations include excruciating torture, are experts on these fronts.

Of course, sensory pageantry is only a means to an end. One reliable method of arousing human beings' emotions is to stimulate their senses. Sensory stimulation, however, is not the only means for doing so. Occasionally religious systems enlist other means. Perhaps the most common is dreams. Or when such substances are available, religious systems can dispense with some of the sensory pageantry and rely on hallucinogenic drugs to induce altered cognitive and emotional states. Baninge introduces another one of the old stand-bys to the Dadul-Maranagi splinter group. Insisting that participants carry out all subsequent ritual activity in the nude introduced an unprecedented level of sexual arousal to the people of Dadul and Maranagi (though see the discussion below about the rapidity with which participants became habituated to these circumstances).

Recognizing that sometimes religious systems achieve the necessary levels of motivation in participants by such alternative means, we shall, none the less, focus throughout on what we have been calling sensory pageantry, i.e., on the stimulation of participants' various sense modalities in order to arouse their emotions. We do proceed, however, with the understanding that, ultimately, talk only of "sensory pageantry" is a convenient shorthand for a variety of means religions employ for inciting elevated emotion in participants in order to increase the probabilities that they will transmit their religious systems. (Indeed, we shall, henceforth, include the nudity of the Dadul-Maranagi splinter group under the category of sensory pageantry, even though we recognize that it involves a different form of arousal.)

We and Whitehouse share three assumptions here:

1 that participants find rituals that are loaded with sensory pageantry emotionally provocative;

2 that, whatever the mechanisms, this emotional provocation tends to increase the probabilities that at least some features of these rituals will prove more memorable than they would otherwise be; and

3 that such emotional provocation also increases the probabilities that participants will be motivated to transmit their religious representations to others.

We agree, in short, about the effects of sensory pageantry and about the two major reasons why rituals incorporate it when they do. Our disagreements mostly concern the "when they do" part of the previous sentence. The empirical question we want to explore is "*which* religious rituals incorporate such high levels of sensory pageantry?" or, given our common assumptions about its effects, "under what conditions do religious rituals turn up the emotional volume?" Why do rituals migrate toward the second attractor?

Two modes of religiosity

Whitehouse's short answer (e.g., 1992, p. 785) to this question and to the more general question of why rituals migrate toward either of the two attractor positions we have described is that this is overwhelmingly a function of rituals' performance *frequencies*. (For the case at hand, when rituals are performed infrequently, they incorporate increasing levels of sensory pageantry and, therefore, migrate toward the second attractor.) Whitehouse embeds this short answer, though, in a far more ambitious theory about what he calls two "modes of religiosity" – the "doctrinal" and the "imagistic" (1995, p. 194, and 2000). Each of these modes has its characteristic "style of codification." The doctrinal style of codification includes the ritual arrangements of our first attractor position, while the imagistic style of codification includes those of the second. Whitehouse clearly thinks of these styles of codification in terms that are quite similar to those describing the migration of ritual arrangements in the directions of these attractor positions, describing them, for example, as "empirically significant trajectories" (2000, p. 1). He explicitly asserts that "the Melanesian traditions examined gravitate strongly towards one or other of the two modes of religiosity, or towards both but within readily distinguishable domains of operation" (2000, p. 2).

Whitehouse acknowledges straightaway that theoreticians of religion from Max Weber (1947) to Ernest Gellner (1969) have proposed such dichotomous schemes. However, his proposal has at least three notable features. First, although he hedges on this point occasionally (see, for example, Whitehouse, 2000, p. 160), his theory is general. It is clear most of the time that his theory applies to religious systems of any shape or size at any place or time. Second, the theory's scope is enormous. Whitehouse argues for substantial correlations among the values of thirteen different variables pertaining to religious systems. (See figure 3.1.) These thirteen variables deal with social, political, structural, historical, ideological, demographic, and cognitive issues. The third and, for our purposes, most significant feature is that at its core Whitehouse's theory (1995, p. 194) contains a cognitively oriented, causal hypothesis – again, Whitehouse's occasional hedges to the contrary notwithstanding (e.g., 2000, pp. 3–4).

More specifically, Whitehouse (1995, p. 220) insists – correctly we believe – that any theory about social and cultural forces that does not refer to the "micro-mechanisms of cognition and communication,"[1] which mediate their interactions, will be importantly incomplete. He (1995, p. 197) labels the four pivotal variables among the thirteen in his theory "frequency of transmission," "cognitive processing, " "style of codification," and "revelatory potential." Whitehouse argues that differential frequencies in opportunities to transmit cultural materials occasion different cognitive (particularly mnemonic) processes, which determine the styles of codification and, in particular, the "revelatory potentials" of religious materials. Those styles of codification (and associated revelatory

Variable	Doctrinal mode	Imagistic mode
1. Style of codification	Verbalized doctrine and exegesis (explanation)	Iconic imagery
2. Frequency of transmission	Repetitive (routinized)	Periodic (at most every few years)
3. Cognitive processing	Generalized schemas (semantic memory)	Unique schemas (episodic memory)
4. Political ethos	Universalistic (imagined community)	Particularistic (face-to-face community)
5. Solidarity/cohesion	Diffuse	Intense
6. Revelatory potential	Intellectual persuasion	Emotional and sensual stimulation
7. Ideological coherence	Ideas linked by implicational logic	Ideas linked by loose connotations
8. Moral character	Strict discipline	Indulgence, license
9. Spread by	Proselytization	Group action only
10. Scale and structure	Large scale, centralized	Small scale, localized
11. Leadership type	Enduring, dynamic	Passive figureheads
12. Distribution of institutions	Uniform beliefs and practices	Variable beliefs and practices
13. Diachronic features	Rigidity (permanent "breaking away")	Flexibility (incremental change/radical innovation)

Figure 3.1   Modes of religiosity, after Whitehouse (1995, p. 197)

potentials), in turn, shape the values of the other nine variables the theory addresses (Whitehouse, 1992, p. 784 and 1995, p. 194). (See figure 3.2.) So, for example, the character of religious experience does not result from the contents of religious beliefs so much as each results from styles for codifying religious materials, which themselves hinge on the details of the underlying cognitive processing and, in particular, on the demands on human memory. Thus, although mediated by codification styles and their emotional impact (or lack thereof), the influence of cognitive processes on these constellations of social and cultural variables is substantial (Whitehouse, 1992, p. 791). Those demands on memory are a direct result of the frequencies of ritual performance. *Performance frequency, then, is the unexplained independent variable at the heart of Whitehouse's theory* (Whitehouse, 1996a, p. 175). Note, our claim is *not* that Whitehouse thinks that rituals' performance frequencies are inexplicable but only that he offers no explanation for them.

Enlisting Tulving's distinction between semantic and episodic memory, Whitehouse notes that these two types of cognitive representation arise, respectively, in connection with frequent and infrequent occasions for the

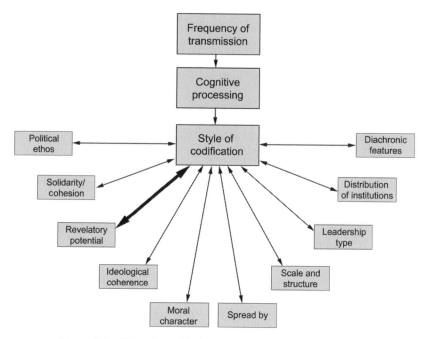

Figure 3.2   Direction of influence among Whitehouse's thirteen variables

transmission of cultural materials. He claims that the divergent principles of codification characteristic of the mainstream Kivung ritual system, on the one hand, and those of the Baktaman and the Dadul-Maranagi splinter group, on the other, simply represent adaptations to these differential demands on memory. Initially contrasting the Kivung and Baktaman systems (1992) and subsequently those of the Kivung and the Dadul-Maranagi splinter group (1995) and of the Paliau Movement and its Noise and Ghost splinter groups (2000), Whitehouse argues (1992, p. 789) that "messages are cultivated, structured and transmitted by two contrasting techniques ... these techniques constitute particular adaptations to differences in the frequency of reproduction and hence in the demands made on memory ..." These two contrasting techniques connect respectively with Whitehouse's two modes of religiosity.

Infrequent transmission dictates an imagistic mode of religiosity, whose style of codification relies on iconic *imagery* and whose revelatory potential turns on "emotional and sensual stimulation" (Whitehouse, 1995, p. 197). Whitehouse suggests that this codification style overlaps substantially with Barth's analogic coding. Both employ "non-verbal imagery."

Whitehouse associates this imagistic mode with indulgent, small-scale, socially cohesive groups that tend to have loosely formulated, flexible ideology.

The imagistic mode arises when the occasions for transmitting religious materials are infrequent and, consequently, participants must depend upon episodic memory. Relying on episodic memories means that the retention of cultural knowledge in such settings hinges on participants' abilities to recollect particular, specific events from their pasts (such as their initiations).[2] The major point is that this imagistic mode relies on the revelatory potential of "emotional and sensual stimulation and cognitive shocks" to engender improved episodic memory (Whitehouse, 1995, p. 198). Whitehouse (1996b, p. 713) stresses that "intense emotional states are a crucial element of the nexus" of factors characteristic of the imagistic mode.

The sort of intense sensory excitation and resulting emotional arousal typical of rituals in the imagistic mode would make little sense if people participated in these rituals frequently. The expenditures necessary to produce the sensory pageantry would be a profoundly inefficient use of resources, since, as Lagawop's conduct during the early stages of her possession indicates, the effects of frequency alone could suffice for memory. In addition, Whitehouse suggests that frequent exposure could result in participants' *habituation* to such sensory stimulation.

The transmission of Baktaman-type messages depends upon the unique and intense quality of ritual experience. It is not conducive to the cultivation of such messages to repeat them very often. Repetition deprives the experience of its uniqueness. Meanwhile, the intensity is largely generated by suffering which nobody would be anxious to repeat and which, if it were repeated, would not yield up its original fruits of revelation. (1992, p. 787; see also 1995, pp. 215–216)

Ironically, substantially increasing the frequency of rituals that are loaded with sensory pageantry will considerably escalate costs while producing diminishing returns. More is not better. To be effective for the long run, religions must administer sensory pageantry in carefully timed doses. So, a religious system that has frequent performances of its rituals will not utilize the imagistic mode. Instead, it will foster Whitehouse's doctrinal mode of religiosity.

In contrast to the imagistic mode, whose style of codification relies on iconic imagery, the style of codification the doctrinal mode exhibits is fundamentally *linguistic*. The so-called "religions of the book" operate chiefly in the doctrinal mode. Common sense, let alone experimental cognitive psychology, counsels, however, that without reading, writing, and available texts, the only way people can gain command of a substantial body of linguistically formulated materials is by means of frequent exposure or rehearsal. Memory in the doctrinal mode depends upon participants building up general schemas in semantic memory on the basis of frequent encounters with religious materials. Transmission does not depend upon participants' recollections of their specific experiences of emotionally stirring religious rituals.

Whitehouse associates the doctrinal mode with proselytizing religions that are not confined to a single locale. Consequently, their orientation is "universalistic" and their communities are mostly "imagined" – with less social cohesion than religious communities that operate in the imagistic mode. With the doctrinal mode the tie that binds is not experiences in common of similar, emotionally provocative rituals loaded with imagery. Its revelatory potential turns on "intellectual persuasion." It arises from disciplined mastery of a unified, logically integrated, inflexible collection of often elaborate, explicitly formulated beliefs that a focused leadership has compiled in a mostly "emotionless way" (Whitehouse, 1995, p. 197).

Properly introducing these bodies of doctrine, let alone insuring their mastery, requires frequent presentations. This is especially so if a culture lacks the tools of literacy. "In an oral tradition, persuasion by the logic and coherence of cosmology and ritual at the same time necessitates frequent repetition . . . their persuasive capacities are in no small degree a function of the extent to which they can be preserved as an entirety through frequent transmission" (Whitehouse, 1992, pp. 787–788; also see 2000, pp. 105–106). Without literacy, gaining command of an extensive system of beliefs and practices is impossible without their continual re-presentation.

Cognitive theories (both Whitehouse's and ours) aim to identify fundamental variables underlying all religious systems. These theories do not distinguish Western religions or the great "world religions" or even literate religions from the rest (Lawson and McCauley, 1993). Both Whitehouse and we claim that the underlying cognitive dynamics are the same in all religions. (We just disagree about some of the salient cognitive details.) So, contrary to a major school of thought within cultural anthropology (e.g., Goody, 1987), both Whitehouse and we hold that, finally, literacy is *not* the fundamental variable in this mix. (See too Donald, 1991.) Although literacy can substantially relieve the cognitive burden that participants' memories must bear, Whitehouse maintains that this does not substantially alter the patterns characteristic of the doctrinal mode. Religions in the doctrinal mode overwhelmingly focus on frequent repetition of highly routinized rituals with little emotional excitement, whether they occur in literate cultures or not.

The crucial point is that a focus on linguistically formulated, logically coherent systems of beliefs and on proselytizing to a wider world marks the religious systems of at least some *non-literate* societies. The Pomio Kivung is but one example. Looking no further than Melanesia, Whitehouse (1996a, p. 191, and 2000) notes others. (See too Severi, 1987 and 1993, and Sherzer, 1983 and 1990.) Whether the tools of literacy are available to aid in the cultivation of religious sensibilities or not, religious systems that operate in the doctrinal mode rely on frequently repeating what are, comparatively speaking, emotionally tame ritual practices.

After advancing these two ideal types, i.e., the imagistic and doctrinal modes of religiosity, Whitehouse indicates that, in fact, they are not always either stable arrangements or uniform ones. As to their stability, some religious systems seem to fluctuate between the two modes. Whitehouse (2000, chapter 7) discusses both the introduction of the doctrinal mode in Papua New Guinea, its tendency to dominate once it arises, and its periodic fluctuation there with the imagistic mode. (As subsequent discussion in chapter 5 will show, a pattern of such alternation will prove the best description of the history of the Pomio Kivung.) Whitehouse also speculates on the evolution of the doctrinal mode. He (2000, chapter 8) agrees with Donald (1991) that it emerged much later than the imagistic.

Regarding their uniformity, Whitehouse concedes that even in New Guinea, where the operations of the two modes are usually fairly discrete, the distinction between the two patterns is not always completely clear. He acknowledges that sometimes the two modes become "so enmeshed that the analytical distinction seems to break down" (2000, p. 149; see also p. 52). He offers routinized practices for inducing ecstatic or mystical states in Hinduism, Buddhism, Taoism, and Islam as apt illustrations of these *mixed mode* phenomena (2000, p. 149).

Such qualifications to his dichotomous scheme are appropriate concessions to the complexities of the real world. In a particular religious system, nothing about alternation between the two modes over time is inconsistent with anything Whitehouse says. However, the ability of the cognitive principles to which Whitehouse appeals to make sense of either *why* a ritual system might alternate over time between rituals characteristic of the doctrinal and imagistic modes or *how* the two modes might become "enmeshed" is entirely unclear.

The ritual frequency hypothesis

Whatever qualifications he considers, Whitehouse never seriously backtracks on his basic hypothesis that the fundamental causal variables shaping the styles of codification that characterize the two modes of religiosity concern cognitive processing. Nor does he hedge his claim that these patterns of cognitive processing result from frequency of transmission. (See figure 3.2.) The ritual frequency hypothesis anchors Whitehouse's overall theory.

The hypothesis is straightforward and clear. It proposes that the amount of sensory pageantry and, therefore, the amount of emotional stimulation any religious ritual involves are inversely proportional to the frequency with which that ritual is performed. Performing rituals frequently correlates with low levels of sensory pageantry and little emotional kick, while the infrequent performance of a ritual necessitates higher levels of sensory pageantry resulting in a bigger emotional bang.

Whitehouse is clear about the crucial role of the underlying cognitive dynamics. The ritual frequency hypothesis delineates the relations between the three most important variables of Whitehouse's larger theory of religious modes. As we have seen, "frequency of transmission" governs "cognitive processing," which drives the "styles of codification" and their associated "revelatory potentials," which, in turn, strongly influence the remaining nine variables. (See figure 3.2.) So, for example, Whitehouse claims to demonstrate (1992, p. 777) that the "differences between Baktaman and 'kivung' religions are related to the relative frequency of cultural transmission or reproduction, and are shown to represent adaptations to the variable demands placed on memory in the respective societies." Infrequently performed rituals call upon episodic memory; hence these rituals include comparatively greater sensory pageantry in order to produce the sorts of emotional responses that will occasion enhanced recall. The power of Baktaman initiation

lies in its remorseless assaults on the physical senses, contrasting and confusing pleasure and pain but above all bombarding the novices with surprising stimuli from multiple directions ... these features are bound together as creative adaptations to the demands which infrequent transmission inevitably makes on memory ... (Whitehouse, 1992, p. 794)

On the other hand, repetitive rituals that occur at the relentless pace the Kivung maintains engage the processes of semantic memory for which sensory pageantry is unnecessary (and, as we saw above, maybe even counterproductive). Whitehouse (1992, p. 781) claims that "kivung ... ritual action tends to be alternately cerebral and routine, and rarely does it construct meaning out of physical sensation or seek to excite or encourage a diversity of such experiences." Since Kivung rituals occur so often, they need not thrill participants in order to insure their recollection.

We shall argue in chapter 5 that, its idiosyncrasies notwithstanding, the Dadul-Maranagi splinter group manifests one pattern of responses to general psychological considerations that constrain religious ritual systems the world over. For now the notable immediate consequence of Whitehouse's theory of religious modes is its apparent ability to make sense of the Dadul-Maranagi splinter group and its emergent rituals. On most relevant dimensions, the Pomio Kivung is a paradigmatic example of a religious system operating in the doctrinal mode. Its rituals clearly epitomize the conditions of the first attractor. In the doctrinal mode a religious system's beliefs and practices undergo considerable elaboration and integration. The resulting system is disciplined in practice and logically unified in belief but also correspondingly less flexible than religion in the imagistic mode. Once participants have worked the relations of ideas and practices out so precisely, a single innovation can be disruptive, since it may have consequences that affect logical and practical relations throughout the entire system. (According to Whitehouse [1996a, p. 191], the Pomio Kivung leaders have explicitly recognized these interconnections in their own system.) Consequently, innovation in religions of the doctrinal sort, unlike that in imagistic religious systems, is less likely to occur piecemeal (Whitehouse, 1992, p. 778).

Whitehouse's account of modes of religiosity, then, predicts that substantial innovation in a religious system like that of the Pomio Kivung will result in the sort of significant practical and ritual upheavals that the Dadul-Maranagi splinter group exhibited. By way of Tanotka's dreams they constructed a supplementary – though not inconsistent – mythology about the parallel origins of the Kivung in the Dadul-Maranagi area and reintroduced both the *awanga* and the *ilotka*. From a practical standpoint, the people of Dadul eventually abandoned their gardens and their homes, while the people of Maranagi built the new roundhouse and welcomed their compatriots from Dadul. The group's ritual innovations were sweeping and dramatic.

Since the splinter group had never performed their new rituals before, these rituals had an initial frequency of zero. According to the ritual frequency hypothesis, they should, therefore, be *saturated* with sensory pageantry – and they were. Whitehouse emphasizes that the splinter group rituals

provoked a diversity of emotions and sensations. The haunting and stirring melodies and rhythms accompanying the dances, the splendor of *awanga* costumes, the athleticism and aggression of the participants, the synchrony and eloquence of collective movements, all contributed to intense feelings . . . The heat, smells, sounds, and visual impact of dances created a dramatic sensual experience . . . The first ring ceremony was . . . profoundly evocative . . . (1996a, p. 186; also see 1995, pp. 195–196)

With no developed tradition of doctrine or practice, the splinter group had to bank on achieving religious inspiration by means of emotionally provocative rituals – just as the ritual frequency hypothesis predicts. The splinter group's eruption amounted to a community collectively overturning a doctrinal religious system in favor of religious experiences and an emergent religious movement both of which functioned in the imagistic mode – introducing rituals packed with sensory pageantry. Ritual arrangements among the Dadul-Maranagi splinter group far more closely approximated the conditions at the second attractor, rather than the first.

Our differences with Whitehouse's views may seem minor. We share objects of study, viz., the transmission of religious systems and the roles that ritual, emotion, and memory play in that process. We have the same convictions about the ability of cognitively oriented research to illuminate these matters. We agree that the manipulation of emotion in ritual is tied to mnemonic issues. We admire Whitehouse's ambitious attempts to formulate so encompassing a theory of human religiosity, and we continue to applaud his focus on cognitive processing as the decisive underlying variable explaining the patterns he ponders. Moreover, we acknowledge that neither admiration nor applause is enough. Any alternative proposal we advance about the cognitive underpinnings of religious ritual had better yield predictions that square pretty well with most of predictions of the ritual frequency hypothesis. That is because they seem, at least so far, to be mostly on target. Whitehouse's ritual frequency hypothesis does a pretty good job, so the more fundamental variables our theory pinpoints had better correlate fairly well with performance frequency. (They do.)

Whitehouse's ritual frequency hypothesis springs from the thoroughly reasonable assumption that the evolution of religious ritual systems is likely to reflect sensitivity to the role that mnemonic variables play in the transmission of those systems. We do not disagree. Our most important difference with Whitehouse, however, pertains to the conditions under which rituals contain the extensive sensory pageantry that produces elevated levels of emotion. We disagree about the critical properties of the rituals that gravitate to each of the two attractor positions. The variable on which we focus, viz., *ritual form*, not only gives a better account of the place of emotional arousal in ritual, it also suggests additional grounds, besides the mnemonic considerations on which we have focused so far, for *why* some rituals are emotionally arousing. We shall also show how ritual form accounts for the *motivational* roles rituals play. Remembering cultural representations is necessary but not sufficient for the transmission of culture. Participants must not only remember their cultural representations, they must also be motivated to transmit them. (We will say much more on this later.)

The question of why some rituals are emotionally provocative connects straightforwardly with a further difference with Whitehouse that we have already noted. In the previous chapter we disagreed with him about the role of heightened emotion in the consolidation of episodic memories. We reviewed psychological research showing that many flashbulb memories are not accurate and that abrupt arousal of emotion is not necessary to produce ones that are.[3] Consequently, we are less sanguine than Whitehouse about a specific, dedicated, Now Print mechanism in the brain triggered by high emotion. By contrast, the cognitive alarm hypothesis suggests that high emotion tends both to marshal and to focus cognitive resources on its apparent causes, which, *if vindicated by subsequent developments*, marks the events as especially memorable.

Connecting sensory pageantry and emotional arousal with religious ritual form

The ritual frequency hypothesis maintains that the infrequent performance of some rituals is what necessitates high emotion in order to produce flashbulb-like, episodic memories. By contrast, we shall defend the *ritual form hypothesis*, which holds that instead of ritual frequency, it is *ritual form* or, more precisely, participants' tacit knowledge about differences in ritual form that determines *which* religious rituals migrate to one or the other of the two attractor positions. As we have already noted, ritual form correlates well with rituals' performance frequencies; indeed, we shall argue that it is one of the principal considerations *influencing* performance frequency. Because of this influence and because performance frequency is the unexplained independent variable of the ritual frequency hypothesis, ritual form is a more fundamental causal variable.

Religious ritual and motivation

Participants' representations of ritual form, explicated in our theory of religious ritual competence, contain the variables that determine which rituals include comparatively higher levels of sensory stimulation and emotional excitement and which do not. Not only does the ritual form hypothesis offer *additional* independent cognitive grounds for why memory is important here, but it also insists that memory is not the whole story about *why* some rituals introduce sensory pageantry and arouse participants' emotions. Motivation (for lack of a better term) matters too.

We shall argue for two conclusions here: first, that those religious rituals that settle around the second attractor, containing increased sensory pageantry, stimulate participants' emotions in order not only to augment their recall for these events but also to motivate them religiously, and, second, that our general theory of religious ritual competence explains why those rituals that must produce enhanced episodic memories are precisely the rituals that must fortify religious motivation.

We do not mean to suggest by all of this that Whitehouse's theory of religious modes has nothing to say about motivational questions. He emphasizes that imagistic practices, grounded in episodic memories of face-to-face interactions with in-group members, promote intense local cohesion, which brings with it all sorts of social and military benefits. Our claim is only that the ritual form hypothesis points to uniquely *religious* questions about motivation and to a deeper account of the cognitive matters at stake (specifically, participants' sensitivities to aspects of ritual form and, especially, to the roles that putative CPS-agents play therein).

Before we develop our own views, though, we must add a sidebar about the notion of motivation. For two related reasons we use the term "motivation" reluctantly here. First, this is not an area where experimental psychology provides much help. Cognitivism has influenced few areas in experimental psychology any less than it has the study of motivation, where in many quarters behaviorist methods and concepts continue to prevail. They confer restrictive connotations on the notion of motivation that purchase it some precision, but do so at the cost of sacrificing the resulting technical concepts' connections with many of our intuitions about the underlying phenomena. We do not intend our informal talk of motivation in what follows to invoke any of these technical uses of the term.

The second reason for our trepidation about this term is the flip-side of the first. The term "motivation" is inevitably vague, and talk of *religious* motivation only magnifies this vagueness. Minimally, motivation concerns the complex connections that link emotion and cognition with action and with one another; *religious motivation* concerns such connections when the emotion, cognition, and action concern religious matters. We will use "motivation" not much more precisely than it is used in everyday discourse, but our use of the term will retain connections to widespread intuitions about these matters. For our purposes, then, "religious motivation" deals with the cluster of feelings, attitudes, beliefs, and behaviors that bear on the probabilities of participants' acting to transmit their religious knowledge or, at least, affirming an intention to do so. On its own that characterization will not clarify matters much, but taken in conjunction with our theory's overall explanatory success, it is a step in the right direction. With these two hesitations in mind, we return to the main line of argument.

The ritual form hypothesis accounts for the interplay between

1 ritual
2 sensory pageantry (and the emotion that accompanies it)
3 memory, and
4 motivation.

It follows as an inference to the best explanation from our larger theory of religious ritual competence and the cognitive alarm hypothesis. We shall explore its connections with each.

The typology of religious rituals revisited

Our theory of religious ritual competence is rooted in the claim that participants' cognitive representations of their religious ritual acts result from the same system for the representation of action that we utilize in representing ordinary actions. The representations of rituals arise from a perfectly ordinary cognitive system expressly devoted to the representation of action, *not* (just) the representation of ritual action.

We mentioned empirical research in developmental psychology that shows that within the first year of life infants gain command of the categories "agent" and "action" and deploy them to make sense of their experience and guide their behavior. Other developmental research reveals that by school age children have mastered a "theory of mind" for managing in the social world – a theory whose basic principles, in the course of cognitive development, seem to undergo elaboration but, otherwise, little change thereafter.

The ability to distinguish agents and their actions, respectively, from other entities and events provides the child with all of the representational resources necessary for the operation of the action representation system that our theory of religious ritual competence proposes. Possessing a full-blown theory of mind permits their thorough-going entry into the world of religious thought and action (Boyer, 2001).

Chapter 1 provided an overview of our theory of religious ritual competence, which we first presented in *Rethinking Religion*. In the next few paragraphs, we provide an even more condensed account of the theory's critical claims.

The action representation system generates structural descriptions of actions. The structural descriptions of religious rituals take some entries for the three action slots that differ from those for ordinary actions. These special entries include CPS-agents (such as gods, ancestors, and saints),

(Culturally Postulated Superhumans)

categories of religious ritual practitioners (such as priests, witches, and bishops), sanctified objects (such as holy water, altars, and cemeteries), and unique ritual acts (such as baptisms, blessings, sacrifices, initiations, investitures, and so on).

If a ritual's immediate structural description does not include an entry for a CPS-agent, then it includes presumptions about enabling actions involving CPS-agents that bring inquiries about the rituals' causal and rational foundations to an end. A ritual's full structural description includes that immediate structural description plus the further structural descriptions of all of the enabling ritual actions the current ritual presumes as well as accounts of their connections with the current ritual's various elements. Recall that enabling actions are simply (earlier) rituals whose successful completion is necessary for the completion of the current ritual.

Knowledge about only two dimensions of participants' representations of CPS-agents' involvement in religious rituals' action structures accounts for a wide array of those rituals' features. The first dimension concerns whether a CPS-agent serves as a ritual element in the current ritual or, if not, to which of the current ritual's elements CPS-agents are ritually connected. Since more than one element in the current ritual may have such connections, the second critical dimension concerns the *number* of enabling rituals each of these connections requires to implicate a CPS-agent in the ritual's description. The connection involving the fewest enabling rituals defines the *initial appearance* of a CPS-agent in a ritual's structural description and, thereby, the element with the most *direct* connection with the gods.

The PSA and PSI provide bases for assessing variation on these two dimensions. These principles classify a ritual according to the *location* of the first CPS-agent implicated in its structural description, assigning each ritual a *type* on the basis of its *profile* and its *depth*. The PSA specifies a ritual's profile. It distinguishes special agent rituals from special patient and special instrument rituals. The important contrast here is between a CPS-agent serving as the agent in the current ritual, or having its most direct ritual connections with the agent of the current ritual, and the CPS-agent serving in one of the current ritual's other roles (such as its patient), or having its most direct ritual connections with one of the other elements that does.

A full structural description of a religious ritual, including all of its enabling rituals, may include many entries for CPS-agents (or the same CPS-agent). Not only are priests who perform weddings ritually connected with God through their ordination, the brides and the grooms are too by way of their confirmations. The PSI states that the element with the most direct ritual connection with a CPS-agent determines that ritual's *depth*.

Principal of Superhuman immediacy [handwritten marginal note]

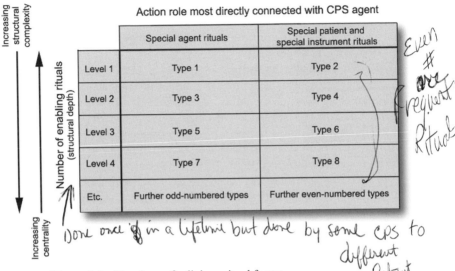

Figure 3.3   Typology of religious ritual forms

(handwritten annotations: "Even # are Frequent Rituals"; "Done once if in a lifetime but done by some CPS to different Patient")

In religious rituals – at least from a formal standpoint – the buck not only stops with the gods, it might be said to stop with the *nearest* god.

Combining these two dimensions (profile and depth) generates the typology of religious rituals' structural descriptions, which summarizes the organization of the resulting system of classification. (See figure 3.3.)

The PSA distinguishes two basic types, designated by odd and even numbers. *Special agent rituals* are always odd-numbered types, since the initial entry for a CPS-agent is ritually connected with the role of the agent who is acting in the current ritual. The most immediate connection with a CPS-agent in the current ritual is by way of its *agent's* ritual history. By contrast, *special patient and special instrument rituals* are always even-numbered types, since the most immediate connection with a CPS-agent is by way of one or the other of the roles represented by the last two slots in the current ritual's structural description, accommodating the entries for the ritual's act and patient, respectively. Since the relevant elaboration of the acts in rituals involves the specification of instruments, this is to say that the gods' most direct connections with rituals of even-numbered types are either by way of the instruments or by way of the patients in the rituals.

The ritual form hypothesis

It is this distinction between special agent rituals and special patient and special instrument rituals that will concern us throughout the remainder of this book. The PSA defines odd- and even-numbered ritual types at each level of structural depth. (For the sake of brevity, we shall henceforth refer to these as "odd-numbered rituals" and "even-numbered rituals," respectively.) At whatever level of depth the initial entry for a CPS-agent appears in a ritual's description, the question can always be raised as to whether it involves a connection with the current ritual's agent or with one of its other elements. If it is connected with the current ritual's agent, i.e., if it is a special agent ritual, then the PSA assigns it to the odd-numbered type for the level of depth in question; if it is connected with another of the current ritual's elements, then the PSA assigns it to the level's even-numbered type.

To keep things simple, we shall assume a scenario that places a wedding at the third level of structural depth. The priest has been ordained by the Church, which in a theoretical ritual is the bride of Christ. (To repeat, *far* more complicated scenarios are possible.[4]) Because the first appearance of a CPS-agent in its structural description arises in connection with the priest, who is the agent performing the wedding, it is a special agent ritual, i.e., a ritual of type five. (Again, see figure 3.3.) Although a priest presides at the celebration of the Eucharist too, an entry for a CPS-agent occurs at the very first level in the structural description of that ritual. When they are consumed, the body and blood of Christ (again – on the orthodox Catholic account) serve as the patients of this ritual. They constitute the initial appearance of a CPS-agent in its structural description. Thus, it is a special patient ritual at the first level of depth, which is to say it is a type two ritual.

That is a quick look at a few of the trees, but, ultimately, only a couple of the major ridges in the forest matter for what follows. To clarify how the ritual form hypothesis makes sense of which religious rituals gravitate, respectively, to the two attractors, i.e., to clarify how it makes sense of the place of sensory pageantry and emotional arousal in religious rituals, we must focus on the distinction between the special agent rituals and the two sorts of even-numbered rituals. Using this formal vocabulary, we can provide a preliminary formulation of the pivotal prediction of the ritual form hypothesis.

For all religious ritual systems, the *comparative* levels of sensory pageantry within *particular religious communities* will be higher in special agent rituals than in rituals whose forms exemplify even-numbered types (i.e., special patient and special instrument rituals) – regardless of the rituals' depths.

Let us unpack this claim.

Beginning with the first of the italicized qualifications, the ritual form hypothesis accounts for *comparative* levels of sensory pageantry between rituals. As our comments in the previous section suggested, quantitative measures of sensory stimulation in something as fluid as a ritual are not easy to obtain and, once had, are extremely difficult to compare across modalities anyway. Emotional arousal is a many splendored thing. An ecstatic response to good fortune is every bit as much a kind of emotional arousal as is the profound sadness that typically accompanies the loss of a loved one. (See Tucker et al., 1990.) Even when they are possible, direct measures of emotional arousal (e.g., self-assessment) are not precise and precise measures (e.g., heart rate) are not direct. What is available for most of us here are a few first-hand experiences and lots of intuitions. But, as we argued before, comparative judgments that are accurate often do not require constituent judgments that are precise, and in this case, in particular, the differences are usually so substantial that the comparisons are non-controversial.

That leads to the second qualification. The ritual form hypothesis makes sense of comparisons of rituals' levels of sensory pageantry *within particular religious communities* only. The hypothesis does not predict differences either between different religious systems or even between different religious communities within the same religious system. Cultures and social classes can vary widely concerning the levels of sensory pageantry and emotional display that constitute the relevant base lines. (Contrast, for example, Baktaman and Scandinavian Protestants' sensibilities.) On this point, local differences matter. The ritual form hypothesis only addresses the comparative differences between the levels of sensory pageantry and emotional excitement that religious rituals possess within a specific religious community.[5]

With those qualifications in place, let us turn to explicating the import of the hypothesis. At the most general level, the hypothesis concerns ritual *form*, because it is participants' tacit knowledge of and resulting sensitivities to the differences in ritual form between two broad groups of religious rituals that are the crucial variables that account for the connections between religious ritual and sensory pageantry. So far, we have provided relatively technical accounts of these differences (within the framework of our theory). It will help to describe these two groups of rituals less formally.

The frequency hypothesis holds that frequently performed rituals require less sensory pageantry. This is the typical (though not universal) profile of even-numbered rituals, i.e., special patient and special instrument rituals. What are these rituals like? The first point to emphasize is that all of the religious rituals that participants perform frequently are even-numbered rituals. We will postpone addressing the question of *why* they perform them frequently until the next chapter, where we will take up the problem of *precisely* specifying the notion of performance frequency.

The forms of these (even-numbered) special patient and special instrument rituals permit participants to do them repeatedly. Participants perform these rites either with instruments or on patients that enjoy special ritual connections with the gods. Often the patient of an even-numbered ritual *is* a CPS-agent – a *special* patient indeed. Most offerings, including sacrificial ones, illustrate this arrangement. Consider, for example, the role of the ancestors to whom the food is offered in the Kivung temple rituals.

To put it the other way around, the agents in these special patient and special instrument rituals are more distant (ritually) from the religious system's CPS-agents than are either the implements they use (e.g., holy water) or the patients of their actions (e.g., the Baining ancestors). Whatever connections they have with the gods occur at a point of greater structural depth than do the connections of one or more of these other ritual elements. (For an illustration of a special instrument ritual, see the extended discussion of the basic Christian blessing in Lawson and McCauley, 1990, pp. 95–121.)

Under these circumstances the agents – whether they are priests or ordinary participants – usually *repeat* these rituals, since from the standpoint of ritual form, whatever connections they have with the gods are, quite literally, of secondary importance at best in these sorts of ritual contexts. The secondary status of their connections with CPS-agents in these rituals means that the ritual agents in special patient and special instrument rituals are not acting in the gods' stead, as they do in all of the special agent rituals. Consequently, these ritual agents do not bring about super-permanent religious effects. As we noted in chapter 1, the effects of special patient and special instrument rituals are always *temporary only*. Getting a second blessing can help; getting initiated a second time is simply redundant. The ancestors may be well fed today, but they get hungry again tomorrow. Note that this explains what is in some ways the theologically puzzling fact that consuming the body and blood of Christ does not absolve participants once and for all. This outcome turns on considerations of ritual form, theological assumptions to the contrary notwithstanding.

Special agent rituals

As we have noted before, even-numbered, special patient and special instrument rituals are *repeatable* (and, usually, frequently repeated). Odd-numbered, special agent rituals are *non-repeated* rituals. We need to say a bit more about what is at stake here. In one sense all rituals in which human beings participate are rituals they do repeatedly. However, because a religious *community* repeats all rituals (given enough time), it does not follow that particular *individual* participants do them repeatedly. Non-repeated special agent rituals are rituals, such as initiations or ordinations, in which participants fill the patient's role in the ritual only once in the course of their lives. By contrast, even-numbered, repeatable rituals are rituals, such as the Puja or the ritual Oban dances for the dead in Japan, in which none of the human participants' roles have constraints of this sort. People participate in these rituals time and time again. Though specific individuals – for example, those who are not priests – may only serve in some roles in these rituals, no role is one that eligible participants characteristically take only once in their lifetimes.

The *same* individuals do what we are calling "repeatable" rituals repeatedly, whereas at least the patients change with each performance of the odd-numbered, non-repeated, special agent rituals. So, although the same rabbi may officiate at scores of them, bar mitzvahs are non-repeated rituals, because the patient's role is one that each participant fills only once. It is different participants who undergo this initiation each time, and in each case it is their one and only bar mitzvah.

Characteristically, these odd-numbered, non-repeated, special agent rituals are rituals that ritually certified religious practitioners perform, which have the profiles that they do precisely because of those practitioners' ritual certifications. Priests can perform baptisms, blessings, weddings, funerals, and more, *because* they are priests. Through earlier rituals, e.g., their ordinations, they have gained a more direct ritual connection with a CPS-agent than most of the people and many of the things that they will act upon ritually. So, when they act ritually in those cases, they act in place of the CPS-agent with whom their ritual certification connects them. They act as ritual intermediaries with no less than what constitutes a CPS-agent's seal of approval. The agents in these rituals *must* have such connections with the gods.

When they are religious rituals (and they usually are), the classic rites of passage are paradigmatic examples of odd-numbered, special agent rituals (Van Gennep, 1960). Typically, the rituals that mark entry into this world at birth, into the adult world during adolescence, and into another world at death are rituals participants only go through once. Exceptions, for example in the case of multiple rituals at death (Hertz, 1960 and Metcalf and Huntington, 1991), invariably involve peculiarities in the accompanying religious conceptual schemes that conform to this general account.

Why does the connection with CPS-agents that religious ritual practitioners possess by virtue of their certification *not* dominate in even-numbered rites? After all, religious practitioners perform sacrifices or

Holy Communion just as they perform initiations or baptisms. Nothing about the even-numbered rituals abrogates these previously established ritual relationships. The difference with special patient and special instrument rituals is that some other element in the current ritual, the patient or the instrument, either has a more intimate relationship with a CPS-agent or, even more straightforwardly, *is* a CPS-agent, for example, in the Puja.

As we noted before, when the gods act, either directly or through their intermediaries, the effects are super-permanent. Of course, the psychological causation could be in just the opposite direction. Participants regard some religious arrangements as super-permanent. Transparently, these are not arrangements that mere humans can establish on their own. Consequently, the human mind inevitably implicates CPS-agents in the rituals that bring about these states of affairs. In either case, the powers of the gods and their abilities to project those powers through their intermediaries are such that these rituals need only be done *once* with each patient to establish such effects. When the gods do something – either directly or indirectly through the agency of their certified representatives – they do it once and for all. There is no need to repeat these rituals. This is why participants undergo these rites only one time. This is also the key to why the rituals filled with sensory pageantry are always rituals of this sort.

If a ritual establishes a super-permanent arrangement, it must *convince* participants that something profound is going on. Since mere humans – limited as they are in time and space – cannot inaugurate super-permanent arrangements, the gods must have had a hand in them. So, in addition, participants need to know that it is the gods who are ultimately responsible for those profound goings on. These special agent rituals often include direct indications that it is CPS-agents who are responsible for what is transpiring. For example, it is no coincidence that so many initiations include opportunities for candidates to confront particular CPS-agents directly, whether as masked dancers such as the *awanga* and *ilotka* or as skulls (Gardner, 1983) or as skulls whose eye sockets are illuminated (Fernandez, 1982) or as icons (Apuleius, 1989) or as figurines (Pfeiffer, 1982) or as images of CPS-agents in cave paintings (Mithen, 1996), etc.[6]

The cognitive alarm hypothesis holds that extreme emotions signal to human beings that the current objects of their attention are particularly significant. That contention has implications for more than just memory. The high emotion of some religious rituals establishes convictions about the significance of both those events and the agents who are putatively responsible for them, especially when they appear to be directly involved. Usually, it is in the grip of such convictions that participants are subsequently *motivated* to transmit such information to others (as appropriate).

Religious rituals' manipulations of sensory pageantry and participants' emotions are not academic exercises about proving the gods' existence. The comparatively high emotion such rituals instigate helps to persuade at least some of the participants involved not only that they have undergone fundamental changes but also that the CPS-agents, who are ultimately responsible for those changes, are *vitally* important to them and, often, to their community as well.

To summarize, then, the ritual form hypothesis differs from the frequency hypothesis both about *which* religious rituals contain elevated levels of sensory pageantry and, at least in part, about *why*. The ritual form hypothesis maintains that heightened sensory pageantry arises only in odd-numbered, special agent rituals, which characteristically spawn super-permanent effects. Ultimately, only the gods can bring about such effects; thus, in these rituals the gods either act directly or certify the action indirectly. Consequently, each individual needs to undergo these rituals only once. Although we have some differences about the details of the processes involved, Whitehouse and we agree that the comparative emotional arousal these rituals produce contributes to enhanced memory for aspects of these events. What we have argued, however, is that enhanced memory is not the whole story here. Rituals of this sort must persuade participants both of the importance of these events and of the gods' involvement. Stirring their emotions so much helps to contribute to this end. The resulting convictions play a critical role in increasing the probabilities that participants will transmit these ideas subsequently.

In the next two chapters we shall compare the merits of the ritual form and ritual frequency hypotheses. We shall examine especially closely their abilities to account for the events in Dadul and Maranagi on which Whitehouse has reported. We shall argue that the ritual form hypothesis provides not only a consistently superior explanation of this specific set of cases but a far more penetrating causal account of much larger patterns that hold both within and among religious ritual systems across cultures and through time. In other words, before we are through with this expedition we aim to stalk much bigger game.

4   Assessing the two hypotheses

Chapter overview

In this chapter we shall argue for advantages of the ritual form hypothesis over the ritual frequency hypothesis. We shall take up a wide array of considerations bearing on the two hypotheses' merits. These considerations are of two broad sorts concerning theoretical and empirical matters. We shall address theoretical and conceptual matters first in the next section, since they will help to set the stage for a fair evaluation in the remaining sections of the hypotheses' empirical predictions.

In the first section we shall defend the greater theoretical depth of the ritual form hypothesis. The argument we make in its behalf has two parts. First, we shall take up some persistent conceptual problems with the ritual frequency hypothesis. We shall argue that precisely the kinds of theoretical distinctions that the ritual form hypothesis makes are necessary to remedy these ambiguities. Second, we will show that the ritual form hypothesis isolates a more fundamental cognitive variable than either the ritual frequency hypothesis or Whitehouse's larger theory of religious modes, since ritual form is a conspicuous factor – probably the principal factor – influencing the unexplained, independent variable of the frequency hypothesis, viz., rituals' performance frequencies.

In the remainder of the chapter we turn to the hypotheses' comparative predictive and explanatory strengths with regard to the empirical facts. On pages 139–146 we shall contend that both Whitehouse's general theory and the ritual frequency hypothesis are less well equipped than our theory of ritual competence and the ritual form hypothesis to handle the explanatory problems we mentioned in the previous chapter concerning the *uniformity* of Whitehouse's doctrinal and imagistic modes. We shall also argue that they are *much* less well equipped to handle the problems surrounding the *stability* of the two modes.

The following section examines the two competing hypotheses' empirical consequences more precisely in those domains where their explanatory and predictive aspirations clearly overlap. There are four relevant types of cases. For two of these the ritual form and ritual frequency hypotheses' predictions coincide. The truth of the coincident predictions seems fairly uncontroversial, and we should note that these constitute the overwhelming majority of the known cases. As we emphasized in the previous chapter, the variables we highlight had better correlate well with performance frequency, since it predicts many of the pertinent data correctly. The correlation *is* good, because, as we argue in the first section of this chapter, ritual form may well prove the most influential variable determining performance frequency. For the other two types of cases, however, the two hypotheses' predictions diverge. We will argue that although the available evidence there is slim, what there is unequivocally favors the ritual form hypothesis. On pages 149–155 we shall consider the first sort of relevant case, viz., even-numbered special patient and special instrument rituals that have extremely low performance frequencies.

On pages 155–171 we shall take up the second sort of relevant case, viz., odd-numbered, special agent rituals that have high performance frequencies. We first examine whether this sort of case involves a contradiction in terms. We shall argue that it need not. In the course of making our case, we shall return to the ritual activities of the Dadul-Maranagi splinter group. They exhibit a means for surmounting this putative conceptual barrier and, thus, provide materials for assessing the two hypotheses' conflicting predictions.

In the final section of this chapter we explore the two hypotheses' abilities to make sense of those materials. Both hypotheses have sufficient conceptual resources to make sense of the contrasting ritual practices of the splinter group and the mainstream Kivung movement. Unlike the ritual form hypothesis, though, the ritual frequency hypothesis proves completely incapable of predicting the more fine-grained developments of the splinter group's ritual system, and, specifically, it makes the *wrong* predictions about the levels of sensory pageantry associated with its frequently performed, special agent ritual. Not only does the ritual form hypothesis make the correct predictions there, it can also explain a variety of other features regarding the splinter group's rituals concerning which the ritual frequency hypothesis remains mute. Consequently, on the basis of the correct predictions of the ritual form hypothesis both where the ritual frequency hypothesis fails and where it supplies no predictions at all, we shall argue, in effect, that it makes better sense of Whitehouse's findings than his own hypothesis does.

Performance frequencies, performance rates, and theoretical depth

The frequency hypothesis holds that injecting emotionally exciting features into rituals is an adaptation to demands on memory that the comparative infrequency of their performance occasions. On this hypothesis, performance frequency is the *unexplained*, independent variable that determines the mnemonic processes involved, which, in turn, determine rituals' styles of codification and their revelatory potentials. (See figure 3.2.) We should emphasize that Whitehouse's theory is *not* deficient for leaving its independent variable unexplained. That is not unusual. The point is, rather, that our own theory gets at even more basic causal processes than Whitehouse's theory does. The evidence for that claim is of two sorts. First, our theory explains all that Whitehouse's theory does and more. Second, and *this is the point here*, it also goes some way toward explaining rituals' performance frequencies, i.e., the independent variable driving Whitehouse's account.

The cognitive principles of our ritual competence theory – to which the ritual form hypothesis appeals – *explain* the *relative* performance frequencies[1] for all religious rituals. They explain the relative performance frequencies for the two broad categories the theory supplies for exhaustively classifying religious rituals, viz., odd-numbered, special agent rituals on the one hand and even-numbered, special patient and special instrument rituals on the other. At this general level at least, the cognitive representation of ritual form is the variable that most significantly influences these comparative performance frequencies. But since rituals' performance frequencies are the crucial underlying variable driving the ritual frequency hypothesis, the pivotal role *ritual form* plays in determining rituals' performance frequencies indicates that the ritual form hypothesis gets at a more fundamental causal variable. Consequently, it possesses greater theoretical depth than either the ritual frequency hypothesis or Whitehouse's overarching theory of religious modes.

No hypothesis explains the independent variable it highlights. The ritual form hypothesis is no exception. But our larger theory of religious ritual competence *does explain* ritual form on the basis of the peculiar properties of the representations of religious rituals that the action representation system generates. And, of course, we have reviewed evidence from developmental psychology suggesting that the relevant features of the action representation system seem to be in place even in human infants.

Although the full story is not so simple, the principal influence of ritual form on performance frequency is clear enough. Even-numbered, special patient and special instrument rituals generally have higher performance frequencies than the odd-numbered, special agent rituals.

But that statement presumes that what qualifies as a *relevant* performance of a ritual – *for the purposes of comparing the two hypotheses' predictions* – is clear. It also presumes that the *proper measure* of those relevant performances' frequencies – again, for the purposes of comparing the two hypotheses' predictions – is clear. Unfortunately, neither is. We must explore these problems, because a fair assessment of the ritual frequency hypothesis depends upon agreement about rituals' performance frequencies.[2] We will have a great deal to say about what qualifies as a *relevant* performance. By comparison, the problem of *measuring* rituals' performance frequencies (i.e., the problem of how we go about *expressing* those performance frequencies) is a somewhat simpler matter.

> *Developing a criterion of relevance for ritual performances: opportunities to observe*

To see the difficulty about what should count as a relevant performance, consider the distinction we drew in chapter 2 between *participating* in an event and merely *observing* one. Observation certainly furnishes ample opportunity to acquire information about a rite. Should opportunities to observe a ritual (but not participate in it) qualify alongside opportunities for direct participation in ascertaining performance frequencies?

The first thing to note is that the differences between the two criteria are not trivial. For some rituals the resulting calculations of performance frequencies would differ substantially, depending upon which criterion we employ. In many religious systems, most people directly participate in special agent rituals (such as confirmations, bar mitzvahs, and berit milas) only once. Unless they become ritual practitioners (e.g., members of the clergy), most do not participate in these rituals ever again, even though they may have scores of opportunities to observe them. Consequently, if direct participation is the criterion for ascertaining performance frequencies, for most participants these rituals would have very low frequencies (such as once in a lifetime). However, if we utilize the more liberal criterion that includes opportunities to observe performances of these rites as well, then their performance frequencies can be quite high.

Two obvious problems lurk with adopting this liberal criterion. First, although a criterion of relevance that includes opportunities for observation will usually yield frequencies equivalent to those that a criterion based simply on the number of occurrences[3] yields, many religious systems prohibit outsiders from observing rituals and some, such as Shintoism and the Church of the Latter Day Saints, even restrict many *participants* from observing some rituals. Consequently, the resulting frequencies these two criteria stipulate will differ. Of course, with mnemonic issues in mind, advocates of the observation criterion may well argue this is just as it should be, since these secret rituals are generally unavailable as aids to recall.

The important problem *for the ritual frequency hypothesis* with including opportunities to observe rituals in the determination of their performance frequencies, though, is that sometimes the resulting version of the frequency hypothesis will yield false predictions. For example, including opportunities to observe rituals such as baptisms and weddings in the reckoning of performance frequencies renders these rituals ones of relatively moderate frequency at least. *Within* the Christian system, though, these rituals are *comparatively* heavy hitters[4] from the standpoint of sensory pageantry and emotional stimulation. If we include opportunities to observe rituals in the determination of performance frequencies, then the ritual frequency hypothesis would make the false prediction that these Christian rituals should not include much sensory pageantry.[5] This suggests that advocates[6] of the ritual frequency hypothesis should avoid this more liberal criterion of performances' relevance. The ritual frequency hypothesis will face fewer problems if the assessment of performance frequencies does not include opportunities for the observation of rituals.

It is worth noting that if considerations of memory are among the salient issues, as both Whitehouse and we have maintained, then eschewing the liberal criterion is consonant with the flashbulb findings we reviewed in chapter 2. Subjects who were literally shaken by the Loma Prieta earthquake (whether they had to do anything in response or not) and, thereby, qualified in their own minds as *participants* in the event had extremely accurate flashbulb memories for their experiences, whereas the mnemonic accuracy for their reception events of subjects who only *observed* the earthquake's effects (on television) was often quite low. Observation does not seem to have the impact that participation does. So, for example, nearly everything about Barth's reports suggests that being initiated as a Baktaman is a very different experience from supervising or assisting in an initiation – let alone merely observing one.

Developing a criterion of relevance for ritual performances:
participation

Even if we set the question of observation aside, arriving at a satisfactory criterion based only on *participation* will prove no less challenging. First of all, the ritual frequency hypothesis supplies no grounds for distinguishing what should qualify as participation.[7] Who, for example, are the participants in a Catholic wedding? The officiating priest? The bride? The groom? The maid of honor? The best man? The bride and groom's other attendants? The ring bearer? The flower girl? The altar boys? The bride's father? The bride's mother? The gr oom's parents? The bride's and groom's extended families? Any members of the parish who are present? Obviously, many rituals could permit numerous, fine distinctions among various levels of participation.

Sometimes, though, multiple ritual roles may present no problem. As the example of Baktaman initiations illustrates, participating in a religious ritual can take many forms. In this case, for example, participants include the initiates, the ritual assistants, and the cult leader, at least. The diversity of these roles notwithstanding, because the Baktaman perform these initiations only once a decade, they pose little problem for an account of performance frequencies that looks to (unqualified) participation. Baktaman males serve as the patients in each of these initiations only once and most initiated males assist in each only once thereafter – in the corresponding initiation of the next age cohort. Given their average life spans, even cult leaders among the Baktaman are unlikely to preside over any more than two or three performances of any particular initiation at most. So, the frequencies for initiations among the Baktaman are low *for everyone involved* (from once or twice in a lifetime for the patients and assistants to, perhaps, three or four times in a lifetime for the cult leaders). Consequently, the frequency hypothesis would correctly predict the high levels of sensory pageantry these initiations contain.

Such odd-numbered, non-repeated special agent rituals are of primary interest here, since for each of these rituals *in any religious system* individuals virtually always take the patient's role *only once* in their lives. Note, this is true whether those rituals can occur either only once per decade, as with Baktaman initiations, or as often as every day, as Christian baptisms, confirmations, and weddings might in a particularly large parish, albeit with different patients each time. This second situation, though, nicely illustrates the problem for the frequency hypothesis with using such a simple, unqualified notion of participation as the criterion for determining the relevance of a performance to the assessment of the hypothesis.

If bare participation is the appropriate criterion of relevance, then it will prove ambiguous in some contexts. For example, the frequencies of these Christian rituals are very low for some participants but relatively high for others. From the standpoint of the rituals' patients, i.e., the baptized, the confirmed, and the wed, the performance frequencies are low, whereas from the standpoint of the rituals' agents, i.e., the ritual practitioners who perform the baptisms, confirmations, and weddings, the performance frequencies can be quite high. When rituals involve multiple

participants serving in different roles, even a simple participation criterion can generate widely varying frequencies for the same ritual.

A more complex approach to the frequency hypothesis

An advocate for what would have to be a *far more complex approach* to
the frequency hypothesis *might* argue that, in fact, a criterion that generates multiple performance frequencies for the same ritual may not be
so bad after all – precisely *because* it generates different values depending
upon participants' roles. The amount of sensory pageantry to which participants are exposed in these rituals often does differ *depending on their
roles*. Some rituals might be said to aim much of their sensory pageantry
at specific participants. Special agent rituals unquestionably direct most
of their sensory pageantry at their patients. For example, in a Christian
wedding, although many people may enjoy the sensory pageantry (the
finery, the flowers, the music, etc.), it seems to be the bride, primarily,
and the groom, secondarily, who are the manifest targets of most of the
special effects. Similarly, in the initiations of the Baktaman, it is only the
initiates, not the cult leaders or their assistants, who undergo the ordeals
and days of torture, even if everyone does participate in the feasts with
which some of these rituals culminate.

We will postpone for a while the question of whether this revised, "far
more complex approach" results in anything legitimately describable as a
version of the *frequency* hypothesis, and focus, instead, on its plausibility.
The first thing to note is that it is not anything Whitehouse intends,
since neither does he take up these problems when presenting either
the frequency hypothesis or his account of the two religious modes nor
does he discuss the possibility of assigning multiple frequencies to the
same ritual depending upon different individuals' roles. But is this revised
approach to the frequency hypothesis plausible, regardless of any specific
theorist's intent?

If the point of this revised approach concerns the *differences in the
frequencies* with which individuals serve in different ritual roles, then we
need go no further than the Baktaman example to see an empirical problem. The very reason the Baktaman initiations posed no problems for the
simple, unqualified participation criterion was that the resulting frequencies were low for all of the participants, *regardless of their roles*. But *that* is
just the reason why these initiations pose a decisive problem for this revised proposal. The levels of sensory stimulation among the different roles
vary markedly (we suspect that torture probably qualifies as sensory pageantry of a fundamentally different order in just about everyone's book),

yet the frequencies *for each of the ritual roles* will differ little or not at all. It is the one and only time the initiates will go through this degree of initiation, but it is also the one and only time the assistants will assist, and it will certainly be no more than one of two or three times at most that the cult leader will preside.

So, if the differences in the frequencies with which individuals serve in different ritual roles are not the point, then, presumably, it must concern the *differences in the levels of sensory stimulation* associated with those different roles. On this front this revised approach would – some of the time – face few problems. As we noted in the sidebar on pages 101–102, *sometimes* the amounts of sensory stimulation two different rituals contain diverge unmistakably. The third degree Baktaman initiation suggests that the same is also sometimes true about the sensory pageantry associated with what certainly look to be (and our theory agrees are) obviously different roles in the same ritual. After all, third degree Baktaman initiation includes different ritual roles with *substantially* disparate levels of sensory pageantry. (Whippings with nettles result in very different sensations for the patients than they do for the agents.) In the cases of many other rituals, though, looking to differences in sensory pageantry associated with different ritual roles can turn on much less obvious distinctions (1) between ritual roles (for example, between instruments and patients rather than agents and patients), (2) between the role's associated levels of sensory stimulation, and (3) between that sensory stimulation's probable effects.

These problems are not insurmountable in principle. The first is not even all that difficult. We have already noted in chapter 1 that very young children have no problems either in distinguishing agents from other sorts of things or in distinguishing actions from other sorts of events. Although we did not take up the topic in detail, presumably the ability to distinguish the patients and instruments of actions as well is concomitant with these capacities. Everything about normal humans' abilities to act in the physical and social worlds suggests that this is so.

It is, however, less plausible that we can make all of the necessary, fine-grained distinctions between levels of sensory pageantry that the evaluation of this "more complex approach" to the frequency hypothesis would require. Although neuropsychology does not provide the requisite insights about these matters now, it is not out of the question that it might someday. Drawing such distinctions is not currently practicable, but, ultimately, we do not wish for our negative argument to turn on this point. The critical deficiency of this more complex approach to the frequency hypothesis lies far deeper – as our discussion in the remainder of this section will demonstrate.

These initial considerations jointly suggest that, however promising on some counts this revised approach to the frequency hypothesis might initially appear, it is not very practicable. Establishing that it is not empirically plausible will take more work.

A brief interlude: reversing a ritual's consequences

To repeat, testing the ritual form hypothesis directly does *not* depend upon obtaining a satisfactory criterion for rituals' performance frequencies. However, because testing the ritual frequency hypothesis does, a *fair* comparison of the two hypotheses' empirical merits will as well. Our aim is to be as fair as possible to the ritual frequency hypothesis. Ultimately, though, it will not matter which criterion of performance frequency its advocates adopt. The ritual form hypothesis makes the better predictions, regardless. That said, it should by now be clear that the requisite criterion must turn on some properly qualified account of participation.

Even-numbered rituals do not pose as many problems for the formulation of an adequate criterion for the relevance of performances as special agent rituals do. That is because, their different roles notwithstanding, ritual practitioners' and normal participants' opportunities to participate in special patient and special instrument rituals do not differ substantially. The overwhelming majority of Eucharists a priest performs are Eucharists of which a normal participant can partake, but even if they do not attend every Eucharist one priest performs, they may still attend other priests' performances.

It is special agent rituals that present the problems. Sometimes with these rituals (for example, with bar mitzvahs) ritual practitioners' opportunities for participation may vastly exceed the opportunities available to those serving in other roles – but (for example, with Baktaman initiations) sometimes not. The critical point is that it is the frequencies with which the *patients* of special agent rituals participate in them that hardly varies. We stated before that *in any religious system* individuals take the patient's role *only once* – at least ideally – in these special agent rituals. (This is the pivotal sense in which these rituals are *non-repeated*.) Even when the real world fails to conform to the ideal, normal participants' opportunities to participate in any special agent ritual (compared with those of ritual practitioners) are few. Even in Hollywood the number of times individuals marry one another (or anyone else, for that matter) is small compared with the number of weddings typical members of the clergy perform.

These observations about real world failures to conform to the ideal occasion some reflections on one theoretically interesting complication with odd-numbered, special agent rituals. We pause to discuss it here because it *bears directly on the formulation of a properly qualified account of participation*, and, as we noted above, *that* is pivotal for developing a satisfactory criterion of performances' relevance to the evaluation of the two hypotheses.

Things sometimes happen that necessitate the undoing of the super-permanent consequences of special agent rituals. Some couples must be divorced; a few participants must be excommunicated; an occasional practitioner must be defrocked; buildings or places must be desacralized. Any rituals by means of which such reversals would be accomplished would themselves have to be special agent rituals, since only CPS-agents have the power to undo what they have done. The reversals concern the first rituals' *consequences*.

We should highlight a distinction here. Throughout we shall distinguish between a ritual's (causal) *effects* and its (religious or logical) *consequences*. The former refers to the ritual's impact on physical, biological, psychological, and social arrangements. It concerns the ritual's place in the causal order scientists study. On the other hand, a ritual's consequences concern its objectives within the framework of the larger religious system and its impact logically on inferences and on the applications of categories from the religious conceptual scheme. So, for example, one of the (psychological) *effects* of ritual scarification is to motivate participants and one of its (logical) *consequences* is the participant's eligibility to participate in communion rituals.

Although, in principle, the consequences of all special agent religious rituals are ritually reversible, in fact, there is little evidence that such *rituals* exist and even less that they are actually performed. Note at once that to say that is *not* to say that the consequences of these rituals cannot be reversed. They can. It is uncontroversial that *juridical* means often exist for reversing the consequences of special agent rituals. Sometimes the authority in question is secular, sometimes it is religious, and sometimes it is both.

This complicates the claim that odd-numbered, special agent rituals are non-repeated, because after a reversal the original special agent ritual can then be re-performed with the same patient(s) a second time. (*Think about marriage and divorce in Hollywood!*) Other than the reversals of marriages, though, such juridical reversals are comparatively rare. Other than remarrying after divorces, second performances of the original special agent rituals *after* a reversal are even rarer still. Yet, *very* occasionally such things do happen. For example, St. Michael's, which stands not too far from the gates of King's College in Cambridge, was originally consecrated, then desacralized, and subsequently consecrated once again.

In the light of such considerations, describing special agent rituals such as consecrations or weddings as "non-repeated" requires a bit more clarification. The point is that additional performances of these rituals with the same patients do not occur, unless in the meantime their consequences have been reversed. Short of these special circumstances, there is no need to perform any of these rituals ever again with these patients. The gods have done what the gods have done.

The least direct connections criterion

Special agent rituals incorporate comparatively high levels of sensory pageantry that they overwhelmingly steer in the direction of their patients. The variation in the levels of sensory pageantry that different participants may experience, as they carry out their roles in these rituals, is typically a straightforward function of their physical proximity to the rituals' patients.[8]

It is in this light that we propose what we shall call the "least direct connections" criterion of performances' relevance (LDC criterion, hereafter) for the purposes of both making sense of the ritual frequency hypothesis and comparing it with the ritual form hypothesis. This criterion for ascertaining relevant performances directs us to look at the number of opportunities for *participation in the ritual* of those who are *eligible* to participate who have the *least direct* ritual connections with CPS-agents. Let us unpack each of the italicized terms in this statement of the LDC criterion.

- "*Participation in the ritual*" concerns those participants (*in the religious system*[9]) who appear in the current ritual's *immediate* structural description, i.e., those religious participants who serve as either the current ritual's agent or its patient(s).
- "Those who are *eligible* to participate" refers to participants in the religious system who meet the minimal (ritual) qualifications for participating in the ritual. (For example, people who have only been baptized as infants, but never confirmed, are not among the subset of participants who are eligible to be ordained.)
- We explicated the relative directness of ritual connections with CPS-agents in chapter 1 and again in chapter 3, pp. 115–117. Briefly, the more successively embedded rituals necessary to connect a participant with a CPS-agent, the *less direct* that participant's connection with that CPS-agent is – keeping in mind, of course, that if participants (infants, for example, in some religious systems) have *no* ritual connections with a

CPS-agent whatsoever, then their (absence of) "connection" would be the least direct connection possible.

The least directly connected participant in an odd-numbered, special agent ritual is reliably the ritual's patient (whose status is often changed by virtue of the ritual's performance). Consequently, the LDC criterion will assign very low performance frequencies (usually once in the participants' lifetime) to such rituals, since most of the time, the participants who serve as the patients of such rituals can do so only once. Since the least directly connected participants eligible to participate in repeatable, even-numbered, special patient and special instrument rituals can participate in them virtually as often as they are done, the LDC criterion would typically assign much higher performance frequencies to these rituals, since they would include *all* of the relevant performances of that ritual in the religious community in question. So, for example, Brahmans are invested with the sacred thread only once, and the LDC criterion assigns this ritual a very low performance frequency, whereas they can offer a homa to a deity time and again, so the LDC criterion assigns this ritual a high performance frequency.

Note that the ritual frequency hypothesis makes predictions about the levels of sensory pageantry in rituals on the basis of their performance frequencies. When we turn in the subsequent sections of this chapter to the comparison of the two hypotheses' predictions about the sensory pageantry associated with various sorts of rituals, the facts about those rituals' performance frequencies will be crucial. The LDC criterion provides the grounds for deciding what the facts about rituals' performance frequencies are.

The problem of measuring rituals' performance frequencies

At the outset of this section we identified *two* problems of clarity in our preliminary comments about rituals' performance frequencies. The first concerned formulating an appropriate criterion for deciding the relevance of performances in calculating the rituals' performance frequencies. In response to that problem, we have argued at length for the appropriateness of the LDC criterion. The second problem we noted in our early comments about performance frequencies concerned how they are properly expressed. We turn to that problem here.

There are two obvious ways in which we might express performance frequencies. We might measure them by simply counting the number of times (according the LDC criterion) that some ritual has been performed. We shall refer to this approach to performance frequency as a "raw count" of the ritual's performances. However, a much better way of measuring a ritual's performance frequency (and the one we have employed throughout the previous discussion) is to calculate its performance *rate*. A ritual's performance rate is the number of times a ritual is performed during some fixed period of time. So, for a given time period, people may perform a ritual hourly or daily or twice a week or (nearer the other end of the spectrum) once every eight years or once in a lifetime.

Sometimes raw counts will suffice for the comparison of two rituals' performance frequencies. But they can often be misleading. It depends upon the differences in the ages of the rituals and the lengths of the relevant time periods. Raw counts will deceive when we compare rituals' frequencies for time periods in which people performed one of the rituals throughout while they performed the other for some small fraction of the time period only, because, for example, it fell into disuse. If we were to express the performance frequencies of the Zulu naming rite and the Zulu circumcision rite for the past three hundred years for some clan in terms of raw counts, we would have a very skewed account of the data, since Shaka eliminated the circumcision rite over a hundred years ago. The same problem could arise in comparisons of long-lived rituals with those that have just emerged.

Expressing rituals' performance frequencies in terms of performance rates will avoid all of these problems. Both naming rituals and circumcision rites were performed once per lifetime. The Pomio Kivung perform the Cemetery Temple ritual daily whereas offerings to the ancestors at Bernard's Temple occur twice a week. *That* is the revealing comparison, regardless of which of the rituals came first.

Sometimes comparisons of rituals' performance rates can be no more helpful than comparisons of raw counts. Both can misdirect us, if the researcher uses too short a time period for the comparison. For example, an annual festival might include the performance of special rituals which during the critical week of the year would have the same raw count and the same performance rate as a ritual performed weekly throughout the entire year. Researchers must exercise some judgment in making such comparisons in order to avoid such unenlightening results.

Why any version of the ritual frequency hypothesis must presuppose the underlying theoretical principles of the theory of ritual competence

Recall that our ultimate goal in this section is to make a case for the greater theoretical depth of the ritual form hypothesis. Augmenting the ritual frequency hypothesis with the LDC criterion for determining the relevance of ritual performances will not render it a robust version of that hypothesis but, instead, a thin version of the ritual form hypothesis. What results is a "thin" version of the ritual form hypothesis for at least two reasons.

First, on *any* version of the ritual frequency hypothesis the importation of the LDC criterion is unmotivated, unexplained, and *ad hoc*. The "more complex approach" to the ritual frequency hypothesis has no more access to the principles of the theory of religious ritual competence than any of the simpler versions do, yet it is precisely those principles that make sense of the ritual connections to which the LDC criterion appeals. In order to test the predictions of the ritual frequency hypothesis, it must employ the LDC criterion. But the hypothesis is utterly incapable of making sense of the comparisons between various ritual elements' *connections* with CPS-agents. Making sense of those connections requires the theoretical apparatus of the theory of ritual competence on which the ritual form hypothesis relies. In short, the ritual frequency hypothesis fails to acknowledge that any tests of its predictions require the theoretically inspired account of performance frequency that our competence theory provides (in terms of the LDC criterion).

Second, the "more complex approach" to the ritual frequency hypothesis remains an exceedingly thin approximation of the ritual form hypothesis, because performance frequency remains its unexplained, independent variable. By contrast, the formal machinery that the ritual form hypothesis recruits from the theory of religious ritual competence specifies the single most important factor influencing performance frequencies, viz., ritual form. Note this is not merely a point about how we choose to calculate performance frequencies. Rather it concerns the variables that are the *causes* of rituals' performance frequencies. The ritual form hypothesis construes the space of possible ritual arrangements three dimensionally. (See figure 4.1.)

If, as we have argued, the LDC criterion is the only viable measure of performance frequency that advocates of the ritual frequency hypothesis can adopt, then the central question of that hypothesis, "is this ritual done more often than others?" largely reduces to the question "is this ritual a repeatable or a non-repeated ritual?" which is equivalent to the question "is this ritual a special patient or special instrument ritual or a special agent ritual?" Since, in effect, ritual form is a discrete variable, the ritual form hypothesis bifurcates the three-dimensional space of religious ritual possibilities into two regions. (See figure 4.2.) Although the repeatability of a religious ritual does not provide the entire explanatory story for that ritual's performance frequency, it is probably the single most important factor to which that story appeals. As we demonstrated in chapter 3, the

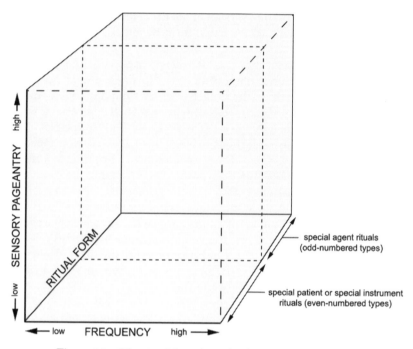

Figure 4.1   The ritual form hypothesis

question of *ritual repetition* is one for which the ritual form hypothesis provides an answer.

Special agent religious rituals, which are odd-numbered in form, have high levels of sensory pageantry and the least directly connected participants participate as the patients of these rituals only once. For each patient these rituals need only be done once, because the CPS-agents in these rituals either act directly themselves or certify their intermediaries' actions indirectly. These rituals contain high levels of sensory pageantry and emotional arousal, both because participants should *remember* these unique rituals and because they should also emerge from them with the *conviction* not only that something profound has transpired but also that the actions of the gods are at least ultimately, if not proximately, responsible for these rituals' consequences.

Aspects of ritual form our theory of ritual competence pinpoints determine whether religious rituals are repeatable or not, which is the principal factor determining ritual frequencies (construed in accord with the LDC criterion).[10] The ritual form hypothesis possesses greater theoretical depth than the ritual frequency hypothesis, then, since it identifies

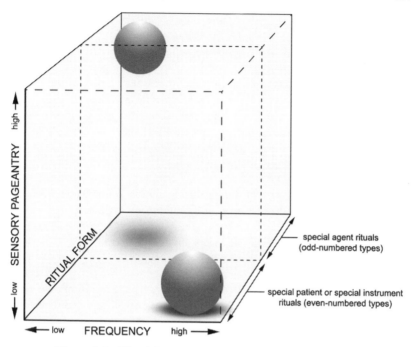

Figure 4.2   Ritual form as a discrete variable

the principal factor determining the values of the independent variable of the latter hypothesis. In the remainder of this chapter we shall turn to the consideration of the two hypotheses' empirical merits.

Empirical evidence: problems of stability and uniformity in the modes of religiosity

Having clarified why we must employ the LDC criterion both to test the ritual frequency hypothesis and to compare its predictions with those of the ritual form hypothesis, we have now set the stage for comparing those hypotheses' explanatory and predictive strengths. At every point we will argue that the ritual form hypothesis either matches or bests the ritual frequency hypothesis on these fronts.

When we noted in the previous chapter that the role of rituals' sensory pageantry and emotional arousal in establishing religious conviction and motivation is not some dry academic exercise about proving the gods' existence, we hinted that a whole constellation of phenomena may ultimately be involved. Whitehouse's theory concerning modes of religiosity explores these matters and more. Whitehouse repeatedly emphasizes (e.g., 1992, p. 783), for example, that, relying on emotionally charged rituals, his imagistic mode of religiosity generates very different sorts of religious experiences and religious messages than does the doctrinal mode with its frequent performances of rituals without much emotional punch.

Whitehouse's theory has sweeping aims that include religious ritual arrangements within its explanatory purview but also much, much more. We shall confine our discussion to the connections among a smaller group of variables bearing on religious ritual only:

1 *performance frequency* and
2 *sensory pageantry* (and emotional arousal), which Whitehouse also discusses (within the frameworks of codification style and revelatory potential), as well as
3 *motivation*, which Whitehouse takes up less systematically now and then, and, finally,
4 *ritual form*, which he discusses not at all.

We confine our proposal in this way for three reasons. First, the variables that our theory aims to coordinate seem plenty complicated enough (without undertaking the incorporation of, perhaps, as many as ten more). Second, our theory accounts for the phenomena behind the *problems of stability* concerning ritual that the theory of religious modes fails to explain. And, third, it captures everything that the ritual frequency hypothesis gets right (as we shall see in this and the next three sections).

In the previous chapter we noted what are, in effect, two telling kinds of explanatory problems for Whitehouse's account concerning the modes' uniformity and stability. We shall take these problems up in order.

Problems of uniformity

Whitehouse offers various routinized practices in Buddhism, Taoism, Hinduism, and Islam that elicit ecstatic or mystical states as illustrations of such problematic, mixed mode phenomena. Presumably, he has activities such as meditation, breathing exercises, yoga, and the whirling of dervishes in mind. He concedes that in these routinized activities the two modes become so "enmeshed" that they seem to undermine the analytical power of his distinction. (See Whitehouse, 2000, p. 149.) Given how Whitehouse characterizes the two modes of religiosity *and their cognitive foundations*, it is *not* obvious how the values for some of the thirteen variables indicative of one of the modes could mix with the values for the other variables indicative of the other.

Activities like meditation and yoga not only create special states of mind, they have, for example, in the case of the Muslim Sufis, also engendered literary and theological projects. Such activities mix Whitehouse's modes in that their *routinization* as well as the generation of theology and literature look like features that are emblematic of the doctrinal mode, whereas the creation of these *special states of mind* seems to realize a revelatory potential indicative of the imagistic mode. These practices mix the doctrinal and the imagistic, because although they are frequently performed to the point of routine, they realize their revelatory potential – at least in part – by inducing extraordinary states of mind rather than by argument and reflection.

Some of these routinized practices (such as meditation, breathing exercises, and yoga) create these special states of mind largely by *quelling* the effects of the senses. Hence, whatever problems they introduce for the overarching theory of religious modes, they do not present any obvious problems for the ritual frequency hypothesis, which connects fewer variables, viz., performance frequency, memory dynamics, and sensory pageantry and its impact on participants' emotions – what Whitehouse calls "frequency of transmission," "cognitive processing," "style of codification," and "revelatory potential" respectively. They present little problem because the ritual frequency hypothesis predicts that frequent, routinized practices will correlate with the low levels of sensory pageantry and emotional arousal that these practices exhibit. These practices may challenge Whitehouse's extended theory of religious modes (in light of its interest in such matters as ideological coherence) but not the more restricted ritual frequency hypothesis that apparently stands at its core.

Two clarifications

Before proceeding further, we need to clarify a couple of points. First, neither the ritual form hypothesis nor the larger theory of religious ritual competence, from which it takes its inspiration, requires that all religious rituals inevitably gravitate to either of the two attractors that we have emphasized within the space of possible ritual arrangements. That multi-dimensional, abstract space includes indefinitely many possibilities, some of which may constitute less frequented attractor positions that are no less stable (though, perhaps, a good deal less easy to approach in the course of a ritual's evolution). We have stressed the predictions of the ritual form hypothesis about the ritual arrangements that result from the two most prominent configurations of the variables it addresses, but, finally, the story we shall tell will prove a good deal more complex.

Other stable patterns can and do exist. (For example, in the next section we shall discuss some rituals that realize one of these stable, alternative arrangements.)

Second, the larger epidemiological framework we have outlined holds that means for ensuring memorability and motivation (to transmit these cultural materials) are two of the decisive dimensions that demarcate stable attractor positions. It follows that any other *stable* ritual arrangements – that enlist neither frequency nor flashbulb effects to help ensure memory reliable enough to maintain a sense of continuity and community – will inevitably employ alternative means for accomplishing these goals. With these points in mind, we can sketch how the ritual form hypothesis – with aid from the theory of religious ritual competence and these epidemiological assumptions – handles the explanation of the other phenomena that raise problems for the frequency hypothesis and Whitehouse's theory.

Problems of stability

Recall that the problems of stability concerned alternation between the modes in some religious systems. In accord with the principles of our theory of ritual competence, the ritual form hypothesis distinguishes among rituals on the basis of their forms. The ritual arrangements characteristic of different forms – specifically concerning the special agent rituals as opposed to special patient and special instrument rituals – *do not exclude one another*. Both commonly arise in the same religious system. But, if it is ritual form (rather than performance frequency) that tracks the underlying cognitive variables dictating the bundles of features that constitute the imagistic and doctrinal modes, then the ritual form hypothesis not only shows how switching modes (in the same religious system) is possible, it can also account for religious ritual systems that simultaneously include rituals peculiar to each. Odd-numbered, special agent rituals and even-numbered, special patient and special instrument rituals address different problems. Fluctuation between rituals characteristic of the two modes (over either short or long time intervals) turns out largely to be *a response to performing rituals of one sort of form rather than another*. Here's how.

Religion, on our view, inevitably involves ritual transactions with CPS-agents. Normal transactions between agents (human or not) are rarely one way all of the time. Both CPS-agents and human agents are capable of (ritual) action. Agents do some things in response to what other agents have done or in order to get other agents to do something else. Nothing about the relations of humans and CPS-agents is any different

(Boyer, 2001). Some circumstances and relations call for one agent to do something; other circumstances and relations call for the actions of different agents. Why should rituals be any different? The gods and human participants *interact*. Sometimes – either directly or indirectly – the CPS-agents act. On the other hand, sometimes they are the patients of human actions (or at least connected with the instruments or patients of human actions). This is a *natural* expectation, given religious participants' conceptions of the gods as *agents* (McCauley, 2000).

The theory of religious ritual competence shows how the action representation system can generate both of the relevant types of ritual representations, i.e., the even-numbered types characteristic of special patient and special instrument rituals and the odd-numbered types characteristic of special agent rituals. Along the lines we have sketched in the previous paragraph, this theory also makes sense of the alternation between "modes" that Whitehouse describes. From a cognitive standpoint, arrangements that involve the ritual patterns typical of Whitehouse's two modes (whether the cycles of alternation are long or short) become a perfectly natural expectation, once it is clear that the CPS-agents of a religious conceptual scheme can infiltrate the human action representation system in more than one way. The theory of mind and the general social intelligence underlying participants' presumptions about the relations between human agents and CPS-agents so overdetermine the production of both sorts of ritual types that what can happen will (McCauley, 2000). For present purposes, the two notable forms of infiltration concern whether the initial entries for CPS-agents yield special agent rituals or either of the two sorts of even-numbered rituals. (We shall suggest in the next chapter that epidemiological considerations reveal that a balanced arrangement involving *both* kinds of rituals will likely prove – for both cognitive and motivational reasons – an especially advantageous option for a religious system to adopt.)

Solutions to the problems

As we saw, the problems of uniformity concern religious phenomena that mix features of the two modes together. Without pretending to analyze the myriad details such activities introduce, a few general observations may still be useful. First, the cases that Whitehouse, apparently, has in mind – from various forms of meditation to breathing exercises to yoga to the dervishes' whirling – involve *esoteric skills* that religious participants literally *practice* in order to induce these special states. Consequently, the participants are the *agents* in these ritualized actions (though they may well be the patients too, since, arguably, they do things to themselves in the exercise of these skills). That they are the agents is why they can *practice* them, and *that* is why these activities are referred to as "disciplines." Their performance frequencies may suffice to support memory, but the *disciplined study* of these skills contributes too.

Given that the same individuals repeat these activities, *if* they are religious rituals in the technical sense our theory defines, then they would apparently be rituals of even-numbered types. Consequently, the ritual form hypothesis would have no more difficulty handling these repeated, mixed-mode activities that quell sensory stimulation than the ritual frequency hypothesis does.

On the other hand, some routinized practices – for example, the famous whirling of Muslim dervishes – seem to turn on producing a host of kinesthetic sensations to induce these special states of mind. *If* this prolonged, rhythmic whirling and the kinesthetic experiences it produces should count as sensory pageantry,[11] then it would not only be inconsistent with the theory of religious modes (like the others), it would also (unlike the others) exemplify patterns that would challenge the ritual frequency hypothesis as well. By contrast, even if the dervishes' whirling qualifies as a ritual involving *elevated* levels of sensory pageantry, it does not automatically pose a problem for the ritual form hypothesis. Whether it does or not would depend upon how its sensory pageantry *compares* with that of the special agent rituals of Islam (such as the rite of circumcision).

The vital question for now, though, is whether or not the religious practices to which Whitehouse alluded even qualify as religious rituals in our theory's technical sense. That an activity is somewhat stable in form and done over and over in a religious community are necessary but not sufficient conditions to qualify as religious rituals according to our theory. Recall that religious rituals in our theory's technical sense must also satisfy a number of additional criteria. Specifically, they must:

1 rearrange something in the religious world and, thereby, have some impact on the licit deployment of the concepts associated with the ritual

   – for example, because someone has practiced meditation in Pure Land Buddhism does not now uniquely entitle them to do some other ritual; however, once a Baktaman male has undergone the fifth degree of initiation, he is now eligible to undergo the sixth;

2 not permit the participation of outsiders except at an entry level

   – for example, anyone can practice yoga, but only a Brahmin can be invested with the sacred thread; and

3 fit into a larger pattern of actions that meet various formal conditions, including the requirement that eventually one of those (enabling) actions directly involves a CPS-agent

– for example, the practice of disciplined breathing involves no presumptions about the *actions* of CPS-agents, whereas no elevation of a pope can occur without presumptions about the (ritual) actions of Christ.

None of the activities we have been discussing seems to qualify as a religious ritual in our technical sense. All of them seem to violate the second and third criteria, and they may all violate the first as well.

It is fairly clear that they do not meet the insider–outsider criterion. Meditation, breathing exercises, yoga, and even whirling are all disciplines in which ritually unconnected outsiders can engage. Scores of Christian churches throughout the United States sponsor classes in Zen meditation and yoga. Whirling has become one of the standard nightclub acts for tourists in Egypt. These religious activities also fail to demonstrate the requisite connections with other rituals that the third criterion specifies. Practicing these activities, studying these disciplines does not inflexibly depend upon successful completion of the various other rituals unique to the pertinent religious systems. It is worthwhile to recall that not all behaviors that religious people do over and over again, even in religious contexts, count as religious rituals on our view.

The considerable explanatory ambitions of the theory of religious modes and the ritual frequency hypothesis may get them into trouble. Since they do not specify exactly what counts as a religious action, let alone as a religious ritual, the range of phenomena their explanatory aims encompass is enormous. To their credit they make a good deal of headway, but as the previous discussion illustrates they also face a number of troubling problems for which they offer no obvious solutions.

Our own theory's delimitation of religious rituals is an asset rather than a liability. This is to say that (1) its ability to contribute to the explanation of the underlying independent variable driving both the theory of religious modes and the ritual frequency hypothesis, and (2) its ability to account more accurately, comprehensively, and systematically for the religious phenomena that fall within its more limited explanatory scope reveal the advantages of our theory's technical characterization of the notion "religious ritual."

The theory of religious ritual competence implies that some things most people call "religious rituals" are in fact something different, just like a bat may look like a bird from a distance but, in fact, turn out not to be one. We will bite the bullet and say that a good theory of religious ritual, which explains what happens with most paradigmatic examples of religious rituals according to our best pretheoretic guesses, *excludes* activities of the sort we have been discussing (such as meditation and yoga). In fact, we have good reasons to think that these are not like the other religious rituals our theory addresses. As we have noted, they involve no membership conditions. Anyone can take part. Second, they seem to have no connection to other rituals in the same systems. They do not have ritual consequences, for example, in the way that serving as the patient in the Zulu *qhumbaza* (earpiercing ritual) leads to the possibility of serving in that same role in the *thomba* (the puberty ritual).

A final point. Although it looks as though the ritual form hypothesis can handle the mixed-mode phenomena to which Whitehouse alluded at least as well as the ritual frequency hypothesis does, we have raised the possibility that these activities may not ultimately fall into the explanatory range of the ritual form hypothesis, i.e., we have argued that they may not even qualify as religious rituals in our theory's technical sense. In fact, assessing the relative merits of the two should rely on uncontroversial cases that unequivocally fall within *both* hypotheses' explanatory purviews. It is to cases of this sort that we now turn.

Empirical evidence: infrequently performed, even-numbered, special patient rituals

To compare the predictions of the two hypotheses we have been considering, we must sort the relevant cases into four groups. The categories of the ritual form hypothesis – "even-numbered" and "odd-numbered" ritual types – are mutually exclusive with respect to one another and jointly exhaustive with respect to the pertinent domain. So are the categories of the ritual frequency hypothesis – "frequently performed" and "infrequently performed" rituals (once informed either by a few of the liberties a little idealization affords or by the practicalities systematic empirical research demands). Cross-indexing the two distinctions generates a two-by-two table that produces four mutually exclusive and jointly exhaustive groups of religious rituals. (See figure 4.3.)

The vast majority of religious rituals fall into two of these four categories, represented by cells I and IV. These first and fourth groups include most of the rituals we have mentioned in this book to this point. Not only the Christian and Jewish rituals we have noted, which are familiar to many Western readers, but those of the Muslims, Hindus, Zulus, Jains, the Kivung, the splinter group, the Baktaman, and the other Mountain Ok groups all look to be rituals that are of the first or fourth sorts.

The four cells of figure 4.3

For the group of rituals in cell I, the two theories' predictions coincide. These rituals are even-numbered, special patient and special instrument

Okay by Whitehouse

Frequency

	Frequent	Infrequent
	I	**II**
Repeatable special patient or special instrument rituals (even-numbered types)	Frequently performed repeatable rituals	Infrequently performed repeatable rituals
	III	**IV**
Non-repeated special agent rituals (odd-numbered types)	Frequently performed non-repeated rituals	Infrequently performed non-repeated rituals

Form

Okay by Whitehouse

Figure 4.3   The four relevant kinds of cases for comparing the ritual form and ritual frequency hypotheses

rituals that are frequently performed. On the basis of their even-numbered types, we can infer that these rituals are repeatable. By virtue of their frequent performance according to the LDC criterion, we can infer that the rituals in question are ones that are actually repeated with some regularity. The ritual form hypothesis predicts that rituals of this sort will have comparatively low levels of sensory pageantry. Since these rituals have relatively high performance frequencies, the ritual frequency hypothesis also predicts that the sensory pageantry will be low. Among the rituals in question are all of the standard Kivung rites we have discussed, the various repeated rituals of the Baktaman performed in the course of routine cult activities, the Jain Puja, the Christian Eucharist, Yoruba offerings, Orthodox Jewish purifications, blessings, sacrifices, and more. Although some of these rituals, e.g., the Kivung temple rituals, may involve a good deal of preparation and work, as Whitehouse emphasizes, they do *not* unduly stimulate the senses or arouse participants' emotions.

For the group of rituals in cell IV, the two theories' predictions again converge. These rituals are infrequently performed, odd-numbered, special agent rituals. Since they are special agent rituals of odd-numbered types, they are non-repeated rituals, so typically their frequency is once in a lifetime. Also, since they are special agent rituals, the ritual form hypothesis predicts that within any particular religious community they incorporate comparatively high levels of sensory pageantry. Since a performance frequency of once in each patient's lifetime surely qualifies as infrequent performance, the ritual frequency hypothesis, again, concurs. Rituals in cell IV include the classic rites of passage, Hindu weddings, Jewish bar mitzvahs, Christian baptisms, Buddhist ordinations, Baktaman initiations, and some of the rituals of the Dadul-Maranagi splinter group, e.g., the mass wedding, among others. Although the last two examples are, perhaps, somewhat extreme illustrations, all do involve levels of sensory pageantry that exceed those of any even-numbered rituals in these systems.

The coincidence of the two hypotheses' predictions for cells I and IV motivates two of our earlier claims. The first was that the ritual form hypothesis captures everything that the ritual frequency hypothesis gets right, viz., the arrangements connected with rituals that occupy the first and fourth cells. This leads naturally enough to the second claim, viz., that since the independent variable our theory stresses (ritual form) is a principal factor driving performance frequency, it goes without saying that it correlates with it well. (See Whitehouse, 1996b, p. 712.) This is to say that most special agent rituals have relatively low performance frequencies and that most special patient and special instrument rituals have relatively high performance frequencies. Consequently, the two hypotheses make roughly the same predictions about the sensory pageantry associated with the overwhelming majority of the pertinent cases.

Ritual form *should* correlate with performance frequency, because the ritual frequency hypothesis makes the correct predictions about most of the relevant cases (viz., those falling into the first and fourth cells). And ritual form *does* correlate with performance frequency, because

1 all of the cases of frequently performed religious rituals involving comparatively low levels of sensory pageantry are special patient and special instrument rituals,
2 all of the cases of infrequently performed religious rituals involving comparatively high levels of sensory pageantry are special agent rituals, and
3 these two sorts of cases constitute the overwhelming majority of religious rituals.

Most of the time, then, the two hypotheses' predictions are the same. But not always – that correlation is not perfect. In fact, the hypotheses' predictions are diametrically opposed in the two remaining cells. (See figure 4.4.) The correlation between the two hypotheses remains high, because far fewer instances fall into these cells. It had better not be perfect, though, because the ritual frequency hypothesis makes the *wrong* predictions here.

It makes the wrong predictions because in cell II at least and, perhaps, even in cell III the rituals are mixed-mode phenomena that concern the basic variables that the ritual frequency hypothesis addresses. We shall devote the remainder of this section to cases that fall into the second cell and the next section to a discussion of what will prove clear cases that

Ritual frequency hypothesis

	Frequent	Infrequent
Repeatable special patient or special instrument rituals (even-numbered types)	I LOW / low	II LOW / high
Non-repeated special agent rituals (odd-numbered types)	III HIGH / low	IV HIGH / high

(left axis label: Ritual form hypothesis)

Figure 4.4 The two hypotheses' predictions about the comparative levels of sensory pageantry for each of the four sorts of cases in figure 4.3

plausibly fall into the third. The crucial point is that it is the ritual form hypothesis – not the ritual frequency hypothesis – that correctly predicts the ritual arrangements accompanying both.

Illustrations of religious rituals that fall into cell II

All of the high frequency rituals from the Pomio Kivung that Whitehouse discusses fall into the first cell. They are even-numbered, special patient rituals that are not only repeatable but frequently repeated. Although people participate in most even-numbered religious rituals frequently, a ritual's repeat*ability* does not require its frequent performance. The repeatability of a special patient or special instrument ritual does not entail that participants, in fact, repeat the ritual frequently. It only requires that these rituals be *repeatable* (full stop). The ritual form hypothesis allows for the possibility that a ritual could be an even-numbered, repeatable ritual – in accord with LDC criterion – yet be performed quite infrequently. These are the rituals that fall into the second cell.

The important point is that the two hypotheses make conflicting predictions about the arrangements accompanying such rituals. The ritual frequency hypothesis holds that since such a ritual is performed infrequently, it will rely on high levels of sensory pageantry to consolidate participants' memories. The ritual form hypothesis maintains that since the ritual is even-numbered, it will not include (comparatively) high levels of sensory pageantry. Moreover, since it is performed infrequently and does not involve many emotionally stimulating elements, it follows on the ritual form hypothesis that some alternative system of mnemonic support

must sustain memory for such a ritual. In a non-literate society, in particular, such an external system of mnemonic support would be difficult to
miss. In fact, such rituals exist in both literate and non-literate settings.

Perhaps the most familiar illustrations of rituals in a literate society
that fall into cell II are the rituals uniquely associated with the hajj, a
faithful Muslim's pilgrimage to the holy sites. The rituals in question are,
in fact, even-numbered, special patient rituals. They are repeatable and
their consequences are incapable of reversal. The salient point for now
is that although it is good for a Muslim to repeat the pilgrimage and
the rituals associated with it, it is perfectly acceptable for the faithful to
perform the pilgrimage only once and that is probably the predominant
pattern of those who perform them at all. On the LDC criterion of performance frequency, these are even-numbered, special patient rituals that
are infrequently performed.

The pilgrimage is almost guaranteed to consume considerable resources, but neither it nor its associated rituals involve extraordinary sensory
pageantry as part of the ritual arrangements. Thus, it mixes Whitehouse's
modes. It is infrequently performed yet low in sensory pageantry.
Although the sheer numbers of pilgrims involved in the past few decades
especially can surely generate stimulating scenes, that is an incidental
feature of the pilgrimage. These effects do not turn on anything intrinsic
to the ritual practices. In short, it is not the result of the ritual arrangements, but a latent effect of the number of Muslims who can manage to
undertake the pilgrimage in these more prosperous, technologically advanced times. The rituals and activities associated with this undertaking
(circling the Ka'bah, kissing the Hajar al-Aswad, climbing Mt. Safā and
Mt. Marwah seven times, offering sacrifices, etc.) are quite time consuming, and they certainly keep the pilgrims busy, but those are not the same
things nor do they produce the same effects as the (targeted) sensory
pageantry characteristic of special agent rituals.

The Kumbha Mela is a triennial pilgrimage to one of four sites in
northern India. All of these sites are on rivers, where the Hindu pilgrims
undertake ritual bathing. Like the hajj this pilgrimage is one that the
faithful can repeat again and again to obtain additional blessings and
merits, but the timing of the Kumbha Melas insures that they cannot
undertake it any more often than once every three years. (The Great
Kumbha Mela, which is reputed to be the largest religious gathering in
the world, occurs only once every twelve years.) The central activities of
the Kumbha Mela involve (even-numbered) special instrument rituals in
which pilgrims bathe themselves in sanctified waters. At one time, they
are also reputed to have bathed pots of seed to be sown the following
planting season to insure a bountiful harvest. The *Puranas* explain that

the four sites support a heavenly pot holding divine nectar, some of which spilled out at each of these locations.

Over the centuries the Khumba Melas have become occasions for Hindu yogis, intellectuals, and theologians to meet as much as they are conclaves for ritual baths. This pilgrimage, though, certainly seems to fall into cell II. It is an even-numbered, special instrument ritual that is performed comparatively infrequently and that seems, like the hajj, to require a good deal of effort from the pilgrims, but ultimately involves no more sensory pageantry than that associated with a ritual bath.

Consuming a great deal of the time of busy participants is a hallmark of the Vedic Agnicayana ritual too. Unlike the hajj or the Kumbha Mela, though, the Agnicayana does not require participants to take – what is for most – the excursion of a lifetime. Nor, like the hajj or the Kumbha Mela, does the recollection and transmission of the Agnicayana always benefit from literacy and texts – at least not among the Nambudiri of the southwestern Indian state of Kerala. The rituals associated with the hajj do not depend exclusively upon oral transmission and human memory. Apparently, among the Nambudiri *the Agnicayana has.*

The Nambudiri performances of the Agnicayana seem to exemplify a non-literate culture capable of sustaining an exceedingly long and elaborate ritual. Of course, Whitehouse provided evidence that, so long as they performed their rituals *frequently,* non-literate peoples were eminently capable of perpetuating religious systems that not only underwent very little change but had all of the earmarks of his doctrinal mode – including precisely formulated doctrines, an extensive ritual system, and elaborate theologies.

Arguably, the Nambudiri performances of the Agnicayana are even more impressive, since this ritual is *far more elaborate* than any of the Kivung rituals and it is performed *far less frequently.* Admittedly, little direct evidence is available for evaluating the uniformity of the Agnicayana across time among the Nambudiri. Still, two things stand out. First, its low performance frequency notwithstanding, this ritual and the larger Vedic religious system of which it is a part have most of the characteristics of Whitehouse's doctrinal mode. Second and more importantly for current purposes, some indirect evidence pertaining to the uniformity of the Nambudiri performances over time does exist. Although virtually *all* of the available evidence suggests that the Agnicayana has persisted completely *independently* of texts among the Nambudiri, literate participants in other parts of India have possessed and consulted supporting texts (*Śrauta Sūtras*) for performances of the Agnicayana for centuries. Frits Staal's intriguing finding was that the similarities between Nambudiri performances of this ritual and those of their literate countrymen, who have consulted the *Śrauta Sūtras* for hundreds of years, are pervasive and substantial. (See Staal, 1983 and 1990.) But the story doesn't stop there.

The Agnicayana is a Śrauta ritual (rather than one of the Grhya rituals associated with the rites of passage). Śrauta rituals are a group of offerings (i.e., special patient rituals) dedicated primarily to Agni and Soma. The first of four significant points to make about the Agnicayana, then, is that, like all such Śrauta rituals, it is an *even-numbered, special patient ritual*. As with all even-numbered rites, there are no procedures for reversing its consequences, and it is repeatable – even if rarely repeated. Since *after the ritual is over* Agni consumes all of the ritual paraphernalia, which is to say that it is burnt in a huge bonfire, the ritual itself embodies a further rationale for why it is repeatable. (As with the hajj, the principal reason the same Nambudiri patrons do not repeat the Agnicayana often, if at all, is the tremendous expense and effort required to perform this ritual.)

The best available evidence indicates that prominent members (*yajamānas*) of various Nambudiri families (all of whom resided in but eight villages in Kerala) sponsored performances of the Agnicayana a total of sixteen times between 1844 and 1975, with intervals between performances as large, perhaps, as twenty-six years (Somayajipad et al., 1983). Its average performance rate over this period was, apparently, about once every eight years. That is nearly as low as that for each of the degrees of Baktaman initiation, which Barth estimates at approximately once per decade. So, the second point is that the Agnicayana is a ritual that is *performed quite infrequently*. It follows from this and the fact that it has an even-numbered type that, like the rituals associated with the hajj and the Kumbha Mela, it too falls into cell II.

The Agnicayana is an extremely complicated ritual requiring extensive, coordinated activity among a large number of ritual participants. Although there are scores of preliminaries, it ultimately focuses on the painstaking process of building a large, bird-shaped altar according to precise specifications and then carrying out sacrifices and presenting offerings to Agni. Altogether the ritual takes twelve days to perform. The ritual has numerous stages that include further offerings, sacrifices, and other smaller rites. Vedic tradition specifies necessary conditions for each of these component rites precisely and at length (including such particulars as the number and placement of sticks for each of the ritual fires).

Like virtually all Vedic rituals, the Agnicayana includes the chanting of verses from the *Veda*. Other than a brief ritual bath on the final day for the *yajamāna* and his wife, who have sponsored the ritual's performance, the Agnicayana neither contains sensory stimulation nor incites emotional arousal that is at all out of the ordinary compared with other rituals in this tradition. Like the rituals associated with the hajj, many people are extremely *busy* during those twelve days, and they accomplish a great deal, including the careful surveying, measurement, and construction of the bird-shaped altar. However occupied everyone is with carrying out these and other chores, the third point is that the Agnicayana contains *no extraordinary sensory pageantry*. On the ritual form hypothesis this is completely consistent with the fact that the Agnicayana is a special patient ritual. By contrast, on the ritual frequency hypothesis this is completely puzzling in light of the fact that the Agnicayana is a ritual that is so infrequently performed. In short, the ritual form hypothesis makes the correct prediction here, and the ritual frequency hypothesis makes an incorrect one.

Of the various Śrauta rituals, the Agnicayana is the most complex, and it is performed the least often (Staal, 1990, p. 69). Furthermore, it involves no uncommon levels of sensory pageantry, compared with other Vedic rites. The fourth point we wish to make is that this ritual confronts participants with a *formidable mnemonic problem*. They certainly seem to recognize the challenge it presents to human memory. Throughout, the ritual includes various ancestral and expiation rites to compensate for possible errors and omissions (Staal, 1990, p. 76). The Nambudiri performances of the Agnicayana demonstrate that not all even-numbered, special patient rituals may gravitate to the first attractor position. At least so long as there are other ways of insuring their recollection, special patient and special instrument rituals may achieve stability in other regions. (See figure 4.5.)

Much of the excitement that accompanied scholars' discovery of the Nambudiri ritual tradition turned on the fact that although texts delineating Vedic rituals exist, the Nambudiri have not used them. Exclusively by non-literate means, they have sustained this elaborate ritual tradition with astonishing fidelity (as gauged by the centuries-old *Śrauta Sūtras*). The ritual form hypothesis correctly holds that infrequently performed, special patient rituals, like the Agnicayana, will not rely on sensory pageantry and, by definition, cannot rely on performance frequency to produce extraordinary memory for such a rite. It follows that other cultural mechanisms must promote the transmission of such a ritual. The transmission of the Agnicayana relies on two, at least.

The first is a mechanism we introduced in chapter 2 when we discussed memory for Baktaman initiations. The Śrauta rituals are ordered hierarchically, and the Agnicayana sits at the pinnacle of this group. That hierarchy exhibits *compositional* relations. Rituals at each level in the hierarchy serve as components in the rituals at the next higher level. Since the Agnicayana sits at the top, it has the most richly detailed compositional structure (Staal, 1990, p. 101). Still, even though these compositional

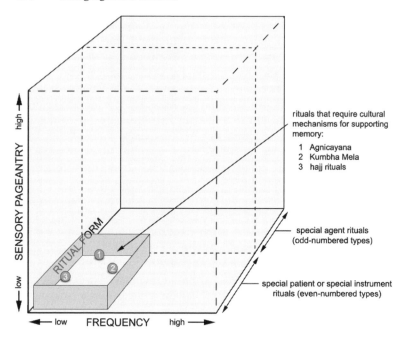

Figure 4.5   Even-numbered, special patient and special instrument rituals with low performance frequencies

relations provide useful landmarks to organize practitioners' memories for the Agnicayana, they constitute but a small percentage of its contents.

Even more important, then, is the extensive, on-going Nambudiri oral training of Brahmin boys to participate in these Vedic rituals. Those who become priests will not only participate in but eventually preside over performances of these rituals. This is a system of external memory support that is – as we put it before – "difficult to miss." Students spend hundreds of hours memorizing the *Vedas* (the *Ṛgveda* in particular) and learning ritual details. The Nambudiri seem to possess one of the world's few lasting oral traditions that enjoys a substantial measure of scholarly authentication (Staal, 1990, p. 68).

The Agnicayana seems not to have changed much among the Nambudiri once this support system was in place. Our theory would predict that that probably occurred fairly early on, seeing how little sensory pageantry the contemporary version of the ritual contains. Among the Nambudiri the Agnicayana has not evolved in the direction of the first attractor, because it did not need to incorporate extensive *internal* aids to memory among its ritual arrangements. A comprehensive, *external* system for preserving participants' memories of their religious system – including the Śrauta rituals – already contributed greatly to its recollection.

The Agnicayana, the Kumbha Mela and the rituals of the hajj are, of course, but a few pieces of empirical evidence. However, since they are repeatable rituals that on the LDC criterion are infrequently performed, they fall into the second cell. Since they do not seem to incorporate comparatively high levels of sensory pageantry even though they are infrequently performed, they qualify as mixed-mode phenomena, and they *refute* the predictions of the ritual frequency hypothesis. Finally, since the Agnicayana, the Kumbha Mela, and at least some of the activities associated with the hajj also qualify as (even-numbered) religious rituals in our technical sense, they *corroborate* the predictions of the ritual form hypothesis. Consequently, these few pieces of evidence are, none the less, valuable pieces of evidence, when sizing up the first of the two situations where the two hypotheses' predictions conflict.

On the possibility of frequently performed, odd-numbered, special agent rituals

The third cell of figure 4.3 represents the other set of circumstances where the two hypotheses' predictions diverge. (See figure 4.4.) That cell represents special agent religious rituals that are frequently performed. Since these are special agent rituals, the ritual form hypothesis predicts that the associated levels of sensory pageantry and emotional arousal should be comparatively *high*. Since these rituals are also frequently performed, the ritual frequency hypothesis predicts that they should be *low*. Like the rituals that belong to the second cell, those in the third constitute useful test cases for evaluating the two hypotheses.

The obvious, next question, then, is "what are the facts?" But a moment's reflection reveals what appears to be a gigantic conceptual roadblock. We have regularly noted that – at least from a practical standpoint (e.g., see note 10) – the most salient feature of special agent rituals, according to the LDC criterion, is the fact that they are *not repeated*. The theory of religious ritual competence holds that they do not need repeating. The gods do things once and for all. The effects of their actions are super-permanent. So, if the items that fall into this cell are special agent rituals, then how can they be performed frequently? The notion of frequently performed special agent rituals seems a contradiction in terms, and if it is, then, presumably, the conditions this third cell requires are incoherent, and if they are, then we will be deprived of one of the two kinds of cases where the empirical predictions of the two hypotheses obviously conflict. (See figure 4.6.) Is this vast region in the space of ritual

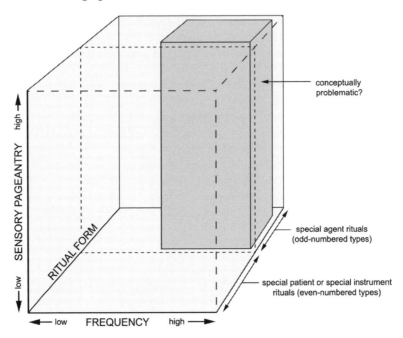

Figure 4.6   Special agent rituals with high performance frequencies

possibilities always empty on conceptual grounds? Or is there some means of breaking through this conceptual roadblock? Previous discussions in this chapter suggest two possibilities.

Two possibilities for breaking through the conceptual roadblock

The first would be to relax the LDC criterion of performance frequency. Recall that when we began to clarify the difference between repeatable and non-repeated rituals in chapter 3, we distinguished between distributed and collective predications. From the standpoint of individual participation, many rituals are non-repeated; however, from the collective standpoint of the community, *all* rituals are repeated – at least all religious rituals in which humans participate. So, even though a priest baptizes each Christian only once, in large parishes they may perform the ritual of baptism a hundred times a year. The point is that if we were to abandon the LDC criterion and measure performance frequency on the basis of the opportunities to observe rituals (or on the sheer number of occurrences), then the notion of frequently performed, special agent rituals need not occasion charges of self-contradiction.

Our earlier discussion on pages 127–128 of possible criteria of performances' relevance clarified why it would *not* be helpful to employ so liberal a criterion with the ritual frequency hypothesis. No survey of exotic religious systems is necessary to see that if opportunity to observe a ritual is the gauge of its performance frequency, then many of these special agent rites (e.g., weddings) might well qualify as rituals that are frequently performed. But that would be bad news for the ritual frequency hypothesis, since it predicts that frequently performed rites have low levels of sensory pageantry, and these odd-numbered rituals obviously do not. So, it would be unfair to the ritual frequency hypothesis for us to employ a more liberal criterion of performance frequency as a means for breaking through this conceptual roadblock.

The second possibility concerns juridical reversals of these rituals' consequences. Once its consequences have been reversed, a special agent ritual could be performed with the same participants once again. Although *theoretically* this cycle of performances and reversals could go on indefinitely and that *could* yield the situation cell III describes, as we noted earlier, in reality – with the exception of divorce – reversals of special agent rituals' consequences are exceedingly rare. After such reversals, performances of the original special agent rites a second time with the same ritual patients are even rarer. They do occur occasionally though. Recall the consecration, desacralization, and re-consecration of St. Michael's at Cambridge. Still, only two consecrations over the hundreds of years that that church has stood should hardly count as *frequent* performance of that special agent rite. With the dynamics of memory in mind, not even Hollywood divorces occur often enough to allow *frequent* re-marriages. If a movie star marries and divorces eight or nine times, this still yields a performance frequency that would average less than once every six years between ages twenty and seventy.

With juridical reversals fairness to the ritual frequency hypothesis is not the issue. After such reversals, re-performances of special agent rituals with the same ritual patients are far too scarce to justify the talk of "frequent" performance that cell III requires, so appeal to juridical reversals will not help. Nor, as we have seen, is it fair to relax the LDC criterion. Is there, then, a third possibility for circumventing this conceptual impasse?

The evolution of the splinter group's ritual system

There is. We shall find how through closer scrutiny of the ritual system of the Dadul-Maranagi splinter group. Because this will require a good deal of work, let us summarize the argument first. We shall note some of the general trends in the evolution of the overall ritual system of the Dadul-Maranagi splinter group and then we shall look at the evolution of the ring ceremony in particular. We shall argue that its evolution largely mirrors the evolutionary trajectory of the ritual system as a whole and especially on one specific front, viz., its frequent repetition with the same patients notwithstanding, it evolved in ways that quickly rendered it a *special agent* ritual. But, of course, if that argument is sound, then we will have established that the third cell of figure 4.3 is not empty after all. Behind the multiple performances of this ritual is a third means for – in this case, successfully – circumventing the conceptual impasse. From there, we shall argue, finally, that – unlike the ritual frequency hypothesis – the ritual form hypothesis not only correctly predicts the ritual arrangements of the materials in cell III, it also makes some sense of the underlying evolutionary trends of both the overall ritual system and the ring ceremony, in particular.

We shall commence by examining some of the general trends that the ritual innovations of the Dadul-Maranagi splinter group embody. The critical period in question commenced on April 6, 1988 with the novel ritual celebrating the construction of the new Cemetery Temple and ended just over six months later in mid-October when the splinter group members from Dadul returned home from Maranagi on the orders of the government health inspector. In addition to this consecration ceremony for the new Cemetery Temple in Dadul, the rituals Baninge and Tanotka introduced included ritual feasts celebrating their various dreams, a ceremony marking the "official opening" (Whitehouse, 1995, p. 137) of the roundhouse in Maranagi and an accompanying "preparation ceremony" for the splinter group members, an initiatory "membership ritual" for newcomers, a mass wedding, and the ring ceremony, which was performed in isolation and, later, in conjunction with the all-night vigils during the splinter group's final weeks. Even though, chronologically, the ring ceremony arises early on, we shall postpone its analysis to the end of this discussion, since it is the most interesting ritual development connected with the Dadul-Maranagi splinter group.

The Cemetery Temple consecration took place on April 6. Although the consecration ceremony for the new Cemetery Temple strayed a good deal from the first attractor position (where the Kivung ritual system resides), it exploited familiar cultural representations, capitalizing on two (the Cemetery Temple and the ancestors) that are absolutely fundamental to the Kivung religious system. It also enlisted forms from the nearly, but not completely, forgotten traditional religion of the Mali Baining.

Because of the ancestors' complaints about the leaks in the roof, the nascent splinter group in Dadul built and dedicated a new Cemetery

Temple, an integral structure in the Kivung ritual system. (Such celebrations of major construction projects were not unusual, but the ritual Baninge and Tanotka staged was utterly unprecedented in a celebration of this sort.) For the purposes of dedicating the new Cemetery Temple, Baninge and Tanotka resuscitated a dance from traditional Baining religion. The splinter group's version of that dance (the *awan*) included elaborately costumed figures (the *awanga* and *ilotka*) representing the ancestors – who, of course, play an integral role both in Kivung cosmology and in that of traditional Baining religion (Whitehouse, 1995, p. 125). Whitehouse notes that the *awan* that the splinter group performed was apparently unique in its inclusion of the *ilotka*, who traditionally figured in the Baining dances associated with the system of non-repeated, special agent initiations.

Whitehouse (1995 and 2000) discusses the pivotal difference between the Kivung and traditional Baining systems at length. Their overlapping interests in the ancestors notwithstanding, the Kivung system relies on frequently repeated (special patient) rituals with little sensory pageantry whereas traditional Baining religion relied principally upon special agent initiations – not unlike those of the Baktaman – loaded with sensory pageantry.

Not only was this consecration ceremony itself a ritual innovation, it included an entire night of feasting and dancing quite unlike anything that goes on in mainstream Kivung rituals. Baninge and Tanotka created a new ritual to celebrate *a specific event*, viz., the construction of the Cemetery Temple, *that the ancestors' recent complaints inspired* yet that was, arguably, within the boundaries of *Kivung* orthodoxy. Unlike standard Kivung rites, though, this new temple consecration contained both the wondrous spectacle of the *awan* and extensive feasting, dancing, and singing. Moreover, since temple consecrations turn on the actions of CPS-agents, they only need to be performed once. This first genuinely innovative ritual was an *odd-numbered, special agent ritual* and included a substantial increase in sensory pageantry.

Shortly after this, on April 11, the first of many extended ritualized feasts occurred celebrating specific dreams Baninge and Tanotka had (Whitehouse, 1995, p. 106). The contents of these dreams, which the witnesses' testimony consistently corroborated, generally emphasized Baninge and Tanotka's special status and their close relationships with the ancestors. Whitehouse (1995, pp. 106–107) does not describe these feasts in sufficient detail to comment on their forms with much confidence, but it is uncontroversial that they constituted a clear elevation in the level of sensory pageantry in comparison with that accompanying the previous regime of strictly orthodox Kivung practices.[12]

The next variation in the ritual system was not to create a new ritual but to add to the already rigorous ritual complement of the Kivung system *more* of the public meetings that occurred in connection with the twice-weekly offerings to the ancestors in Bernard's Temple. Henceforth, these meetings would occur every day (Whitehouse, 1995, p. 112). From the standpoint of ritual form, this was not an innovation so much as an extension of conventional Kivung practices, which permitted the injection of new religious materials during what were now daily meetings of the entire community.

The significant development here concerns these meetings' contents, rather than their forms. These new meetings were overwhelmingly devoted to presenting Tanotka and Baninge's new revelations and, through reports about the testimony of the witnesses, the ancestors' endorsements of their veracity. The focus had shifted from the mastery of a system of standardized (Kivung) doctrines in semantic memory to the on-going presentation, authentication, and consideration of the ancestors' (often *particular* ancestors') current states of mind and recent activities. And, of course, the ancestors' two specially chosen representatives, viz., Tanotka and Baninge, were the principal conduits for communicating this information (as the witnesses in the ritual at Bernard's Temple corroborated). Although these standard Kivung meetings never did assume forms likely to produce episodic memories themselves, their contents turned from canned sermons about *long-standing doctrines* to reflection on the ancestors' recent activities. Subsequent variations not only in ritual contents but also *in ritual forms* would only magnify this trend away from semantic memories not only toward the consideration of *recent episodes* but toward the production of episodic memories through the incorporation of increased sensory pageantry.

Continuing to set the ring ceremony aside for the moment, all of the remaining ritual innovations, viz., the consecration of the round-house (a traditional Baining structure), the membership ritual, and the mass wedding, exhibited the same patterns that the consecration of the Cemetery Temple manifested. Each fulfilled three conditions:

1 the production of a new *non-repeated, odd-numbered, special agent* ritual,
2 a focus on the *ancestors' current actions* and their connections with Tanotka and Baninge, instead of on orthodox Kivung doctrines (see note 13 below), and
3 an infusion of *increased sensory pageantry* – often by way of exploiting traditional materials (such as the *awan*, the *ilotka*, and the roundhouse) associated with the Mali Baining system of special agent initiations.

Of course, items (1) and (3) are the characteristic arrangements of our second attractor. Thus, from a diachronic perspective, the Cemetery

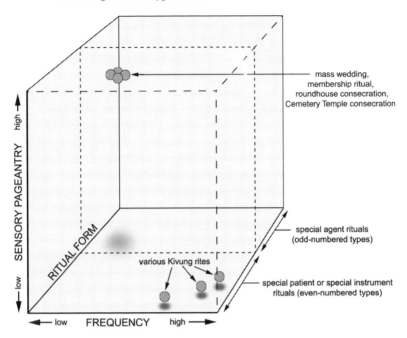

Figure 4.7   Kivung rites versus splinter group innovations

Temple consecration and most of the other new splinter group rituals
embody a shift of ritual arrangements away from the first attractor
position (where the community's ritual practices had settled with the
standard Kivung rites) to the second. (See figure 4.7.) The shift was
toward infrequently performed, special agent rituals with substantially
higher levels of sensory pageantry that constituted encounters with the
local CPS-agents' actions.

When outlining the ritual frequency hypothesis in the previous chapter,
we noted that it seemed to make sense of most of the arrangements
surrounding the splinter group's rituals. The temple and roundhouse
consecrations, the initiatory membership ritual, and the mass wedding
are certainly rituals with low performance frequencies, and, in fact, the
splinter group performed each one of these rituals only once. Consequently, the ritual frequency hypothesis predicts correctly that these rituals should have exhibited high levels of sensory pageantry, at least in
comparison with the mainstream Kivung rites.

Because each of these rituals depended upon CPS-agents[13] bringing
about changes in the religious world (consecrating structures, creating
new members, joining partners in marriage), i.e., because *all of these*

rituals were special agent rituals, the ritual form hypothesis makes the same prediction. In sum, both hypotheses get this part of the splinter group's story right, since these rituals introduced unprecedented levels of sensory pageantry, in comparison with standard Kivung rituals (which the splinter group also continued to perform). The mass wedding, for example, included a "feast to end all feasts" and "singing and dancing throughout the night" (Whitehouse, 1995, pp. 141 and 143).

Our aim in the preceding paragraphs has been to substantiate and clarify the overall pattern of ritual innovation among the Dadul-Maranagi splinter group. The principal evolutionary trend in the splinter group's rituals was to introduce many new rituals that shifted from the first attractor position to the second, i.e., from even-numbered, frequently performed, special patient rituals with low levels of sensory pageantry to the odd-numbered, non-repeated, special agent rituals that included sensory spectacles that were unique to the splinter group.

The ring ceremony

Our aim in the following paragraphs is to demonstrate how one of the splinter group rituals, viz., the ring ceremony, instantiates essentially the same pattern. Among the splinter group's new rituals, the ring ceremony certainly possesses the greatest theoretical interest. Unlike all of the other *new* splinter group rituals, the ring ceremony is the only one that the Dadul-Maranagi splinter group *clearly repeated* and, therefore, it was the only one that could have undergone *evolution*. We shall divide its evolution into two periods, distinguishing between performances of the ring ceremony *before* and those that occurred *after* the mass migration to Maranagi.

Our principal task in what follows will be to demonstrate that, at least eventually, this ritual satisfied condition (1) on page 160, i.e., that it was a special agent, non-repeated ritual, *its frequent performance with the same ritual patients notwithstanding*. If we can make the case successfully that it evolved into a special agent ritual, then we will have secured an illustration of the ritual arrangements that cell III represents and, therefore, a test case for evaluating the two hypotheses (by examining whether it also satisfied condition (3), i.e., whether it underwent an infusion of increased sensory pageantry).

In fact, the splinter group did not merely repeat the ring ceremony; they repeated it frequently. Especially during what we have identified as the second period, i.e., during the last five weeks of the splinter group's life in Maranagi, members repeated the ring ceremony and its culminating all-night vigils virtually every night. How could a ritual that the splinter group repeated so frequently with the same patients be a special agent ritual? It is to that question that we now turn.

It is not unreasonable to expect, particularly in the early stages of a religious movement, that when religious innovators – even those who proceed as self-consciously as Baninge did (see, for example, Whitehouse, 1995, p. 115) – carry out some religious act, they may not be at all clear about what conditions, if any, might call for its subsequent repetition. *A fortiori*, they may have no idea whether it is a repeatable or non-repeated ritual – in the senses we have used these terms throughout. Moreover, the possibility that a collective, repeated practice may undergo change across a series of performances does not seem too far-fetched. This latter assumption is functionally equivalent to Sperber's comments on the transformations of representations and to our own comments on the evolution of ritual arrangements with which we opened chapter 2. In short, ritual matters may be somewhat obscure at the outset of a religious movement. Exactly what Baninge or Tanotka or the other participants thought about the ring ceremony when they performed it the first time is not completely clear. We can only examine Whitehouse's reports about their ritual practices and comments on them.[14]

One of Baninge's timely dreams inspired the ring ceremony too. In it he and Tanotka were in one half of a circle bisected by a fence. Dainge, the *ancestral* "boss" of the Cemetery Temple, was in the other half of the circle on the other side of the fence. He ignored Tanotka's pleas in behalf of the splinter group members, whom (it was presumed by the dream's interpreters) Tanotka and Baninge were to lead (in one version of the resulting ritual) into their "earthly semicircle" and, thereby, into both a morally purified state and considerably closer proximity to the ancestors. Soon thereafter, "the fence would be broken and all of the people within the ring would be united on earth (i.e., in the Period of the Companies)" (Whitehouse, 1995, p. 111). Baninge related this dream to both the orators and the witnesses and (sure enough) those same witnesses subsequently reported that the ancestors certified its contents. After a week of concentrated activity aimed at achieving sufficient moral strength across the entire community, the first ring ceremony occurred at dawn on May 28.

From the outset, the ring ceremony exhibited increased levels of sensory pageantry relative to performances of the familiar Kivung rituals *up to then*. Specifically, it introduced what was probably the single most attention-grabbing innovation that, in comparison with what the community was used to in its previous rituals, unequivocally raised the level of sensory pageantry. At the first performance of the ring ceremony, participants wore genital coverings only (Whitehouse, 1995, pp. 113–114).

Prima facie, this elevated sensory pageantry may seem obvious evidence for the ritual's odd-numbered form, but not only would that reasoning commit the fallacy of affirming the consequent, it might also distort the facts.

Although this initial performance of the ring ceremony included the various sensations associated with rising together in the middle of the night and experiencing daybreak outdoors in the nude, the nudity, *per se*, may not have concerned memory for this rite specifically. The first reason for this conjecture is that, although this practice began with the first performance of the ring ceremony, splinter group members subsequently performed *all* rituals, including the familiar Kivung rites, "in a state of virtual nakedness" (Whitehouse, 1995, p. 114). It may have simply been the manifestation of *an increase in sensory pageantry*[15] *across the board* that came with the birth of a splinter group movement in which Tanotka and Baninge had become CPS-agents in the community's midst. (See note 13.) In fact, this became the preferred state of (un)dress not only for all of the other rituals (innovative splinter group rituals *and* standard Kivung rituals alike) but for everyday activities as well.

If, henceforth, everyone was virtually nude all of the time, marking odd-numbered, special agent rituals off by means of their sensory pageantry would require even higher levels of emotionally arousing materials. Whitehouse (1995, p. 114) remarks that "the initial visual and psychological effects of this practice rapidly decayed, and nakedness was increasingly taken for granted." *Relative to this new baseline*, then, the sensory pageantry accompanying the ring ceremony during the first period from late May to early September was a little higher, but certainly not startlingly higher, than that accompanying the performances of the standard, even-numbered Kivung rites during the same stretch. (See Whitehouse, 1995, p. 151.)

The second reason that the nudity in the ring ceremony may not have concerned memory for a special agent rite is that it is not at all obvious from Whitehouse's account that this initial performance of the ring ceremony was a special agent rite. The ring ceremony seems to have *begun* as a ritual through which participants acknowledged Tanotka and Baninge's special connections with the ancestors (and their outright apotheoses) by greeting them and providing them with offerings. Whitehouse (1995, p. 113) describes the first ring ceremony: "Tanotka stood alone in the middle of the ring and, one by one, the people came forward solemnly to shake his hand and give him money..." The point is that, at least initially, it looks as though it was the people who served as the agents in this ritual and it was Tanotka who functioned as the ritual's *patient*: "they presented him with an offering (of money) and their allegiance (expressed through handshakes)" (Whitehouse, 1995, p. 113). If Tanotka was not

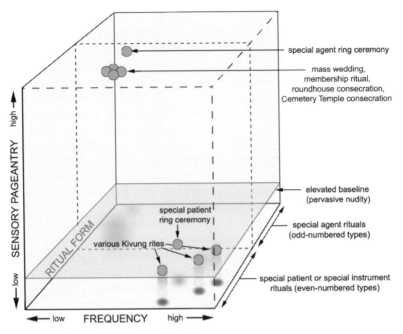

SENSORY PAGEANTRY — high ↑ / low ↓

RITUAL FORM

← low   FREQUENCY   high →

special agent ring ceremony

mass wedding,
membership ritual,
roundhouse consecration,
Cemetery Temple consecration

elevated baseline
(pervasive nudity)

special agent rituals
(odd-numbered types)

special patient
ring ceremony

various Kivung rites

special patient or special instrument
rituals (even-numbered types)

Figure 4.8   Elevated baseline

yet a full-fledged CPS-agent himself, he was still clearly in this version
of the ring ceremony the participant with the most direct connection
to the ancestors. Therefore, this ritual's patient seemed to be the participant who had the most immediate connection to the relevant CPS-
agents.

At least this description of the first ring ceremony suggests that it began
as a special patient ritual. The fact that the splinter group repeated this
ritual many times over the next three months would be fully consistent
with its even-numbered status (as would the absence of any eye-popping
levels of sensory pageantry relative to the new community baseline).
(See figure 4.8.)

Perhaps we should not make too much of this, though. Whitehouse's
account of the ring ceremony does not include all of the details we would
wish (though he can hardly be faulted for not having written his ethnography with our theory in mind!). He notes (1996a, p. 186), for example, that
after this performance of the ring ceremony, it was "subsequently adapted
for other purposes connected with protection against evil." Like confessions and offerings, rituals to protect against evil must be done again and
again. So, it looks as though in this version too the ring ceremony retained
an even-numbered form.

It is unclear from Whitehouse's text whether from the outset or eventually, the initial even-numbered, special patient version of the ring ceremony either was to have a second part involving a special agent rite or was to be supplemented by an alternative special agent version or was simply to be replaced by a special agent version of odd-numbered form. In any event, we can infer from other remarks in Whitehouse's discussion that by the time the Dadul splinter group was ready to migrate to Maranagi, something like one or more of these options had come to pass.

This special agent second half or alternate version or outright replacement for the initial special patient version of the ring ceremony was not about participants giving Tanotka and Baninge offerings and allegiance nor about the members doing things to keep away evil, but rather about the ancestors presenting Tanotka with "the key to the fence" to open it and bring the splinter group members and the ancestors together to inaugurate the Period of the Companies *here and now* (Whitehouse, 1995, p. 115). Now the ritual's agents were either the ancestors themselves who were aiming to launch the new age or Tanotka doing so as their representative. Not only do CPS-agents only act once, new ages, once begun, do not need restarting. So, how, according to the ritual form hypothesis, could the splinter group perform this special agent version of the ring ceremony again and again, if, on the LDC criterion, special agent rituals are non-repeated?[16]

Breaking through the conceptual roadblock

Whitehouse's discussion of why the splinter group *repeated* this version of the ring ceremony over this first period provides us with a key too, viz., the key for unlocking cell III of figure 4.3. Whitehouse states that

Following the first ring ceremony, there was a period (lasting about three months) in which the same emergent ideas . . . were reiterated over and over, and the emergent rituals were repeated again and again . . . progress towards the miracle during this period entailed the pretence of having taken a step back so that it appeared that everybody had entered the ring for the first time (again) or Tanotka had obtained the key from Kolman (again). . . .
   Baninge justified the absence of progress in terms of the *failure* on the part of the community to maintain a secure position within the ring. This, of course, was also the justification for repetitions of the ring ceremony. (1995, pp. 115–116, emphasis added)

Baninge's persistent appeal to this justification for the ritual's repetition constitutes evidence of its odd-numbered, special agent status. It also provides the pivotal insight about how special agent rituals can sometimes be repeated with the same patients many times. We take these points up in turn.

Baninge's repeated justification for re-performing the ring ceremony suggests that in at least one of its versions, it was a special agent rite. It may be that performances of even-numbered rituals are no less likely than performances of special agent rituals to fail and, therefore, to require repetition; however, *their repetition requires no justification*. They are, after all, *repeatable* rituals by virtue of their forms. Moreover, it would be even more extraordinary if ritual practitioners felt the need to justify *every* subsequent performance of an even-numbered ritual after the first! By contrast, of course, this is just what we would expect if the ritual being repeated were a special agent ritual. Whitehouse continually emphasizes how Baninge and the others subsequently seized upon every conceivable excuse that came along to explain the failures of this (apparently) special agent version of the ring ceremony. (The problems usually stemmed from the community's moral failings.) It is only the frequent repetition of a special agent rite that demands such overt, *methodical* justification.

Even more importantly for our purposes now, we can see not only how a special agent ritual can be repeated with the same patients, but how it can be repeated with them frequently, viz., when each and every one of those repeated performances *fails*. When special agent rituals fail, they must be done again, and when they fail repeatedly, they must be done again and again and again. The splinter group members apparently performed this special agent version of the ring ceremony "several" times before their migration to Maranagi in September. (See note 16 above.)

It appears that cell III is not empty. Arguably, though, some ambiguity may have surrounded the performances of the ring ceremony in the first few months, and Whitehouse's discussion of these events is too sketchy to draw any firm conclusion about the implications for the contents of cell III of these performances of the ring ceremony before the migration to Maranagi. A brief examination of the ring ceremony during the second period, i.e., after the migration to Maranagi, however, should remove all doubt.

The migration to Maranagi coincided with more ritual innovations. These included the combination of the ring ceremony (1) with the official opening of the roundhouse and the preparation ceremony both on September 9 – the day after the migration was complete and (2) with the membership ritual on September 13 (see Whitehouse, 1995, pp. 134 and 142). (Although Whitehouse's descriptions do not make it clear which version of the ring ceremony they employed, with the preparation ceremony at least, it was almost certainly the special agent version.) The most important of these innovations, though, was the combination of the special agent version of the ring ceremony with night-long vigils in which the people awaited the ancestors' arrival (see Whitehouse, 1995, pp. 149 and 150). Beginning on September 14 and on at least seventeen occasions over the next five weeks, they performed this ring ceremony-vigil complex.

There are two points to make about these developments straightaway. First, *all* of the ritual complexes in question were special agent rituals. Second, during this second period the performance rate (and, perhaps, even the raw count of performances) of this special agent version of the ring ceremony that was now incorporated into this larger ritual complex exceeded the rate (and, perhaps, even the raw count of performances) it exhibited during the previous three months before the migration. It may have even exceeded the performance rate of the ring ceremony (in all of its manifestations put together) during the first three months, but since Whitehouse's texts do not provide precise counts of ritual performances, we cannot know for sure.

Baninge marked the opening of the roundhouse and the preparation ceremony that followed that evening with performances of the ring ceremony. In the first case Baninge ended the ring ceremony with the consecration and "official opening" of the roundhouse. Again, official openings (of Cemetery Temples or of roundhouses) are rituals that only need to be done once. Whether the ancestors needed to officially open the roundhouse or whether an apotheosized Baninge's actions sufficed on their own, this was clearly a special agent rite.

Baninge ordered two pork feasts that day, one to accompany the opening of the roundhouse and the other with the standard Kivung Cemetery Temple ritual that preceded the preparation ceremony that was to be held that night. It would "pay off a backlog of debts to the ancestors" in final preparation for their return (Whitehouse, 1995, p. 137). If this enhanced sensory pageantry was not enough, the witness's report that day from the Cemetery Temple ritual that "the people will see proof of their work in the Kivung" stirred even greater expectations about the preparation ceremony that evening. Whitehouse reports, "the mood in Maranagi almost reached fever pitch," and people brought their garden tools to be locked away since "they would not be needing these 'foreign' tools again" (Whitehouse, 1995, p. 138). Clearly, they expected this ceremony to provoke the ancestors' return (if not usher in the Period of the Companies and their prosperity straightaway).

The expectation surrounding the preparation ceremony was that it would be the final ritual that would initiate the new age.[17] By virtue of this ritual, the ancestors (serving as the ritual's agents) would transform the splinter group community once and for all. This ceremony was simply a performance of the special agent version of the ring ceremony again, but this time it culminated in everyone crowding into the newly opened roundhouse to await the ancestors' return. Consequently, it was, in effect, the first performance of what would emerge four days later as what we shall refer to as the "ring ceremony-vigil complex." Along with the pork feasts that day, the overcrowded roundhouse, in which people could hardly even shift positions, added to the sensory pageantry... but it brought no miracle. Like the others before it, this performance of the special agent version of the ring ceremony had also failed. The ancestors had not returned.

Four days later on September 13 Baninge responded to the obvious let-down following the failure of the preparation ceremony to mark any dramatic change with two new rituals. He presided over a membership ritual (also based on the ring ceremony) for some newcomers *and* a mass wedding ceremony for all of the unmarried members of the splinter group. He responded, that is, with two more special agent rituals. The high levels of feasting, dancing, and singing that day had the right effect, producing "a suitable impact on morale in Maranagi ... nobody seemed to be troubled any more about the apparent *failure* of the first vigil" (accompanying the preparation ceremony) (Whitehouse, 1995, p. 143, emphasis added).

On the very next day (September 14), Baninge began what would prove to be a series of at least seventeen performances of the ring ceremony-vigil complex over the next five weeks. Each night Tanotka opened the fence and the splinter group members crowded into the roundhouse to await the ancestors' return. The ancestors refused to return on the night of September 14, because other uninvited newcomers also entered the roundhouse. Consequently, Tanotka called the vigil off not too long after it began.

Members were so confident of the ancestors' return with the next night's vigil that they consumed pork fat on the assumption that the ancestors would arrive soon enough to transform them before they fell ill. Unfortunately, yet again their prognostications were off, so the miseries associated with the overcrowding of the preparation ceremony vigil were seasoned this night with frequent exits in order for the consumers of pork fat to vomit. (That, of course, became the perfect excuse for why *this* performance of the ring ceremony-vigil complex failed, since the ancestors did not appreciate such unseemly behavior.)

Every night (excepting a three-day and a two-week interruption to drive out Satan and to gather food, respectively) the members of the splinter group performed the ring ceremony-vigil complex and waited for the ancestors to return and transform both them and their world. Each day following the ancestors' failure to appear, Baninge and Tanotka and the participants themselves sought explanations for the failure of the previous night's vigil. For example, the third vigil on the night of September 16 brought Lagawop's possession, which along with her eventual exorcism, dominated the vigils for the next four nights. In retrospect of course, Satan's possession of Lagawop provided excellent reasons for the failure of these vigils to culminate in the ancestors' return.

Whitehouse reports (1995, p. 148) that the ring ceremony-vigil complex did not occur for three consecutive nights (September 20–22). Instead, they performed the even-numbered version of the ring ceremony for warding off Satan. It is worthwhile to stress that on these occasions they performed this version of the ring ceremony *without the vigils and the sensory pageantry that accompanied them*. But the subsequent performances of the ring ceremony-vigil complex on the next five consecutive nights (September 23–27) also failed (Whitehouse, 1995, p. 148).

Two features of considerable theoretical significance stand out about these events. First, when the ring ceremony (aimed at ushering in the Period of the Companies) indisputably exhibited an odd-numbered, special agent profile during the second period, its *levels of sensory pageantry were substantially higher* than those associated with performances of any of the other versions of the ring ceremony (*including* the version devoted to driving evil out of the community that they performed on September 20–22). "Undoubtedly the most powerful and enduring images to come out of the splinter group were generated toward the end of its life, through a program of climactic rituals intended to usher in the Period of the Companies" (Whitehouse, 1996a, p. 187). Whitehouse (1995, p. 151) notes that, by comparison with anything that occurred before the migration to Maranagi, (what we are calling) the ring ceremony-vigil complex during this second period was "far more traumatic."

Second, over this five-week span, the level of sensory pageantry associated with the ring ceremony-vigil complex generally *increased*. (See figure 4.9.) During the ensuing performances, people were eventually forbidden to leave the roundhouse to relieve themselves, and thus, they did so where they stood or sat. Later no one was permitted to sleep, even though the vigils regularly went on until three or four in the morning, and near the end – with food running short – the discomforts of hunger often replaced the nausea that accompanied the combination of full tummies and conditions so uncongenial to digestion (Whitehouse, 1995, p. 151 and 1996a, p. 188). In short, they steadily ratcheted up the sensory pageantry (almost all of it negative now). The point is that during this second period, when no doubt remains about the ring ceremony-vigil complex's special agent status, the ritual also just as straightforwardly incorporated ever-increasing levels of sensory pageantry (satisfying condition (3) above).

In sum, then, during this period after the migration to Maranagi, the special agent version of the ring ceremony, in which the relevant CPS-agents were to carry out actions that would change things once and for all,

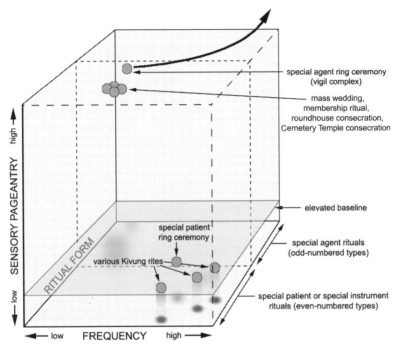

Figure 4.9   Special agent version of the ring ceremony

became loaded with sensory pageantry that was extraordinary *even by the standards of the previous splinter group rituals*, such as the Cemetery Temple consecration and the performances of the even-numbered versions of the ring ceremony. It was also directly associated with traditional Mali Baining materials, viz., the newly constructed roundhouse in Maranagi. (See condition (3) above.) Moreover, because of diverse developments that interfered with the success of these ritual performances, the splinter group repeated this special agent ritual complex frequently for over a month. In short, cell III is not empty.

Empirical evidence: frequently performed, odd-numbered special agent rituals

We are, then, finally ready to examine at least one relevant set of facts that bear on the assessment of the two hypotheses' competing predictions about the relative levels of sensory pageantry in special agent rituals that are frequently performed. Since all of these predictions are *comparative*, we must examine both changes in the levels of sensory pageantry that accompanied the ring ceremony in its odd-numbered, special agent version over time and the levels of sensory pageantry that accompanied *even-numbered* rituals that this religious community performed during the *same* interval.

Both of these comparisons will pose substantial problems for the ritual frequency hypothesis but not for the ritual form hypothesis. Ultimately, regardless of whether we employ a fine-grained or a coarse-grained analysis of the ring ceremony's form, the ritual frequency hypothesis correctly predicts neither its evolutionary trajectory nor its associated levels of sensory pageantry (compared with those accompanying the splinter group's performances of rituals of even-numbered types). Once we clarify the relevant period of time for doing these comparisons, we can turn to these topics.

Clarifying the proper time period for comparing the two hypotheses

It is not obvious that the ritual frequency hypothesis predicts *any* of the ring ceremony's evolutionary trajectory correctly – depending upon what is to be made of the introduction of the near nudity in its first performance. When the splinter group performed the first ring ceremony, its performance frequency at that point was very low, indeed, viz., zero. Whitehouse repeatedly emphasizes that the ritual frequency hypothesis predicts that the ceremony should have had a substantially increased level of sensory pageantry, relative to the existing baseline. Of course, whether or not it does count as incorporating enhanced sensory pageantry *depends upon which baseline constitutes the relevant standard for comparison*, the one before or the one after the splinter group began to perform new rituals. Whitehouse clearly has the former alternative in mind.

Generally, Whitehouse's defense of the ritual frequency hypothesis and of his theory of religious modes emphasizes the substantial increase in sensory pageantry of the rituals that the splinter group performed – presumably including their performances of the standard Kivung rites – in comparison with that which accompanied performances of the Kivung rituals in Dadul and Maranagi *before* the splinter group erupted. If, as Whitehouse maintains, the eruption of the Dadul-Maranagi splinter group constitutes a transition in religious practices from the doctrinal to the imagistic mode, then his theory of religious modes certainly does predict this general elevation of sensory excitation correctly. One question, though, is whether or not the ritual frequency hypothesis correctly predicts the increase in sensory stimulation associated with the splinter group's performances of the familiar Kivung rituals, in particular. We shall argue in the second section of chapter 5 (pages 183–184) that it does not. We postpone this question for now, because it does not bear on the comparison at hand.

In this and the previous section we have been seeking to evaluate the hypotheses' *conflicting* predictions about the comparative levels of sensory pageantry connected with frequently performed, special agent rituals. The principal question before us, then, is "which of the two hypotheses makes the correct predictions about the special agent version of the ring ceremony?" *This* comparison of the two hypotheses' empirical credentials demands attention to the finer-grained details of the splinter group's various ritual practices during their six months of ritual innovations. This is the period when – on the basis of their aberrant *ritual practices* – the Dadul and Maranagi communities genuinely deserved to be characterized as a "splinter group," since they no longer pursued orthodox Kivung rituals only. We should also add that it is the demands of making these finer-grained comparisons about this time of ritual innovation among the Dadul-Maranagi splinter group, not prejudice in favor of our theory, that require the use of the later baseline. (In fact, adopting the new baseline does not unequivocally favor the ritual form hypothesis.)

Once we move to the very next level of specificity regarding developments *within* the ritual system of the splinter group, the ritual frequency hypothesis immediately faces problems. The overall trend in the sensory pageantry associated with the rituals the splinter group performed (including the standard Kivung rites) across the pivotal six months in question was *upward* even though the performance rate and the raw count of the rituals were *increasing* too. (Recall, for example, that – in addition to the performances of the innovative rituals [including the many performances of the ring ceremony in its various versions] – one of the other ritual innovations was to increase the number of public meetings coordinated with the Bernard's Temple ritual from two to seven times a week.) So, although the theory of religious modes correctly predicts the collective elevation of sensory pageantry in the Dadul and Maranagi communities' transitions from standard Kivung practices to the era of the splinter group's ritual innovations, *within* that era, the ritual frequency hypothesis fails to predict the most obvious general trend correctly.

The evolution of the special agent version of the ring ceremony during the splinter group period

As we stressed above, however, it is its predictions about *the special agent version of the ring ceremony* that are our current concern. (Our aim is still to sort out the two hypotheses' diverging predictions about cell III of figure 4.3.) The predictions of the ritual frequency hypothesis about that specific ritual's evolution are even less satisfactory. Not only do the levels of sensory pageantry associated with its performances from late May through mid-October undergo the single greatest leap, compared with those associated with any of the other rituals unique to the splinter group, *the trend of that variation is in exactly the opposite direction from what the ritual frequency hypothesis predicts.*

During the first period, from late May until early September, White-house gives no indication that performances of the special agent version exhibited any more sensory pageantry than did performances of any other versions of the ring ceremony. He also concedes that the levels of sensory pageantry in question are *not* extraordinary, given the new baseline. Acknowledging that "the routine observance of nakedness...undermined its initial impact," Whitehouse (1995, p. 151) describes the level of sensory pageantry associated with the performances of (all versions) of the ring ceremony during this first period as "no more impressive as a sensory experience than the satisfaction of day-to-day desires."

By contrast, Whitehouse describes (1995, p. 151) the ring ceremony-vigil complex during the second period as "involving severe deprivations, miseries, and even physical assault . . . conducive to a particularly intense experience of physical and emotional suffering . . . providing some of the most memorable religious revelations of all splinter-group activity." In short, after holding steady at intermediate levels for five months, the sensory pageantry associated with the special agent version of the ring ceremony and accompanying vigils climbed to extremely high levels during the final five weeks. But this was just the period when the ritual's raw count continued to mount and its performance rate substantially *increased.*

The crucial point is that the basically *steady* level of sensory pageantry during the first period but especially the rapidly *mounting* levels during the second are not consistent with the predictions of the ritual frequency hypothesis. According to that hypothesis, the gradual rise of the raw count and, therefore, of the performance rate of the special agent version of the ring ceremony during the first period and their brisk increases during the second suggest that its level of sensory pageantry should have noticeably *decreased* throughout when, in fact, it remained *steady* for five months and then greatly *increased* at the end.

For two reasons, perhaps, we should not press the problem of explaining the ritual arrangements surrounding the special agent version of the ring ceremony during the first period. First, we should grant that on this front the competition may not be a complete wash in favor of the ritual form hypothesis. If, from late May to early September, one version of the ring ceremony *was* a special agent ritual (as seems to be the case), then the ritual form hypothesis predicts that its associated sensory pageantry should have been higher than that of even-numbered rites performed during the same time period. In conformity with that prediction, it did exceed the levels connected with performances of the standard Kivung rites. However, that it did not, apparently, exceed those attached to performances of the special patient versions of the ring ceremony (involving the presentation of offerings and greetings to Tanotka) during this first period is contrary to the prediction of the ritual form hypothesis. Second, at least some of the time, the performances of the ring ceremony during the first period may have been ambiguous with regard to questions of ritual form. Finally, Whitehouse's discussion of these matters does not provide all of the necessary details for adjudicating the relevant questions definitively. These considerations might justify suspending the responsibility of the ritual frequency hypothesis for accounting for the ritual arrangements surrounding the performances in question.

In response we should make two points clear. First, appeals to any lack of clarity about these matters in the first period also indemnify the ritual form hypothesis. Second, our argument against the ritual frequency hypothesis need not rely on the events of the first period at all. Its more serious predictive failures about associated levels of sensory pageantry concern developments during the second period when performances of the ring ceremony-vigil complex unequivocally exemplified a special agent ritual that falls into cell III by virtue of its frequent performance. The ritual form hypothesis wins that round hands down.

Comparing the sensory pageantry associated with special agent as opposed to special patient rituals during the splinter group period

That success, however, is the less important half of the story. How the ritual arrangements surrounding performances of the special agent version of the ring ceremony may have evolved over the six months in question does not matter much, if its comparative levels of sensory stimulation did not exceed those connected with the even-numbered, special patient rituals that the community performed during the same time period.

We stated on page 174 that the ritual frequency hypothesis does not correctly predict these comparative levels of sensory pageantry either. By *any* measure, across the time period in question (from late May to mid-October) neither the special agent ring ceremony's raw count nor its performance rate was low. Over this six-month stretch the splinter group members had performed the special agent ring ceremony at least a couple of dozen times. The point is that during this interval its raw count and performance rate *exceeded* those of the standard Kivung absolution

rites that were performed monthly or the garden rituals performed fortnightly (or, before this new era of ritual innovation, even the offerings
in Bernard's Temple which had been performed twice a week prior to
the splinter group's eruption). During the final five weeks they exceeded
them substantially. Note that although its average rate for the approximately thirty-five days in question was one performance every other day,
if we subtract the two "interruptions" when the community was occupied with other activities (viz., driving out Satan and searching for food),
then its performance rate was as high as that of the most frequently performed Kivung ritual (viz., daily)! The problem for the ritual frequency
hypothesis, of course, is that the special agent ring ceremony's levels of
sensory pageantry *far* exceeded those associated with performances of
any of these Kivung rituals, even those with considerably *lower* counts
and rates during the period in question.

This is not the only failure of the ritual frequency hypothesis on this
front. The first interruption in the continuous string of performances
of the special agent ring ceremony-vigil complex (that commenced on
September 14) came on September 20. After the surprising realization
that it had been Satan, rather than her deceased grandfather, who had
taken possession of Lagawop the three previous nights, Baninge de-
nounced her and performed an exorcism during the vigil of September 19.
As a result of this stain on the community's integrity, instead of continuing
to perform the special agent ring ceremony-vigil complex, they decided
to perform "several ring ceremonies to drive Satan out of Maranagi" over
the next three days (Whitehouse, 1995, p. 148). Although Whitehouse
provides no details about the version of the ring ceremony in question, by
virtue of (1) its aim (viz., driving out evil), (2) its repetition over the entire
six-month period, and (3) the occasions when it was performed (viz., after
periods of continued ritual failures), it certainly looks as though it was a
version of the ring ceremony with an even-numbered form.

But now here is the rub. These performances of this even-numbered
version of the ring ceremony were *not* accompanied by the vigils that accompanied the performances of the special agent version on the previous
six nights and the subsequent five nights, nor does Whitehouse give any
indication that they were accompanied by any other sort of extraordinary
sensory pageantry (relative to the new community baseline).

The ritual frequency hypothesis is unable to explain these patterns
in two respects. First, ascertaining and even expressing these claims requires all of the theoretical apparatus behind the ritual form hypothesis
to make sense of these distinctions between types of ritual forms and
different versions of the ring ceremony. Second and more importantly,
though, even if we allow the hypothesis to borrow those distinctions,

unquestionably across the five-week period at hand and perhaps even across the overall six-month era, this even-numbered version of the ring ceremony was not performed much, if any, more often than the special agent version was. Yet, whatever ambiguity may surround these matters during the first five months, during the final five weeks, at least, the sensory pageantry connected with the *many* performances of the special agent version *far exceeded* that associated with these *few* performances of this even-numbered version.

At this point supporters of the ritual frequency hypothesis might simply argue that the sample of ritual performances in this ethnography is too small and the time periods in question too short to draw any firm conclusions. That argument seems fair enough. Cell III may have contents, but we have not surveyed enough of them across a long enough period of time to draw any conclusions confidently. Still, it seems reasonable to examine the direction in which the available evidence points. The ritual form hypothesis correctly predicts virtually all of the findings we have reviewed (some of which, as we have just demonstrated, the ritual frequency hypothesis cannot even address without its aid) and is at least as consistent as its competitor with the one potentially recalcitrant item.

Consider the evolutionary trajectories of the various versions of the ring ceremony, i.e., the comparative levels of sensory pageantry between performances of these various versions across the era of the splinter group's ritual innovations. In two of its versions, viz., when it focused on an offering and a demonstration of allegiance to the splinter group leaders and when the members used it to drive out Satan, it appeared to be an even-numbered rite. That, according to the ritual form hypothesis, meant that participants could repeat these rituals but that they should show no substantial change in sensory pageantry over time and no substantial increase in sensory pageantry compared with the other repeatable rituals (such as the standard Kivung rites). Just as the hypothesis predicts, the participants did and the rituals did not. (Recall that once the ring ceremony was performed the first time, even the standard Kivung rites were performed in the same state of near nudity.)

Whatever ambiguities surround performances of these two even-numbered versions and of the special agent version of the ring ceremony during the first five months, the special agent ring ceremony-vigil complex's profile was not at all ambiguous during the final five weeks. All it would take was one successful performance to inaugurate the new age. Therefore, according to the ritual form hypothesis, its sensory pageantry should have been noticeably higher than that associated with any even-numbered ritual (standard Kivung rite or innovative splinter group ritual) performed during the same time period. Like the sensory pageantry attached to all of the other special agent rituals that the splinter group performed (successfully) only once, viz., the consecrations of the Cemetery Temple and the roundhouse, the membership ritual, and the mass wedding, the sensory pageantry attached to the performances of the special agent ring ceremony was far higher, indeed.[18]

The generally increasing levels of sensory pageantry of the special agent version of the ring ceremony across the final five weeks are perfectly consistent with the repeated failures of this rite. If the initial level of elevated sensory pageantry elicited neither a convincing encounter with the ancestors nor evidence of the desired ancestral actions, then the logic of our account about the connection between sensory pageantry and motivation suggests that more sensory pageantry would. Presumably, the capacities of our sensory systems for stimulation set the only limits here.

Finally, the ritual form hypothesis makes perfect sense of why the performances of the ring ceremony for the purposes of purging Satanic influences on September 20–22 could be performed "several" times and why those performances were not accompanied by the elevated levels of sensory pageantry that had characterized all of the other performances of the ring ceremony for both the previous days and the subsequent weeks. In short, unlike those performances, these were performances of a ritual of an even-numbered type.

We have argued in this chapter that the ritual form hypothesis stands up to empirical tests far better than its principal cognitively inspired competitor. We have also maintained that it embodies more penetrating theoretical insights about the role of cognitive considerations in making sense of a wide range of religious rituals' features. Ultimately, we have argued in this section that the ritual form hypothesis makes better sense of Whitehouse's ethnography of Kivung and splinter group rituals than his own hypothesis does. In the final chapter we shall argue that with respect to such developments our overall theory makes good sense of even larger historical patterns too.

5 General profiles of religious ritual systems: the emerging cognitive science of religion

Chapter overview

We aim to show how the considerations of ritual form our theory emphasizes motivate an account of general evolutionary trends in religious ritual systems that affect the distributions of these cultural representations. Toward that end, our principal goal is to show how a small set of psychological variables exert selection pressures on *all* religious ritual systems, and how those systems' resulting properties insure that they meet the mnemonic and motivational demands necessary for their transmission. Well-adapted ritual systems are ones that cope with the constraints these psychological variables impose.

Nothing about this analysis will depend upon any of the details about either the Pomio Kivung or the Dadul-Maranagi splinter group. We continue to devote attention to them, because they serve as a means for highlighting differences between our and Whitehouse's views and because they so splendidly illustrate one of the *dynamical profiles* our analysis identifies. Although, finally, we will maintain that the materials from Whitehouse's ethnography constitute an exceptional case in some important respects, it is for just that reason that they will serve so well in explicating other patterns. Studying atypical cases in order to illuminate the workings of the typical ones is a standard research strategy in science.

It is uncontroversial that the general evolution of both the Dadul-Maranagi splinter group's ritual innovations and its innovative rituals was toward higher levels of sensory pageantry. It is one thing to predict this general trend, as the theory of religious modes does, but quite another to account for the changes in specific rituals. The ritual frequency hypothesis *cannot* account for the changes in the performances of the Kivung rites during the splinter group period. Thus, the larger theory of religious modes should not depend upon the ritual frequency hypothesis. These rituals' increasing sensory pageantry arose in response to the tedium effect, and it seems to solve that problem. But elevated sensory pageantry attached to such special patient rituals presents problems of its own. The most important is how the resulting ritual system can avoid habituation.

On pages 183–192 we point out that in order to relieve tedium and avoid habituation, the resulting innovations also evolved toward a ritual system in which special agent rituals predominated. The ritual form hypothesis straightforwardly explains the connection between these two trends, i.e., the trend toward greater sensory pageantry in rituals and the increasing prominence of special agent rituals. So, the ritual form hypothesis can explain not merely the features and evolution of specific rituals (as we did in the previous chapter) but the general trends the splinter group's ritual innovations exhibited as well. The ritual frequency hypothesis, however, does not possess the necessary conceptual resolution even to view the second of these trends, let alone the resources necessary to connect it with the first. By contrast, the cognitive alarm hypothesis accounts for the fact that the splinter group introduced higher levels of sensory pageantry into rituals, and the ritual form hypothesis accounts for why it introduced new special agent rituals and why the most extreme forms of sensory stimulation became attached to those rituals.

The Pomio Kivung ritual system is unusual in that it includes *no* special agent rituals. By contrast, the introduction of special agent rituals dominates the splinter group's ritual innovations. Of course, splinter groups have arisen not just in Dadul, not just among the Kivung, not just in Melanesia, but through the ages and across the world. On pages 192–212 we consider the connections between the Dadul-Maranagi splinter group and larger Kivung patterns and, following Whitehouse (2000) (and, ultimately, Max Weber, 1947), between those larger patterns and *trends in the evolution of religious systems generally.*

Our focus, of course, remains on ritual. We will advance two general profiles that arise among religious ritual systems and speculate about a third. Religious ritual systems can exemplify either of at least two dynamical profiles that recur in the space of possible ritual arrangements. Although each profile involves a characteristic pattern of change that traverses many of the same regions in the space of possible ritual arrangements, they also differ in some important respects. Explicating these two profiles enables us to clarify how micro-processes at the psychological level are responsible for these alternative distributions of cultural representations and for the phase portraits they produce. The pivotal variable discriminating between these two dynamical profiles is whether the ritual systems include odd-numbered, special agent rituals in addition to even-numbered, special instrument and special patient rituals or whether they possess rituals of the latter sorts only.

The complement of rituals in a *balanced* ritual system is a bivalent configuration that includes rituals from *both* of the two major categories our theory discusses. This is a familiar configuration that virtually all of the world's most successful religions exhibit; consequently we suspect that the pattern of cultural representations balanced systems represent is a good deal more widespread today than that of unbalanced systems.

We actually discuss the profile of one sort of *unbalanced* religious ritual system first on pages 192–201. That is because this profile captures the dynamics of the Pomio Kivung ritual system as well as other religious developments in Melanesia that Whitehouse (2000) discusses. We describe such systems as "unbalanced" because of their complement of rituals during the longest and most stable stage of their characteristic phase portraits. That complement of rituals is unbalanced because special patient and special instrument rituals *overwhelmingly* predominate. Special agent rituals play little, if any, role. Unbalanced ritual systems manifest a limit cycle, i.e., a dynamical pattern that cycles between these longer stable stages and periodic outbursts of prophetic, splinter group activity of much shorter duration. In this shorter splinter group stage the ritual system comes to focus on special agent rituals with substantially greater levels of sensory pageantry. We have argued that these special agent rituals that dominate during these short intervals enhance participants' motivation. They typically do so, however, without undermining participants' fidelity to the mainstream religious system and its unbalanced complement of rituals that prevail during the longer, stable periods. Ultimately, these splinter group episodes do not result in any fundamental changes in participants' religious identities. When these splinter groups crash, their members are readily reassimilated back into the mainstream group.

We argue on pages 201–212 that unbalanced ritual systems and the splinter groups they spawn differ, respectively, from balanced ritual systems and the many splinter groups they engender. As we noted above, balanced systems consist, on the one hand, of routinized performances of special patient and special instrument rituals and, on the other, of performances of special agent rituals whose heightened sensory stimulation energizes participants and motivates them to transmit these systems anew. One of the factors that is critical to any stability that balanced systems might achieve is their conceptual schemes' capacity to retain *control* of the interpretations of the special agent rituals that periodically inject these stimulating experiences. Referring to these systems as "balanced" does not imply that they are any more stable than unbalanced systems. The balance (or imbalance) in question simply concerns whether or not a religious ritual system includes rituals of both odd- and even-numbered types. Balanced religious systems must possess conceptual resources sufficient to insure that the interpretations of these experiences conform to constraints that rule out *empirically detectable* transformations that are beyond their control, if they are to attain any stability.

If balanced ritual systems retain both *markedly* higher levels of sensory pageantry with their special agent rituals and conceptual schemes capable of controlling those rituals' interpretations, they *can* prove quite stable. Still, the pivotal role that conceptual matters play in preserving that stability introduces abundant opportunities for (conceptual) variations and, therefore, many new grounds for generating splinter groups. Consequently, the long-term stability of balanced ritual systems also turns on their power to discourage such variations and enforce their interpretations.

Achieving conceptual control of special agent rituals is also critical to the fate of groups that splinter off from balanced systems. Not every splinter group is as powerless to attain such control as the groups Whitehouse documents. Unlike the Melanesian groups that have splintered from unbalanced systems that have no means for controlling special agent rituals, *since they have no special agent rituals*, groups that have broken from balanced systems may adopt most or all of the apparatus for the conceptual control of special agent rituals from the parent system. If they can survive the parent system's exercise of its power to suppress variation and enforce orthodox interpretations, these splinter groups can emerge as new religious systems whose participants undergo a fundamental change in their religious identities. On the basis of divergences in (1) their systems of origin (unbalanced versus balanced), (2) their levels of conceptual control over special agent rituals, and, (3) most obviously, their fates, we shall maintain that the splinter group phenomena on which Whitehouse reports (exhibiting one stage in the phase portrait of unbalanced systems) differ from *all three sorts of splinter groups that can arise from balanced systems*. Appreciating their differences from the third sort, in particular, depends upon understanding our theory's distinction between special agent rituals, on the one hand, and special patient and special instrument rituals, on the other.

Reflections on the history of culture and on the natural history of human cognition suggest that special agent rituals play a more fundamental role in the transmission of religious systems than special patient and special instrument rituals do. Our analysis of religious ritual *systems* and their underlying psychological dynamics corroborates this proposal. We argue that the periodic performance of special agent rituals with elevated levels of sensory pageantry is a critical constraint on the fitness of all religious ritual systems. All of this raises the possibility of a third sort of religious ritual system that is unbalanced in a different way. The complement of rituals in these sorts of unbalanced ritual systems is dominated not by special patient and special instrument rituals but by rituals of special agent form. The ritual system of the Baktaman *may* be an example.

Trends in ritual innovation

Much of our discussion in the previous chapter dealt with specific rituals Tanotka and Baninge created. One pervasive trend in these rituals was their substantially increased levels of sensory pageantry relative to that surrounding the community's earlier performances of Pomio Kivung rituals. We shall show that such elevated levels of sensory pageantry inevitably become associated with special agent rituals and how Whitehouse's reasoning about some of the psychological issues at stake goes some way toward explaining why.

The problem of explaining the levels of sensory pageantry associated with the splinter group's performances of Pomio Kivung rituals

By introducing virtual nudity to all dimensions of community life, Baninge clearly raised the bar with respect to what we have broadly called "sensory pageantry." One of the consequences of this innovation was that the splinter group's subsequent performances of the standard Kivung rites were more arousing than they had been before. Therein lies a revealing problem.

Neither our theory of religious ritual competence nor the ritual form hypothesis addresses such broad, overall trends in religious ritual systems directly. However, since the transition from conventional Pomio Kivung practices to the splinter group is one from a religious ritual system that performed special patient rites only to one in which special agent rituals dominate, it does follow that the predictions of the ritual form hypothesis about particular rituals would collectively entail an elevation in the *average* amounts of sensory pageantry present in the community's rituals. We should be clear, though, that

1 the ritual form hypothesis makes no predictions about the overall elevation of sensory stimulation in daily activities other than religious rituals, and

2 its only prediction concerning the subsequent performances of the Kivung rites is comparative, viz., that they would contain less sensory pageantry than performances of special agent rituals during the same time period, *and that prediction is correct.*

In contrast to our theory and to both the ritual form and ritual frequency hypotheses, it is precisely such community-wide phenomena that

Whitehouse's theory of religious modes addresses. The emergence of the Dadul-Maranagi splinter group marks a transition from the doctrinal to the imagistic mode on Whitehouse's account, and his theory correctly predicts a general increase in sensory pageantry under such circumstances. It predicts the elevation of the community's baseline.

But *that* is just what is so revealing. The theory of religious modes' explanatory success here indicates that the ritual frequency hypothesis cannot be telling the right story about that theory's cognitive foundations, because the predictions of the ritual frequency hypothesis about the splinter group's performances of the Pomio Kivung rituals are *false*. The problems are clear. First, the performance frequencies of the Cemetery Temple ritual, garden ritual, and absolution ritual did not change. Hence, the frequency hypothesis predicts that neither should their associated levels of sensory pageantry. Second, although the performance frequency of the ritual connected with Bernard's Temple did change, it *increased*. Consequently, the ritual frequency hypothesis predicts that its related sensory pageantry should have, if anything, *decreased* – but, of course, it did not. So, the ritual frequency hypothesis does not explain why the sensory pageantry associated with all of these rituals increased during the splinter group's era of imagistic religious practices.

Our suggestion, in short, is that although both hypotheses get at critical cognitive variables, religious ritual form proves the more fundamental of the two and, thus, the ritual form hypothesis constitutes a sounder cognitive foundation for any theory about larger religious ritual patterns.

Psychological constraints on religious ritual systems and the emerging prominence of special agent rituals

Whitehouse argues that such splintering in religious systems arises as the result of the tedium effect. The logical rigor and ritual routines of his doctrinal mode may purchase uniformity of belief and practice (though see Boyer, 2001), but it comes at the price of tedium and boredom and, sometimes, disaffection (Whitehouse, 2000, p. 147). It does, at least, if these doctrinal religious systems do not include some means for insuring their reinvigoration, i.e., for insuring a periodic injection of imagistic practices to counteract the impact of the tedium.

A religious system whose rituals congregate exclusively (or nearly so) around the first attractor is what we are calling an *unbalanced* system. Sooner or later such systems *will* induce boredom. Such ritual tedium will provoke creative reactions sufficient to spring ritual systems out of this position. Those reactions will generate enough energy to break the ritual system free from the first attractor. (See figure 5.1.)

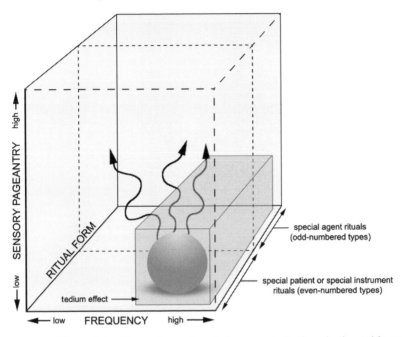

Figure 5.1   The tedium effect induces perturbations in the stable stage
of unbalanced systems

The introduction of such energy, though, is critical to these religious
systems' survival. Without avenues for such reinvigoration these religious
systems risk decline. Participants' motivation to transmit these systems
wanes. The generation of ecstatic splinter groups becomes a standard
means for reinstilling participants' enthusiasm and for resuscitating their
religious representations' cognitive relevance in Sperber's sense. The tedium effect shows why these sorts of unbalanced ritual systems, i.e., ones
that exclusively possess rituals located near the first attractor during their
longest, most stable stages, will either experience periodic instability or,
if constrained by other cultural factors, slowly decline until they become
extinct. (See pages 201–212.)

Of course, we have already seen that rituals associated with Whitehouse's imagistic mode carry psychological hazards of their own. The
high levels of sensory pageantry connected with rituals of this sort must
be dispensed in measured doses. Otherwise, as Whitehouse has warned,
participants will become habituated to such conditions, raising the threshold necessary to induce strong emotional effects the next time around and
that (typically) requires increasingly greater expenditures of resources.

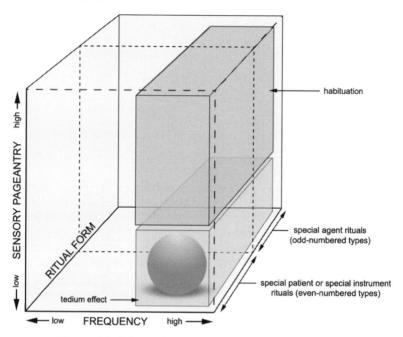

Figure 5.2   The problem of habituation

So, with sensory pageantry as well as with rituals, more is not always better.

Habituation seems to be just what happened in the Dadul-Maranagi splinter group after Baninge introduced pervasive nudity to the community. It ended up doing nothing more than elevating the community's collective threshold for arousal. All of this suggests that, regardless of cultural mechanisms, at least one region in the space of possible ritual arrangements will be unlikely to support stable systems at all. Religious ritual systems simply cannot rely on rituals that simultaneously have high levels of sensory pageantry and high performance frequencies (regardless of their forms). (See figure 5.2.)

The frustrations that tedium provokes and the constraints that habituation imposes go a good deal of the way toward explaining the evolutionary trajectory of the Dadul-Maranagi splinter group's innovations. The former makes sense of the sudden outburst of ritual activities with substantially increased levels of sensory pageantry. The latter accounts for the trend toward more and more sensory stimulation associated generally with the emerging ritual system and especially with the performances of the special agent version of the ring ceremony after the migration to Maranagi.

All of the innovative rituals and all of the ritual innovations that *unequivocally* involved extraordinary sensory pageantry and emotional arousal were *special agent rituals*. Since what counts as unequivocal involvement of "extraordinary" sensory pageantry and emotional arousal here are levels elevated *relative to the new baseline*, all of the splinter group's performances (save one[1]) of the standard Kivung rites and all of their performances of the two special patient versions of the ring ceremony (for acknowledging Tanotka and Baninge and for driving out Satan) do not qualify.

The ritual form hypothesis predicts that the increases in sensory pageantry in a ritual system (in response to the tedium effect) *will inevitably become associated with special agent rituals*, where CPS-agents or their representatives do something that they need only do once (such as inaugurate a new age). The splinter group introduced greater pageantry (nudity) into the special patient rituals of the Kivung. But since these rituals are repeatable and, indeed, frequently repeated, the inevitability of habituation insures that these are not the rituals that can carry the pivotal emotional punch that will increase the probabilities that participants will transmit their religious representations. The introduction of nudity in these rituals and in everyday activities simply raised the floor of the entire system. (See figure 4.9.)

Even if it does not predict it, the ritual frequency hypothesis is certainly consistent with the fact that *new* rituals must shoulder the motivational burden. New rituals, after all, will be ones with the lowest possible performance frequencies. The ritual frequency hypothesis, however, is utterly mute about those new rituals' *forms*. By contrast, the ritual form hypothesis holds that – new or not – the rituals that incorporate the most flashy sensory effects (for both motivational and mnemonic purposes) will be special agent rituals. These sorts of unbalanced ritual systems are bereft of special agent rituals, so the ritual form hypothesis predicts that their splinter groups will eventually *invent* such rituals when they are not available.

Rituals that serve to resuscitate a religious system choking on tedium must inspire many participants. As we have seen, the way to do so is to make them the patients of some highly arousing special agent rituals in which the actions of CPS-agents mark a fundamental moment in their lives that brings about a super-permanent change. Consequently, it seems a reasonable prediction that not just any special agent ritual will do. These new special agent rituals must be ones in which all or most participants can serve as ritual patients. Ordaining a new religious practitioner, for example, is a special agent ritual, but it probably has limited motivational effects beyond that newly certified practitioner who served as the ritual's patient. The psychological considerations we have examined suggest that if the tedium is widespread, then the motivational effects had better be as well.

It is important to recognize that this is not the only possibility. Repeatable, but infrequently repeated, special patient rituals that are arousing do, in fact, exist (e.g., human sacrifices of in-group members). But such variants are rare, and they are even more rarely (if ever) the rituals splinter groups invent – and not just because they are extreme. First, any participant who serves as the victim in such a ritual will not be in a position to transmit representations at its conclusion. In addition, such rituals must necessarily relegate most other participants in the religious system to the status of observers (at best), which seems far less likely to produce either vivid or accurate memories or high levels of motivation. In short, these rituals just aren't up to the job.

Their comparatively high levels of sensory pageantry notwithstanding, special agent rituals are – not coincidentally – also well suited to prevent habituation, since they are non-repeated. Participants serve as their patients only once. For each of their patients, they constitute a unique event. This point is critical.[2]

The cognitive alarm hypothesis holds that, at least initially, participants will regard rituals containing *unprecedentedly high levels* of sensory pageantry as ones that mark potentially significant events in their lives. These events will prove worthy of unique episodic memories, if participants' subsequent experiences corroborate that initial assessment. The ritual form hypothesis maintains that these rituals will inevitably take the profile of special agent rituals. The fact that special patient or special instrument rituals with such high levels of sensory pageantry can be done repeatedly – even frequently – will lead to habituation, and habituation will require steady increases in the resources devoted to producing sensory pageantry and, eventually, push participants up through what we might call a "sensory overload ceiling." (See figure 5.3.) Ever greater levels of sensory pageantry will inevitably push human beings beyond their abilities to endure it. Whether the sensory manipulation involves deprivation or excess (e.g., hunger or gluttonous feasting), human beings reach their limits and shut down by either falling asleep or experiencing shock or (if things get really bad) dying. It is clear enough that initiates cannot go indefinitely without water or endure endless torture. But it is no less true that they cannot continue to feast indefinitely or sustain extraordinary ecstatic states forever.

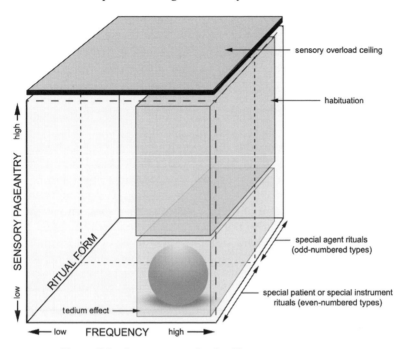

Figure 5.3   A sensory overload ceiling

The region in the space of possible ritual arrangements in which habituation presents a problem is large. Like an invisible hand, it pushes ritual innovations that wander into this region upward toward the sensory overload ceiling, where memory and motivation and, thus, transmission may all be in jeopardy.

If a religious ritual system clearly undergoes an overall increase in sensory pageantry and is to avoid the problems of habituation, its most extreme expressions will reliably arise in non-repeated, special agent rituals, and, as we noted above, if the system has no such rituals, *it will invent them.* A substantial increase in sensory pageantry in a religious ritual system overall will always correlate with a growing prominence of special agent rituals, even if they have to be fabricated precisely for that purpose.

The theory of religious ritual competence specifies that such special agent rituals are the ones in which CPS-agents take the initiative in human affairs. In interactions with fellow agents we sometimes serve as the agent and sometimes as the patient of actions. The theory of religious ritual competence shows how participants can represent CPS-agents as operating in either role in religious rituals. Presumptive *trans*actions with the gods imply that, at least occasionally, they have some things to do too. Special agent rituals result when the logic of those transactions calls for such initiatives on the part of the gods. Special agent rituals contain higher levels of sensory stimulation, because they cue participants to the fact that they have experienced life transforming events wrought by the gods (that should also have the effect of increasing their motivation).

Perhaps the better way to put this, though, is that special agent rituals contain higher levels of sensory stimulation precisely because there is little or nothing about these experiences in themselves that would signal their putative importance. If the underlying psychological dynamics have some of their roots in reactions to the tedium effect, then what is called for are (ritual) measures that will overcome that effect and motivate participants to transmit the system in question. If such motivation results from the stimulation of human passions, then these rituals must contain materials sufficient to that task. This undoubtedly includes the myriad ways religious ritual practitioners have struck upon to stimulate participants' senses. (Baninge's experimentation with this arsenal is an ideal case in point.)

On this view, making sense of all of this excitement in terms of a conceptual overlay that the religious conceptual scheme supplies concerning the putative actions of the gods is not the *cause* of these events but, perhaps quite literally, an *afterthought*. It may not be so much that special agent rituals demand new heights of sensory pageantry in response to dreams, possessions, unexpected events, timely theological reflections, and the like, but rather that rituals involving new levels of sensory pageantry erupt (in order to overcome the tedium effect) and that they are inevitably propelled away from the first attractor. Construing the resulting rituals in terms of special agent form is how the conceptual scheme *accommodates* rituals with such high levels of sensory pageantry. In ritual expressions of reaction to ritual tedium, the constraints that habituation imposes (represented in the upper right-hand region of the space of possible ritual arrangements) and the demands that mnemonic requirements sometimes place on the construction of cultural mechanisms (in the circumstances represented by the lower left-hand region of that space) tend to channel these creative energies. They typically generate cultural representations that evolve in the direction of the second attractor. (See figure 5.4.)

Although the constraints that habituation and mnemonic requirements impose are substantial, they are not even jointly sufficient to drive ritual innovations toward the second attractor. As we noted above, highly arousing, infrequently performed, special patient rituals, after all, are not a mere logical possibility. A few, such as the sacrifice of selected religious participants, have certainly existed. But for what we assume are obvious reasons, they are unlikely to generate much motivation, and as

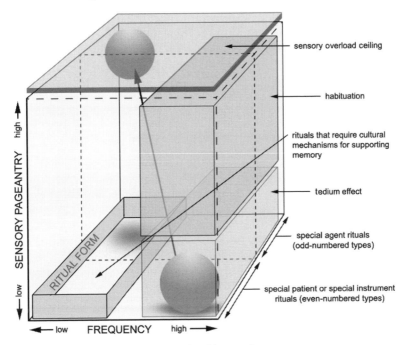

Figure 5.4   Constraining ritual innovation

special patient rituals, both their psychological effects *and their religious consequences* are clearly the results of *human* undertakings. Typically, in such rituals human agents are doing (extreme) things to appease the gods. So, not only are these rituals less likely to motivate participants, *they have the wrong forms*, since the richest motivational benefits that arise should, presumably, not appear to result from human artifice. The rituals should have forms in which *the gods get the credit*.

The action structures of special agent rituals in which each participant can serve as the ritual's patient are more likely to generate religious consequences and psychological effects consonant with both enhanced memory and motivation. CPS-agents' actions will bring about a super-permanent change in each specific ritual patient. That ritual change is culturally significant, emotionally arousing, and *construed as the result of the gods' actions*. The reintroduction of full immersion baptism by the Dissenters in seventeenth-century England illustrates this pattern. It is not by chance that splinter group innovations often take the profile of special agent rituals. This is the first reason to think that considerations of ritual form are not quite so causally inert as the proposal outlined in the previous two paragraphs seems to suggest. There is another.

The imposition of special agent profile on these rituals plays a decisive causal role on a second front. In the course of introducing our two dynamic profiles of religious ritual systems, we shall show how conceiving of these rituals in this way requires that religious conceptual schemes fulfill quite specific functions in order to ensure the long-term stability of the larger religious systems.

One sort of unbalanced religious ritual system

It is difficult to imagine a ritual system that illustrates all of this any better than that of the Pomio Kivung, because few persisting religious systems put so little emphasis on special agent rituals. (See, however, Severi, 1987 and 1993 and Sherzer, 1983 and 1990.) All of the rituals of the original Pomio Kivung system are special patient rituals. The two most central rituals, viz., the Cemetery Temple ritual and the ritual associated with Bernard's Temple, involve elaborate preparations of offerings to the ancestors. The garden ritual and the absolution ritual involve sharing resources (at least indirectly) with the ancestors too.

In the first years many who joined the Pomio Kivung had undergone traditional Baining initiations earlier in their lives, and they were well aware of the confrontations with the ancestors and the resulting revelations such rites evoked. So, too, were the leaders of the Pomio Kivung. They seem to have shared Whitehouse's insight that such imagistic practices do not resonate well with the sort of rigidly structured, logically coherent, doctrinal system they were propounding. Consequently, they explicitly prohibited members from participating in *any* sort of initiation (Whitehouse, 1992, p. 794). Originally, the system included *no special agent rituals*. So, there are no unique Pomio Kivung rituals associated with the traditional rites of passage. The Pomio Kivung ritual system does not mark long-term pair bonding or death ritually (Whitehouse, 1996a, p. 174). The ritual system of the Pomio Kivung includes none of the special agent rituals that typically recur across most religious systems. Participants simply continue to enact traditional Baining practices in connection with such events.

Subsequent developments necessitated one minor exception to this pattern. The Pomio Kivung system is now entering its fifth decade and it has become a victim of its own success. According to Whitehouse's theory of religious modes, the principal form of transmission in doctrinal systems such as these is proselytization. But since the ancestors have not returned, the Pomio Kivung conceptual scheme has had to accommodate persons who are born into the faith. Eventually, Kivung leaders permitted a perfunctory baptism ritual for members' infant children (Whitehouse, 2000, p. 74). It is not clear that this ritual even qualifies as a religious ritual in our technical sense, since it is not clear that it involves any appeal (direct or indirect) to the actions of any CPS-agents. That take is consistent with what, according to Whitehouse's own account, is its completely peripheral status in Pomio Kivung ideolo₃y.

Instabilities in some religious ritual systems

It is not too difficult to see, in the light of the psychological considerations summarized in figure 5.4, that the overall success of what Whitehouse calls "doctrinal" religious systems to the contrary notwithstanding, a ritual system like that of the Pomio Kivung will inevitably prove unstable. As we have seen, it will be unstable because eventually it will induce tedium. Ritual systems in which special patient rituals receive the overwhelming (if not exclusive) emphasis involve the uninterrupted repetition of rituals that have unremarkable levels of sensory pageantry and involve participants doing things to satisfy the CPS-agents time and time again. Although they may enjoy long periods of comparative stability, as we have seen, tedium is inevitable. If current cultural arrangements do not permit creative responses and the generation of new cultural representations, that tedium will gradually diminish the popularity of the prevailing cultural representations. Religious systems will not last in which such tedium goes forever unrelieved.

In any ritual system like that of the Pomio Kivung, the rituals that must address this motivational deficit must be rituals of a new and different sort. Since infusing special patient rituals with added levels of sensory pageantry rapidly risks habituation, the only successful response to tedium is either to revive or to invent special agent rituals. Again, it is not sheer coincidence that Tanotka and Baninge tried both. In their initial forays into ritual innovation, they rehabilitated not only the *awanga* from traditional Baining religion. They reintroduced the *ilotka* as well. The *ilotka* were central figures in traditional Baining initiations, i.e., in traditional, non-repeated, special agent rituals. They revived cultural representations associated with the most prominent (and very nearly the only) special agent religious rituals they knew of.

Of course, they created *new* special agent rituals too. Their first experiment on this front was to invent a dedication ceremony for the new Cemetery Temple the ancestors had demanded. This was a special agent ritual, since the ancestors, through their intermediaries, Tanotka and Baninge, consecrated this building. The ceremony included feasting and dancing (involving the *awanga* and *ilotka*). Compared with the standard Kivung rites, it was filled with sensory pageantry, but it was not a special agent ritual that marks a fundamental change in the lives of individual participants. (The patient of the ritual, after all, was the Cemetery Temple.

From the standpoint of religious ritual form, the splinter group participants were simply observers.)

Again setting the ring ceremony to the side for the moment, the next
three ritual innovations addressed this deficiency with improving precision. Not only were the second and third special agent rituals, they
were ones that aimed straightforwardly to bring about super-permanent
transformations in members' lives. That may be true of the first as well,
since the roundhouse consecration was incorporated into a larger ritual
undertaking, viz., what Whitehouse calls the "preparation ceremony."
Unlike the consecration of the Cemetery Temple, the roundhouse consecration was a preliminary to what, apparently, was the first time the
special agent version of the ring ceremony was performed *with a connected
vigil* aimed at bringing about the ancestors' return *that night*. (Recall that
this ritual was deemed unsuccessful early on because of Baninge and
Tanotka's inability to get intruders to leave the roundhouse.) The second
of this trio, the membership ritual, was, in effect, an *initiation* for new
members who joined the splinter group along the way. The third, the
mass wedding, was a special agent ritual in which the ancestors, through
Baninge and Tanotka, brought about a super-permanent transformation
in many members' lives. This special agent ritual too was marked by feasting and dancing and must have resulted in new forms of sexual arousal
for many members.

It was, however, the performance of the special agent version of the ring
ceremony connected with the vigil that was most climactic. After the
intruders had finally left and the new members were initiated, Baninge
and Tanotka could now use the key to unlock the gate in the fence that
bisected the ring, opening the way for the ancestors to join with the splinter group members and launch the Period of the Companies *that night*
(again). We have examined two important features of this ritual at length.
First, because each time the ancestors did not return, the splinter group
members construed each performance as a *failure*, which required that
they perform the ritual again the next night. However, second, because
the levels of sensory pageantry were so high from the outset, each performance had to include more and more measures for creating new
sensory experiences in order to *prevent habituation*. This set this ritual
off on a trajectory toward a psychologically "dangerous" region in the
space of possible ritual arrangements where considerations of habituation will inevitably push the ritual up through the sensory overload ceiling.
(See figure 5.5.)

There seems no doubt that this is just where the Dadul-Maranagi splinter group was heading, but external intervention precipitated the group's
crash not long before it would have punctured the sensory overload

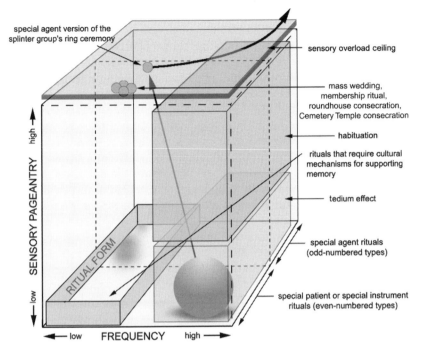

Figure 5.5   Entering psychologically "dangerous" regions

ceiling. Our suggestion is that even if the government health inspector had not intervened, the psychological dynamics we have discussed reveal how the internal developments of the Dadul-Maranagi splinter group would have produced the same result anyway. The crucial points so far, from the standpoint of our theory, were that

1 this resulted from the repeated performance of a (new) *special agent ritual*,
2 those repeated performances demanded justification in terms of the repeated *failures* of all of the previous performances, and
3 although those failures permitted repeated performances of this special agent ritual, each performance included ever-increasing levels of sensory pageantry in order to *prevent habituation*.

The phase portrait of splinter group cycles in Dadul

Not only Whitehouse's ethnography but also his subsequent research provide the most compelling evidence for the truth of two claims. The first is the counterfactual conditional that if the government health inspector had not intervened, the splinter group would still have crashed. The second is our theory's prediction that abrupt elevations of sensory pageantry across an entire religious ritual system inevitably become associated with existing special agent rituals (or provoke the invention of new ones).

A notable point is that the splintering from Pomio Kivung practices and beliefs in Dadul and Maranagi in 1988 was not an isolated set of events. Whitehouse (1995, pp. 172–173) shows that similar events occurred in Dadul in the mid-1970s, in 1977, and in the early 1980s. He remarks that "climactic millenarian rituals have a tendency to re-emerge every few years in Dadul." Whitehouse's estimate (1995, p. 172) that such splintering occurred in Dadul on average about once every five years provides the first – admittedly, very rough – quantitative measure of the time it takes the tedium effect to provoke creative responses with ritual implications, though it is by no means obvious precisely what the relevant set of impinging social variables is here.

The 1977 splinter group introduced at least two new rituals, both of which involved elevated levels of sensory pageantry and, corroborating our prediction in the previous section, both of which were rituals with special agent profiles. This splinter group carried out mass baptisms and the already familiar all-night vigils (that Baninge would copy eleven years later) designed to bring about the return of the ancestors then and there. Then, too, this activity attracted people from the surrounding area, including Sunam, and when the Period of the Companies failed to materialize "the non-residents of Dadul became discontented and were in turn blamed by the original community for obstructing the miracle through degeneracy and scepticism" (Whitehouse, 1995, p. 172). But, of course, because the vigil failed, they performed this special agent ritual again . . . and again . . . and again. The 1977 splinter group manifested the same pattern of justifying the repeated performance of a new special agent ritual on the basis of claims about each previous performance's failure.

The 1977 group was shorter lived than the 1988 group on which Whitehouse reports. It too ceased – because of substantial external criticism from neighboring communities – before the repetition of the vigils punctured the sensory overload ceiling. So, the phase portrait of such splinter group cycles shown in figure 5.6, like all models in science, is a somewhat idealized account that embodies various *ceteris paribus* assumptions. Obviously, a range of variables (such as external criticism or the intervention of government health inspectors) may influence this dynamic pattern. Still, this phase portrait is a good approximation of the characteristic pattern of the religious ritual system in Dadul over the two decades in question.

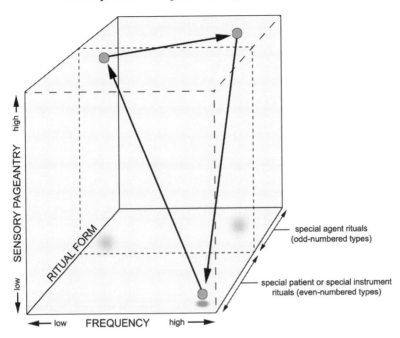

Figure 5.6   The characteristic phase portrait of splinter group cycles in Dadul

It is a limit cycle through which the community's ritual system circulated four times during the period in question.

Each time, after five years or so of comparatively tranquil pursuit of orthodox Kivung belief and practice, new ritual activities (provoked by new revelations) emerged which involved far higher levels of sensory pageantry and emotional arousal. Because the Kivung system lacked special agent rituals, the splinter groups had to invent *new* ones to accommodate this heightened religious excitement. Apparently, during each of these episodes the salient goal was to entice the ancestors' return. For the two of these episodes for which Whitehouse provides detailed information about the evolution of ritual patterns, the pivotal new special agent ritual, viz., the vigil, ends up being repeated because of the ancestors' refusal to cooperate. In order for these ritual performances to carry a provocative emotional punch, though, they must include ever greater levels of sensory stimulation. But, as we have noted above, that pattern cannot be sustained indefinitely, so – absent the ancestors' return – the system will inevitably crash, either because of exceeding the sensory overload ceiling, exhausting available resources for producing sensory pageantry, or because of external intervention. After the splinter group system crashes, the community returns to the familiar, comparatively stable, unbalanced pattern of orthodox Kivung religion.

Widespread but short-lived patterns and the profile of one sort of unbalanced religious ritual system

Ultimately, what makes the phase portrait in figure 5.6 particularly suggestive is that it looks like it is a good first approximation of cycles of ritual systems in a far wider range of religious communities. First, many Kivung communities on New Britain Island in addition to Dadul have displayed the same pattern. Whitehouse (1995, p. 172) cites research by Tovalele (1977) that reports eight other outbursts in Kivung communities between 1964 and 1972 of splinter group movements involving ritual innovations designed to prepare for the ancestors' imminent return inaugurating the new age.

Even more telling, though, is the extended discussion in Whitehouse's *Arguments and Icons* of similar patterns throughout Melanesia. Although he discusses many groups, he devotes particular attention to the Paliau Movement (2000, pp. 126–146; also see Schwartz, 1962). The Paliau Movement mirrors the Kivung system in all relevant respects. It too depends on the frequent repetition of special patient rituals with low levels of sensory pageantry. It too relies on "sober orations and highly repetitive ritual" (Whitehouse, 2000, pp. 141–142). All the evidence suggests that with this system too the tedium effects sets in. Whitehouse (2000, p. 142) comments that "it was not that people doubted...Paliau's doctrines but simply that they had become platitudinous, and could only be rescued...by being recast in a more revelatory form." So six years after the founding of Paliau's Movement the Second or "Ghost" cult arises with new rituals with higher levels of sensory pageantry (such as impassioned confessions, erotic bathing, and ring ceremonies of their own) and explicit expectations about the imminent return of the ancestors.[3] Like the splinter groups among the Pomio Kivung, the Ghost cult also eventually withers with members returning to conventional forms and rejoining the Paliau Movement. Of course, one striking feature about the Ghost cult's timing relative to the founding of the Paliau Movement is that it closely approximates Whitehouse's estimate of the cycles of splintering among the Pomio Kivung in Dadul.

Our suggestion, then, is that the phase portrait in figure 5.6 is a profile for a set of religious ritual systems. It follows from our discussion of the ties between special agent rituals, sensory pageantry, and emotional stimulation that participants in unbalanced ritual systems of this sort will regularly face motivational deficits. They will inevitably face the tedium effect but have no obvious ritual resources for ameliorating its impact (not, at least, without rapidly risking habituation). If such religious systems prove intolerant of innovative reactions to this tedium, they will succumb to it. If, on the other hand, they prove flexible in the face of such reactions, then (as we have already noted) various psychological variables will impose constraints that tend to direct these innovations toward ritual forms that cluster near the second attractor position. This leads to the creation of new special agent rituals (or the revitalization of ones that were previously available).

We have suggested that if the tedium is widespread, the motivational impetus must be as well. Consequently, not only will these events likely produce performances of special agent rituals, they are also likely to produce performances of special agent rituals in which most, if not all, participants will serve as ritual patients. These rituals must motivate enough participants – on the basis of their confrontations with the resident CPS-agents – to ensure the transmission of the religious system to new participants.

The critical issue, though, is that if the consequences of these rituals are supposed to be empirically detectable and their performance is unable to deliver the goods, then these ritual innovations face the prospect of *systematic* failure. For special agent rituals are non-repeatable. So, if they do not prove convincing the first time through, there must be some mechanism that will permit their repetition.

For reasons we reviewed in the previous chapter, construing these ritual performances as failures is the only viable alternative. But that presents a dilemma. Construing these performances as failures will work only so long as participants are able to withstand the sensory bombardment, but avoiding habituation virtually guarantees that the sensory pageantry in the ritual system will rise steadily toward the point where they cannot, i.e., toward the sensory overload ceiling. That is the first horn of the dilemma. The alternative is to back off on the sensory pageantry, which means that participants will be *far* less likely to have emotionally inspiring experiences and, hence, they will be less likely to emerge motivated to transmit the system anew. Moreover, this second horn of the dilemma requires participants to embrace explicitly the system's *persistent failure for the long term*. Since that horn is conceptually unacceptable (religions that insist all of their gods are either ineffective, unresponsive, or dead have never had much staying power – see Boyer, 2001), the conditions generating this dilemma insure that these systems are inevitably short-lived.

At least in Melanesia it appears that the standard route is for these splinter groups to risk penetration of the sensory overload ceiling. By seizing the first horn, ecstatic splinter groups exhaust themselves (quite literally) and crash. Hard-core intellectualists about religion might maintain that these systems crashed not because of the psychological dynamics we have noted but because, in fact, the ancestors simply did not return. One obvious response to this objection is to observe that frustrated prophecies are not sufficient to explain the crash. *Unfulfilled expectations, after all, often do not do a religion in.* (We shall argue below that such questions turn on the control a religious system can impose on the interpretations of its special agent rituals.)

These considerations point to a far more interesting explanatory problem with these cases that this hard-core intellectualist account misses. Given the repeated failure of the ancestors to return, i.e., the repeated failure of the innovative special agent rituals, why do the participants *not* abandon the orthodox religious beliefs of the mainstream movements from which they sprang? In fact, the members of these Melanesian splinter groups do not surrender their beliefs that the ancestors will eventually come back; at most, they only relax their expectations about their imminent return. With both the Pomio Kivung and the Paliau Movement, whole splinter groups – after they crash – reenter the orthodox systems with little or no fuss.

Groups facing persistent ritual failure that do not have ready access to special patient or special instrument rituals have nowhere to go and no one to turn to. It is easy enough to see how the crash of such a ritual system may well lead to the group's extinction. By contrast, if splinter groups have arisen in response to the tedium effect inherent in this sort of unbalanced system, participants are already familiar with special patient rituals to which they can return and which *provide them with avenues for reconnecting with the CPS-agents who seemed to have abandoned them.* In fact, the logic of (social) transactions with the gods demands it. In short, the availability of their old special patient rituals enables them to walk away from the scene of the crash unscathed. They can simply resume the ways of the comparatively stable unbalanced system with which they were already familiar. Their ritual system will return to the first attractor. This shift in their ritual practices completes the limit cycle illustrated in figure 5.6.

So, for example, although the members of the Dadul-Maranagi splinter group had to spend some time mending fences (both literally and figuratively) after the government health official ordered them to return home, neither had they abandoned orthodox Pomio Kivung ways nor were they returning as cynical or disaffected participants. Quite to the contrary, their splinter group experience *enhanced* their devotion to Kivung doctrines and practices. Whitehouse (1995, pp. 169–170) reports that "many of those who had participated enthusiastically in the splinter group experienced no discernible disillusionment with regard to basic Kivung ideas . . . Far from undermining commitment to Kivung ideology, the climactic rituals at Maranagi had rejuvenated that commitment in important ways."

Whitehouse holds (2000, pp. 129–130 and 143) that the splintering that goes on primarily concerns issues of *codification* as opposed to *content*. The splinter group phase does not result in revolutionary religious thought but simply the temporary *"recodification"* of orthodox beliefs in religious practices involving greater emotional arousal – clusters of religious practices that, we argue, overwhelmingly consist of special agent rituals. The uneventful reassimilation of splinter group members seems to have been the way all of the religious upheavals in Dadul played themselves out. The reinvigoration and reassimilation of splinter group participants as orthodox Kivung believers was their common outcome.

Balanced religious ritual systems

Whitehouse maintains (2000, pp. 128 and 143) that the mainstream movements, viz., the Pomio Kivung and the Paliau Movement, probably could not survive without the reinvigoration that issues from these periodic splinter group outbursts. Finally, both he and we are suggesting that the phase portrait in figure 5.6 simply captures the various stages of what is best construed as a *single* religious system. This point of agreement is important, because Whitehouse (2000, pp. 150–159) *also* holds that these patterns are not confined to recent Melanesian religious movements but appear just as clearly in Christianity worldwide, at least since the late Middle Ages and the Protestant Reformation. We are not so sure.

The varieties of religious splinterings

Historians of religion know full well how often splintering has occurred in the history of religion generally. For example, breakaway groups pepper the history of Christianity. Scholars have documented the activities of legions of such groups that have arisen since the Middle Ages. (See, for example, Lanternari, 1963 and Cohn, 1970.)

Just like the Dadul splinter groups, most of these splinter groups have also crashed. However, their crashes rarely lead to precisely the same results that the phase portrait in figure 5.6 predicts. The unbalanced systems of the Melanesian cases Whitehouse highlights differ from the balanced ritual systems that most of the world's widespread religions exhibit. Consequently, it should come as no surprise that some important features of the splintering phenomena differ too. We are not convinced that most splinter groups in most other religious systems – and especially in the history of Christianity since the Middle Ages – either arise from the same conditions or exhibit the same profile as the Melanesian cases that Whitehouse aims to group with them within the framework of his doctrinal mode.

We hold this view on the basis of three broad considerations. First, the *causes* of the splinter groups in these other religious settings are often not the same. Second, the *outcomes* of splinter groups arising from these other religious systems are often not the same, and third, the values of one of the principal variables influencing those outcomes, viz., the levels of *conceptual control* over their special agent rituals these splinter groups possess, are often not the same. It follows from the second of these considerations that rarely would anyone be tempted to treat the throngs of splinter groups in question as but a cyclical stage in a *single* religious system in the way that we and Whitehouse have agreed was true about the Melanesian cases he examines. *It follows from these three considerations collectively that our theory provides a far richer and finer-grained account of the general sorts of religious ritual systems than the one implicit in Whitehouse's theory of religious modes.*[4]

Regarding the first of these three reasons, then, the *causes* need not be the same. It is quite clear that many of the mainstream movements from which these groups break away are not unbalanced systems (like the Pomio Kivung) possessing no special agent rituals. By contrast, these mainstream religious systems – virtually all known versions of Christianity, for example – are *balanced* systems. (See figure 5.7.) These are ritual systems that not only contain special patient and special instrument rituals but *also contain special agent rituals*. So long as the sensory pageantry associated with those special agent rituals does not drastically diminish, the tedium effect is unlikely to arise. Because they include special agent rituals, they have ritual resources available for enhancing participants' motivation. Not only need tedium not set in, it is unlikely to do so in religious systems that include performances of special agent rituals that incorporate decidedly (as opposed to trivially) higher levels of sensory pageantry and that touch all or most participants at one time or another in the course of their lives.

Splinter groups arise for a host of reasons in these balanced situations, not just or even usually because of tedious rituals. Historically, the most prominent reasons seem to be *conceptual* and *political*, but at least occasionally the causes just seem random. (The gods, after all,

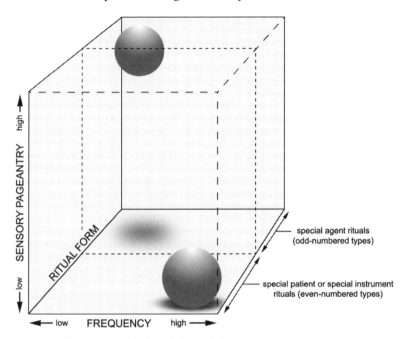

Figure 5.7   Bivalent balanced ritual systems

sometimes work in mysterious ways, and there is just no telling how *some* folks will respond.) At the conceptual level, religious systems have splintered over everything from arguments about lines of descent from Muhammad (in Islam) to disagreements over the character of enlightenment (in Buddhism) to squabbles about the language in which the mass should be said (in Catholicism) to disputes about the possibilities of ice in August in the American South (in the Southern Baptist system). On the political front, breakaway groups have arisen over issues such as who is the head of the church in England, who is the most recent incarnation of the Dalai Lama, and whether members of a variety of Protestant denominations lived in the Confederate States of America. Apparently, with balanced systems splintering is at least as likely to concern the *interpretation* of rituals as it is the performance of new or different rituals. By contrast with the Melanesian cases, splintering in these instances seems primarily to concern *content* rather than *codification*.

The second reason we think that most splinter groups from balanced systems differ from the Melanesian cases is the differences in their outcomes. Groups that split from religions that have balanced ritual systems usually result in one of three outcomes – none of which exactly matches the phase portrait of the Dadul-Maranagi splinter group or the Ghost cult that figure 5.6 captures and at least one of which does not resemble it in the least.

Recall that the Melanesian splinter groups crashed and were readily reassimilated into the mainstream movements soon thereafter. Two kinds of splinter group outcomes in other religious contexts (and especially in the history of Christianity) involve splinter group crashes as well. *Like the Melanesian cases,* one kind of splinter group crash also involves the dissolution of the breakaway group yet the survival of its individual members. Of the three outcomes with balanced systems, this is the one most like the Melanesian cases. Even this outcome, though, differs from these cases on some fronts. First, as we have already noted, these splinter groups will usually *not* have arisen in response to ritual tedium. Balanced ritual systems are far less likely to generate tedium in the first place. (Near the end of this section we will discuss circumstances within contemporary Christianity where ritual tedium may arise.) Second, because existing balanced systems typically include a variety of conceptual and political resources for discouraging such variations and for enforcing their orthodox interpretations, former splinter group members are *often not* readily reassimilated into the mainstream religious movement and certainly not *en masse* the way the members of the Melanesian groups were. Mainstream religions with balanced ritual systems usually do not unconditionally welcome an unsuccessful breakaway movement *as a group* back into the fold.

These more straightforward political considerations play a role in explaining the second sort of outcome, which is even less like the Melanesian cases. The crashes of groups that have splintered from religions with balanced ritual systems have often entailed not just the demise of the group identity but the demise of many, if not all, of the group members. The most extreme form of *external* intervention has been violent confrontations with group members. In America the early treatment of the Church of the Latter Day Saints comes to mind. (The government health inspector's demands in Maranagi seem quite measured by comparison.) The wholesale slaughter of the members of dissenting religious groups, though, is by no means an American invention. It was standard practice throughout Europe during the Middle Ages and the Reformation.

It remains a point of contention among partisans whether the tragic events in Waco, Texas turned on such external intervention or on *internal* collapse in the face of external pressure. The most extreme form of internal collapse is the startlingly frequent occurrences of mass murder and mass suicide. Jonestown and Heaven's Gate are probably the best-known recent examples, but as even a casual perusal of the literature reveals, dozens of breakaway religious groups have committed collective suicide over the centuries.

The myriad examples in the history of Christianity not only of splinter groups that have gone extinct but of ones whose individual members shared the same fate suggest that these groups are following a trajectory that is different from the one that the patterns among the Pomio Kivung and the Paliau Movement exhibit. The number of fatal crashes of such systems in the history of religions indicates that breaking away from balanced systems can easily spin out of control. Whether it is their threat to orthodoxy or the perception of their lack of control that leads members of mainstream groups, neighbors, or central authorities to carry out preemptive strikes against them or whether it is their own self-destruction, such groups have all too often been occasions for horrific violence.

Conceptual control, new religions, and the replication of the balanced pattern

Sometimes such splinter groups, even some that introduce new levels of sensory pageantry to existing special agent rituals (e.g., Baptists) or introduce completely new special agent rituals (e.g., Latter Day Saints), neither collapse nor return to the mainstream religious systems like the cases Whitehouse discusses. This third outcome of splintering from balanced systems does not even remotely approximate the profile of the Melanesian cases. In this scenario, these splinter groups emerge as *independent* religious systems on their own. Why? The critical variables seem to be whether such systems can both avoid extermination and obtain what we shall call "conceptual control" over their ritual innovations. Among the many cases of breakaway groups that reinvigorate special agent rituals or introduce new or additional special agent rituals, those that survive as independent religious systems (such as the Baptists and the Latter Day Saints) in contrast to those that do not (such as the Pomio Kivung splinter groups and the Ghost cult in the Melanesian context or the followers of Jim Jones in the Western Christian context) are the ones that gain conceptual control over these new ritual means for motivation.

What does conceptual control of innovative special agent rituals amount to? In short, these new religious groups must possess *religious conceptual schemes that can avert these rituals' failures.* They must not only provide enough sensory pageantry to increase the probabilities that participants will deem the ritual a convincing manifestation of the actions of the gods, they must also provide ready means for construing performances of these non-repeated rituals as successful, so that individual participants will not serve as their patients too often in too short a time (and risk habituation and the exhaustion of group resources).

And *how* is such control achieved? These religions' conceptual schemes must provide conceptual resources for characterizing the consequences of these rituals as fundamental transformations that result from the actions of CPS-agents *without necessitating any empirically detectable changes in the world that the religious system cannot control.* Otherwise, they are stuck with ritual failure, repetition of the critical special agent ritual(s), and the dilemma we outlined at the end of the previous section that guarantees that they will be short lived.

Some special agent rituals are particularly difficult to control. Ecstatic millennial movements are especially vulnerable here, if they include new climactic special agent rituals whose putative consequence is the CPS-agents' inauguration of the new age. A ritual so conceived is out of control from the outset unless the religious system's conceptual scheme can do-mesticate its millennial expectations the way Christianity did very early in its history. (Of course, even a millennial movement like Christianity that has this sort of conceptual control over its special agent rituals faces the perpetual problem of generating new millennial spin-off groups!) The domestication of these rituals is critical, since new ages, in which, for example, Jesus is (yet again) supposed to return to set up his kingdom on earth or to gather up all believers into heaven are the sorts of events that splinter group participants consistently expect to be able to *detect!* (Consider the pervasiveness of bumper stickers throughout America warning other drivers of the traffic dangers that will ensue in the event of the Rapture.) Without conceptual control of specifically millennial special agent rituals, ritual failure is inevitable as is the gradual ascent from the second attractor, i.e., the simultaneous increase in the special agent millennial ritual's performance frequency and in its levels of sen-sory pageantry. This much of many splinter groups' stories can closely resemble the patterns among the Dadul-Maranagi and Ghost cult splin-ter groups. But, as we emphasized when we discussed the first two sorts of splinter group outcomes, tedium is not usually the precipitating circum-stance and these outcomes rarely involve ready reassimilation of splinter groups and often involve their demise.

The point about this third possible outcome is that neither splinter groups generally nor millennial splinter groups in particular must in-evitably crash. Millennial movements that do not include *rituals* designed to foment heaven on earth *today*, i.e., ones that can gain conceptual con-trol of their special agent rituals, and that include some special patient or special instrument rituals can achieve the same balance in their ritual complements that so many successful religions manifest. (See figure 5.7.)

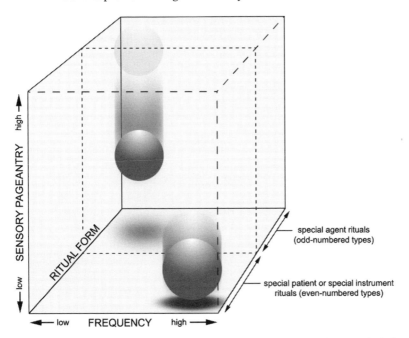

Figure 5.8 The consequences of excess conceptual control: deflated balanced systems

Unlike the Melanesian splinter groups that constitute one stage in the phase portrait of the one sort of unbalanced system we have, so far, examined, these breakaway movements retain conceptual control of their non-repeated special agent rituals. Ritual failure does not threaten their stability – though the power and influence of the mainstream balanced system from which they parted may.

How tedium may arise in balanced ritual systems

If anything, recent developments in the industrialized Western world in particular (but also, we suspect, in many parts of Asia) suggest that the greater threat to these bivalent, balanced systems may come from their conceptual schemes gaining what might be called *excess control*. Excess conceptual (in most cases – reflective, theological) control seems to reduce sensory pageantry *pervasively* in a religious ritual system, i.e., in *all* of its rituals.[5] Not only does the system's baseline seem to decline but the difference between the levels of sensory pageantry associated with special agent rituals as opposed to special patient and special instrument rituals decreases too. (See figure 5.8.)

208 Bringing ritual to mind

What do we mean by "excess control?" This is our term for what looks like a growing and widespread preoccupation with theological and intellectual concerns among participants in a religious system. The resulting arrangements involve what we referred to above as "drastically diminished" levels of sensory pageantry associated with these systems' non-repeated, special agent rituals.

These *deflated* balanced systems superficially resemble the earlier unbalanced systems in two respects. First, because they have wandered away from the standard balanced configuration, they too manifest a dynamical phase portrait (though, since they retain their special agent rituals, it differs from the phase portrait associated with the unbalanced systems we described above). Second, like unbalanced systems, they seem to be caught in a stage in which their principal engine of ritual motivation, viz., special agent rituals, is neutralized – though, again, in a different fashion. In these deflated balanced systems, this neutralization results from the drastically diminished sensory pageantry associated with their special agent rituals. In unbalanced systems, by contrast, it results from the systems returning to the first attractor position exclusively, i.e., to a position that simply *excludes* special agent rituals. The point, in short, is that whether special agent rituals are stripped of most of their extraordinary sensory pageantry or simply eliminated altogether, the result is the same – gradual generation of the tedium effect. (So, it is no surprise that Whitehouse ended up treating these two patterns as if they were the same.)

We hypothesize that widespread concerns with broadly intellectual matters in religious systems, resulting in what we have called excess conceptual control, may be the principal variable driving this decline of sensory pageantry in special agent rituals. Over the past four centuries in the West this increasing concern with theological niceties and intellectual nuance may have arisen in the face of challenges from a larger secular society armed with modern science. In the past century, especially, in which education sufficient to insure widespread literacy has become the norm in northern Europe and North America, the mainstream denominations of Christianity that prevail in these regions have grown increasingly uncomfortable with their more emotionally stimulating religious practices.

If, under such broader cultural influences, the balanced systems figure 5.7 represents tend to evolve in the direction of the deflated balanced systems figure 5.8 portrays, then we have good reason to expect one or both of two outcomes. If these systems uphold unyielding constraints on energetic, emotional outbursts in response to the tedium they induce (preventing their "re-inflation"), then they may decline to the point that they eventually face extinction. They may also lead to a second outcome as well. They may provoke splinter group movements[6] with balanced ritual systems themselves that either

1 re-energize special agent rituals that already exist in the parent system (as, for example, have the many evangelical Protestant groups that have arisen in America over the past hundred and fifty years), or
2 permit additional performances of available special agent rituals (as, for example, have the Latter Day Saints), or
3 create new special agent rituals (as again, for example, have the Latter Day Saints)

over all of which they retain satisfactory conceptual control.

The Church of the Latter Day Saints introduced new special agent rituals and it allowed for additional (though not an uncontrolled number) of performances of existing special agent rituals. Concerning the latter, marriage rituals are comparatively easy to manage and, for that reason, are especially good candidates for enhancing motivation. In many societies no special agent rituals contain any more sensory pageantry than weddings do, and their success as rituals, i.e., the success of the gods' actions, does not turn on bringing about any empirically detectable changes. The possibility of multiple marriage, then, gives the best of both worlds. At least some participants enjoy the motivational stimulation of multiple special agent rituals without the religious system losing conceptual control.

Multiple marriage is not the repetition of the same wedding over and over. Although two people need wed each other only once, one or the other (where it occurs it is usually the men) may be free to experience this special agent ritual again with another partner in a different wedding. Multiple marriage permits at least some participants to undergo this one special agent ritual more than once without undermining its special agent status and without facing the problem of ritual failure. The practical exigencies of married life insure that for any particular participant performances of this ritual are still unlikely to occur very rapidly or very often, so the gradual ascent from the second attractor toward the hazardous region of habituation is effectively forestalled.

The Church of the Latter Day Saints provides an interesting case in point of a splinter group that hit upon this solution for preventing evolution from the balanced profile to the deflated profile that figure 5.8 describes. It not only survived but thrived, despite early attempts to eliminate the group violently. Although external political forces required the ecclesiastical hierarchy to prohibit this practice, it has, in fact, persisted now for more than a century *sub rosa*. This very fact is an indication of just how adaptive this solution is.

If current trends persist, some of the mainstream Protestant denominations in the developed world may prove candidates for the first of these two outcomes. During the second half of the twentieth century most of the mainline Protestant churches in contemporary northern Europe and North America have witnessed precipitous declines in both their official membership and their actual participation. In the meantime evangelical and charismatic groups, which constitute a reaction to the tedium that arises in deflated balanced systems, and Southern Baptists, whose special agent rituals have not declined in their levels of sensory pageantry, have been enjoying increasing popularity. (Theological elites in the languishing mainstream denominations have been in particular turmoil over these cultural developments, given both their religious allegiances and their commitments to rational reflection. See Wiebe, 1991.)

Whether splinter groups arise from a standard balanced system or a deflated one, if

1. they retain their parent systems' balanced configuration and their conceptual control over their special agent rituals, and

2. they either survive violent attempts at their suppression or face none (like most contemporary evangelical splinter groups), and

3. they insure that their special agent rituals involve a good deal more sensory pageantry than their special patient and special instrument rituals,

then, *ceteris paribus*, they are likely to be successful – at least in the modern Western world.

Transmission, fitness, and religious ritual systems

What do these analyses show about the factors that contribute to the comparative fitness of religious systems? Another way of putting that question is to ask about the sorts of ritual arrangements that tend to increase the probabilities of participants transmitting their religious system.

We argued that, whatever else may be required for the transmission of a religious ritual system, accurate recollection is necessary in settings where religious leaders do not have Orwellian levels of power to coerce compliance. Early on we pointed out that religious rituals tend to gravitate toward either of two attractors in the space of possible ritual arrangements. At the first of these attractors, the high performance frequencies typical of special patient and special instrument rituals tend to insure their recollection. We also argued that with the appropriate cultural and conceptual support, the higher levels of sensory pageantry characteristic of special agent rituals at the second attractor will tend to enhance participants' recollections of those rituals.

Recollection of rituals, however, is only a necessary condition for their transmission. It is not sufficient. The possessed maiden Lagawop's three-night performance demonstrated the ability of this one sort of unbalanced system to burn doctrines and rituals into the memories of even the most humble participants. But the exclusive focus of such unbalanced systems (during their unbalanced phase) on rituals at the first attractor seems to have an extremely negative impact on participants' motivation, provoking the tedium effect. Recollection is not enough. Religious ritual systems survive only if they also motivate participants to transmit them.

To increase the probabilities that participants will transmit their religious systems, some religious practices must pack enough emotional wallop to convince them that they have had dealings with the divine. This, it seems, is overwhelmingly where special agent rituals enter the picture. We demonstrated why such climactic rituals always end up having special agent forms. For reasons having to do with the apparent phylogenetic primitiveness of episodic – as opposed to semantic – memory, both Whitehouse (2000) and Merlin Donald (1991) argue that such rituals have more ancient origins in our species' prehistory than do those that rely on frequency effects. Jared Diamond (1998) and Boyer (2001) suggest that the development of a priestly caste and the preoccupation with elaborate, rigidly codified doctrines (and the special patient and special instrument rituals that the accompanying ritual systems include) probably arose only in the past ten thousand years or so with the invention of agriculture, the growth of urban centers, and the consolidation of political power.

If these various scholars have these chronological relations right and if religion existed prior to the invention of agriculture, large human groups, and centralized political power (and virtually everyone agrees that it did), then forms of religion existed in which special patient and special instrument rituals may have played little or no role. If so, then at least under what Diamond (1998, especially pp. 268–269) refers to as the conditions of early "bands" and "tribes," religious ritual systems may have exhibited a third general pattern, viz., *a second (but very old) and different sort of unbalanced system* that included *only* special agent rituals at the second attractor position or, at least, one that overwhelmingly emphasized such rituals.

Do such religious ritual systems exist anywhere today? Barth's account of the Baktaman suggests that such systems may have survived into the twentieth century. It is difficult to know, though, whether to describe the Baktaman system this way is to characterize it accurately or merely to characterize accurately what Barth chose to emphasize about it. It seems clear from Barth's book that the Baktaman *do* have some repeated special patient and special instrument rituals. (See the discussion of compositionality in Baktaman rituals in chapter 2.) That Barth gives them almost no attention may indicate nothing more than that he approached these materials with different questions in mind. We should note straightaway that even the notion that the Baktaman have a standard, balanced ritual system is fully consistent with Barth's text. Still, granting all of this, both Barth's discussion and the theoretical considerations that both Whitehouse's analysis and our own raise all suggest that the Baktaman ritual system may at least approximate this second sort of unbalanced arrangement.

If this proposal is right, then Barth's account of Baktaman religious knowledge suggests that maintaining tight conceptual control over special agent rituals is less important in this second sort of unbalanced ritual system. Noting that the Baktaman do not engage in theology, Barth repeatedly emphasizes how little conceptual elaboration they provide for any of their rituals and symbols. If participants' experience is as radically limited as that of the Baktaman, they are going to imagine neither new ages like the Period of the Companies nor new rituals that will bring them about. In settings such as these conceptual control is not an issue.

Diamond's and Boyer's views of the history of culture and Donald's, Boyer's, and Whitehouse's views of the natural history of human cognition all suggest that some religions have existed that have had no special patient or special instrument rituals. This suggests that *special agent rituals must play a more fundamental role in the transmission and persistence of religion than do special patient and special instrument rituals.* At least under some social conditions, special patient and special instrument rituals are not necessary for a religious ritual to persist. Arguably, the patterns we have explored in this chapter suggest the same. What the three profiles we have discussed indicate is that, ultimately, whatever the status of special patient and special instrument rituals, no religious ritual system can survive without at least the periodic performance of special agent rituals capable of energizing participants and motivating them to transmit their religious systems. If various social conditions have tended to squelch those special agent rituals' levels of sensory pageantry (in the modern Western world) or even to suppress those rituals outright (in at least one phase of recent Melanesian religions), then participants will inevitably experience new insights or revelations and either revitalize performances of existing special agent rituals or invent new ones. Such are the ways of the gods.

Notes

1 COGNITIVE CONSTRAINTS ON RELIGIOUS RITUAL FORM: A THEORY OF PARTICIPANTS' COMPETENCE WITH RELIGIOUS RITUAL SYSTEMS

1 A caution, however, is in order. This formal system should not be mistaken for the theory; *it is only a means for elucidating many of the theory's claims.*

2 We shall use the terms "instruments" and "patients" to refer to what in *Rethinking Religion* we referred to (less efficiently) as the ritual's "action conditions" and "logical object" respectively. Technically these terms pick out action roles. We will sometimes use them to refer to the items that serve in these roles as well.

3 For evidence in even more closely related species of such "cognitive fluidity" and of the deployment of social intelligence in other domains, see Mithen, 1996.

4 The process of identifying underlying, impersonal causes is far more difficult and far more costly for humans generally (McCauley, 2000). Concepts such as agency may come naturally, but scientific explanations of human behavior are achieved, if at all, only with great difficulty because they seem to require that we transcend common sense.

5 We are grateful to Pascal Boyer for suggesting this term.

6 ... nor even when the CPS-agent is most directly connected with the current ritual's instrument or patient by means of enabling ritual actions.

7 Although it does require appeal to enabling actions in order to make sense of the substitution of the bread and wine for the body and blood of Christ. See the discussion of ritual substitution above.

2 RITUAL AND MEMORY: FREQUENCY AND FLASHBULBS

1 Advocates of punctuated equilibrium (Eldredge and Gould, 1972) insist that not all evolution is gradualist in the way that Darwin seemed to envision. They characterize evolutionary change, primarily, in terms of brief moments of speciation – in as few as a hundred generations – erupting within what are otherwise long periods of comparative stability.

2 Like Sperber, we want no truck with what he calls "empty materialism" in the study of culture, i.e., analyses of cultural forms by putative materialists who do not even pretend to sketch how those forms are, in fact, material. The simultaneous popularity within cultural anthropology of materialist metaphysics and the autonomy of culture thesis generates a profound dilemma that goes mostly

unrecognized and almost completely unaddressed. (Shore [1995] is a welcome exception.) None the less, we see no compelling grounds to adopt Sperber's abstemiousness about cultural forms, precisely because we see some broadly cognitive considerations that suggest that these notions enjoy some stability and, therefore, some explanatory integrity (and, thus, possibly some metaphysical muscle too). Our differences with Sperber on these fronts, ultimately, turn on our different views about some of the pertinent mnemonic processes, about models of cross-scientific relations, and about the mechanisms of mental representation. (See McCauley, 1996 and 1998.) The last two differences, though, are not vital to our aims in this book.

3 On parallel distributed processing accounts of mental representation of the sort we broadly favor, minor, subtle changes of the sort that concern Sperber are virtually inevitable in light of the influences of both the external and internal contexts, i.e., the influences both of the environment during acquisition and of cognitive dispositions that the organism's previous experience has already engendered (Clark, 1997).

4 We examine the notion of *performance frequency* at length in chapter 4, pp. 126–139.

5 We discuss the distinction between repeatable and non-repeated rituals at length in chapter 3, pp. 120–123.

6 See chapter 4, pp. 139–155.

7 This and many other important points of agreement notwithstanding, Rubin's analyses will prove of limited usefulness for our purposes here. First, his study focuses on subjects' memories for linguistic materials, whereas we are primarily concerned with their memories for (ritual) actions. These two types of cultural materials are often closely related, but sometimes they are not. What interests us most are precisely the non-linguistic considerations that contribute to enhanced memory for *actions*. Second, Rubin holds that memory in oral traditions is usefully thought of as a "well practiced skill dependent on extensive experience" (1995, p. 146). Rubin states, for example, that ballads and counting-out rhymes are considerably overlearned. However, extensive and elaborate rituals are performed only once per generation in some non-literate cultures with only limited preparation and rehearsal. For example, in the case of the Baktaman (Barth, 1975), it appears that neither extensive experience nor overlearning is even possible for initiations.

8 Not all flashbulb memories are connected with events that are unexpected or startling. Subjects in some studies report, for example, flashbulb memories for Richard Nixon's resignation. Although unusual, by the time Nixon actually resigned that event was neither unexpected nor startling. Rituals are often perfect illustrations of the same thing. Weddings, for example, regularly involve substantial planning and preparation. This ritual hardly comes as a surprise to the participants, yet it often proves one of the most memorable days in the lives of the bride and groom.

9 It has turned out that Neisser's memory may not have been as inaccurate as he thought – see Thompson and Cowan, 1986 and Neisser, 1986.

10 William Brewer (1992) argues, though, that the inaccuracies of Neisser and Harsch's subjects may not be as grievous as their analysis suggests. He

maintains that those inaccuracies probably reflected retrieval problems rather than erroneous reconstructions. He suspects that many subjects were accurately remembering events from the day when they heard about the *Challenger*. They were just not remembering the events they described in their initial questionnaires. They were recalling "the wrong time slice."

What Neisser and Harsch (1992, p. 25) called "TV priority" may be evidence for this conjecture. The difference between the large number of subjects who misremembered that they had first heard about the *Challenger* on television and the small number who misremembered that they had not was statistically significant.

11 Approximately a third of the California subjects were from Santa Cruz. Logistical difficulties prevented data collection with these subjects until the third week after the disaster. By Rubin's estimate (1992), this would be enough time for them to have consolidated their stories. Of course, conformity to narrative conventions may have subtly distorting effects on those stories' accuracy.

12 These initiation rituals contrast with the various repeated rituals the Baktaman perform in the course of their routine religious activities.

13 However, not from Barth, who was so clearly an outsider. The principal cult leader "bent rules" to make Barth "a participant in his religion" (1975, p. 5). Sharing knowledge with Barth was, apparently, regarded as relatively harmless, after Barth had gained the seniors' trust and made it clear that he would only reveal their knowledge to "others who had passed through all *our* initiations" in Barth's "distant homeland" (1975, p. 7). Finally, the only world that possession of the secrets of Baktaman initiations need stratify is their own (and, perhaps, those of the only neighbors they knew of – though even on this front the evidence is scanty). The crucial point was to keep these secrets from uninitiated Baktaman.

When Barth returned to the region in 1981, other Ok groups proved comparably cooperative, once it became clear to them that Barth already knew a great deal about Baktaman rituals and cosmology.

14 For a discussion of the role of compositionality, productivity, and systematicity in symbolic systems, see Fodor and Pylyshyn, 1988.

15 Although much that he says could be construed as evidence for the claim, Barth does not consider the possibility that such symbolic relations simply do not exist. (See Sperber, 1975.)

16 Barth (1987, pp. 66–67) states that these themes mostly concern Nature.

17 At least one Baktaman senior seemed to think not (Barth, 1975, p. 101): "You know how it is during your initiation: your *finik* (spirit, consciousness) does not hear, you are afraid, you do not understand. Who can remember the acts and the words?"

18 We are grateful to David Rubin for this proposal.

19 Whitehouse (1992, p. 786) notes: "Although complex ideology could not be accurately reproduced in an oral tradition once every decade, it could conceivably be invented or re-created in a profoundly modified form at each, rare performance. But in an imaginary system of this type, which would not emphasize continuity, it is hard to imagine how the authority of religious ideas could be generated or upheld."

20 Frits Staal (1979 and 1990) and Merlin Donald (1991) argue that rituals (if not religion) predate not merely literacy but language as well and that they play a direct role in its invention.

3 TWO HYPOTHESES CONCERNING RELIGIOUS RITUAL AND EMOTIONAL STIMULATION

1 He quotes Sperber (1996, p. 64): "[it is no longer adequate to formulate] causal explanations of cultural facts...at a fairly abstract level, ignoring thereby the micro-mechanisms of cognition and communication. This is certainly what anthropologists and sociologists have tried to do, linking, for instance, economic infrastructure and religion. However good it might be, any such explanation would be incomplete. For economic infrastructure to affect religion, it must affect human minds."

2 Merlin Donald (1991) argues that both the episodic memory system and rituals that rely on it have earlier origins than the system of semantic memory and the rituals that rely on it.

3 Recall that near the end of chapter 2 we argued that although the transmission of rituals can leave them substantially transformed, the accuracy of memory cannot be completely irrelevant in this process, short of Orwellian forms of social coercion.

4 Like most religions, the resources of the Christian system on these fronts are substantial. For example, some Christians may prefer an account of this connection that turns neither on the bridal metaphor nor on the personification of the Church but rather looks, for example, to Christ's declaration about St. Peter and the subsequent succession of ecclesiastical authority and ritual acts. Specified in all of its detail, this scenario would certainly affect this ritual's depth and the depths of most other Christian rituals, but it would have no impact on the odd or even numberings of their types. The crucial point for present purposes is that this ritual's primary connection with a CPS-agent is via the presiding religious authority's ritual certification and, consequently, it is a *special agent* ritual, which will always be an odd-numbered type.

5 In light of the fact that Whitehouse does not qualify the ritual frequency hypothesis in this fashion, it would seem that the hypothesis's predictions about comparative levels of sensory pageantry should hold across both religious communities and religious systems. His focus on mnemonic considerations as the primary underlying variable shaping many features of cultural (i.e., religious) detail is consistent with this conclusion. We suspect that this consequence of the frequency hypothesis is devastating, as it appears that contrary evidence abounds. We will not belabor this point, though, since it is easy enough to reformulate the frequency hypothesis with such a qualification in place. Moreover, we suspect that this was Whitehouse's intention all along, though we find no direct textual support for that claim.

6 Stewart Guthrie (1993) has built an entire theory of religion around our proclivities for anthropomorphism, which results from what he takes to be a hyper-vigilant human perceptual strategy of detecting human forms in the visual (and acoustic) arrays. Baron-Cohen (1995) argues that children's developing a full-blown theory of mind depends, in part, on the proper functioning

of what he calls an Eye-Direction-Detector. If such hypotheses are correct, then these sorts of stimuli include precisely the sorts of cues that prime human beings for the detection of agents.

4 ASSESSING THE TWO HYPOTHESES

1 Undoubtedly, a host of extraneous factors – including everything from the availability of resources to the weather – can affect how often rituals occur. Although we suspect that planning and preparation usually insure that the impact of such factors is negligible, nothing about our account does or should rule out such contingencies. Still, performance frequencies do not usually depend in any decisive way on these factors.

2 The relevance of the ritual form hypothesis to performance frequency is *indirect*. The ritual form hypothesis simply predicts whether a religious ritual is *repeatable or not*. That surely goes most of the way, but it does *not* go all of the way toward explaining rituals' performance frequencies. We undertake the following discussion because clarifying the notion of performance frequency is necessary for *the comparison* of the two hypotheses.

3 Of course, a criterion for the relevance of performances in the assessment of the two hypotheses based on the sheer number of occurrences is the most liberal of all. We do not discuss this criterion separately, though, since it will face all of the problems that the (only slight less liberal) observation criterion faces and more.

4 Two points: first, this is *not* to suggest that all Christian baptisms or weddings are particularly arousing emotionally compared with the rituals of many other religious systems. Second, the differences between Christian denominations that practice infant baptism and those that do not are often substantial on these fronts. Nevertheless, *within* each kind of system, baptism is a ritual with comparatively high levels of sensory pageantry.

5 The ritual form hypothesis does not face any of these problems. With respect to these particular rituals, it correctly predicts that – by virtue of their special agent profiles – they should include relatively high levels of sensory pageantry compared with the levels in even-numbered rituals in the pertinent Christian communities.

6 Although Whitehouse does not address the distinction between participation and observation directly, various comments (e.g., 1995, pp. 215–216) indicate that he recognizes the distinction and opts for a criterion of performance frequency more conservative than one based on opportunities to observe rites.

7 By contrast, the structural descriptions of rituals that our theory of religious ritual competence generates provide the ritual form hypothesis with quite precise bases for defining what counts as more and less direct forms of participation in a religious ritual.

8 This principle seems to hold even when those patients are infants or the dead. Although *they* will not emerge from these rituals with either memories or motivation, they are, none the less, the objects on which others' attentions focus. Consequently, by aiming the sensory pageantry in their vicinities, these rituals increase the probabilities of influencing the largest number of those participants who *can* emerge with both knowledge about what the gods have wrought and motivation to transmit it.

9 The distinction between *participants in the religious system* and *participants in a religious ritual* is important. The latter (for any given ritual) is a subset of the former. To repeat, this distinction, in effect, serves to explicate the notion of "eligibility" for a ritual.

10 When explicating the distinction between even- and odd-numbered types, we have focused much of the time on whether religious rituals are repeatable or not. Now it should be clear why this is a telling and useful heuristic. To find out whether a ritual is odd- or even-numbered, simply determine whether or not it is repeatable (in the technical sense in which we are using that term – see chapter 3, pp. 120–123). If a religious ritual is repeatable, then it is an even-numbered, special patient or special instrument ritual; if not, then it is an odd-numbered, special agent ritual. Of course, the most straightforward, but not the only, evidence that it is repeatable is that all of the same human participants serving in all of the same ritual roles have repeated it and that its consequences have not been reversed in the meantime. (In fact, no procedures for the reversal of its consequences should even exist.) It is much easier (and quite sufficient for *current* purposes) to rely on the diagnostic power of this feature. The extended argument we have offered for the LDC criterion of performance frequency clarifies why this heuristic provides a telling indication of the fundamental cognitive variables at stake.

11 It is not obvious that it should. Arguably, this disciplined, rhythmic exercise and the concentration it requires also tend to suppress attention to all of the other inputs to the senses.

12 These may have been rituals of even-numbered types. Whitehouse explicitly notes (1995, p. 107) that a special performance of a special patient Kivung ritual donation occurred in conjunction with the second celebration of a dream on April 15. If these rituals were, in fact, even-numbered in form, then the elevation of sensory pageantry they embodied is best understood in terms of a general elevation of the community's baseline that the new regime of splinter group rituals initiated.

13 The CPS-agents in question, depending upon the ritual, were either the ancestors or Baninge and Tanotka acting as their intermediaries or Baninge or Tanotka acting on their own. The splinter group's activities resulted in the apotheosis of both. For example, Whitehouse (1995, p. 116) notes that while "Baninge's divine powers were being crystallized, the idea arrived from Maranagi that Tanotka was Jesus Christ."

14 Whitehouse offers an elaborate and detailed interpretation of the ritual's significance, but our goal is to track variables that explain patterns in religious ritual systems that do not depend upon any particular interpretive scheme.

15 Recall that we are employing the term "sensory pageantry" quite broadly to cover a wide range of emotionally stimulating phenomena including mind-altering drugs and sexually arousing stimuli.

16 Whitehouse (1995, p. 115) reports, for example, that "[b]y the end of May 1988 Tanotka had been given the key to the fence (several times in fact)..." This indicates that this special agent version of the ring ceremony had occurred repeatedly too before the migration to Maranagi in early September. (It is not obvious, though, how this claim squares with Whitehouse's claim

two pages before that the splinter group performed the first ring ceremony on May 28 – inspired by a dream shortly before that in which the image of the fence bisecting the ring arose.)

17 Whitehouse (1995, p. 137) agrees with this reading of these events: "once in Maranagi . . . Baninge and Tanotka were confronted with . . . the organization of a new programme of rituals, premissed upon the rapid production of the miracle."

18 Note that this is true *regardless* of which of the two baselines we adopt. Indeed, the more striking contrast between the initial baseline and the subsequent splinter group innovations works no less to the advantage of the ritual form hypothesis than it does to that of the ritual frequency hypothesis. We have, of course, argued for the appropriateness of the second of the two baselines – for which pervasive nudity raised the stakes across the board. Even then, with the nudity all of these rituals had in common factored out, the suffering during the vigils was extreme compared with anything that happened in the even-numbered, orthodox Kivung rituals or the even-numbered versions of the ring ceremony – even those that had *lower* performance frequencies and rates!

5 GENERAL PROFILES OF RELIGIOUS RITUAL SYSTEMS: THE EMERGING COGNITIVE SCIENCE OF RELIGION

1 The one possible exception is the performance of the Cemetery Temple ritual on September 9 that preceded the preparation ceremony that night. Recall that Whitehouse said (1995, p. 137) that it included an especially large pork feast, as it was designed to "pay off a backlog of debts to the ancestors" in final preparation for their return.

2 Maurice Bloch's *Prey into Hunter* (1992) captures this same insight.

3 Whitehouse also discusses the First or "Noise" cult. However since it erupted within the first three months of the Paliau Movement itself, it is less clear that it should be treated as a distinct phenomenon. Both in origin and in timing it looks much more like a continuous elaboration of the Paliau Movement itself – an elaboration that plays a significant role in its consolidation. (See Whitehouse, 2000, p. 145.)

4 As we argue in the next section, the analysis of religious ritual systems our theory supplies will require rethinking Whitehouse's account of the four variables from his theory of religious modes that our theory also addresses, viz., style of codification, frequency of transmission, cognitive processing, and revelatory potential. Incidental comments in the remainder of this section certainly pertain to other variables his theory addresses as well.

5 The speculations that follow conform with much that Whitehouse says concerning his doctrinal mode. Contrary to his account, though, the religious systems in question still have plenty of (special agent) rituals with very low performance frequencies. The developments in question in many Christian settings in northern Europe and North America do not depend on increasing rituals' performance frequencies but on declines in sensory pageantry across

the board – both in frequent special patient and special instrument rituals but especially in infrequent special agent rituals as well. In short, these are not phenomena that the ritual frequency hypothesis can make sense of.

6 Note that under the conditions of contemporary civil society in the countries in question, the sort of violent suppression of splinter group responses to tedium by mainstream communities – described earlier – is no longer a logistically plausible nor politically viable outcome. Consequently, it is no coincidence that it was agents of the state that were on the front lines in Waco.

References

Abbink, J. (1995). "Ritual and Environment: The *Mosit* Ceremony of the Ethiopian Me'en People," *Journal of Religion in Africa* 25, 163–190

Apuleius (1989). *Metamorphoses* (volume II). J. A. Hansen (ed. and trans.). Cambridge, MA: Harvard University Press

Baranowski, A. (1994). "Ritual Alone." PhD dissertation. University of Toronto
    (1998). "A Psychological Comparison of Ritual and Musical Meaning," *Method and Theory in the Study of Religion* 10, 3–29

Baron-Cohen, S. (1995). *Mindblindness: An Essay on Autism and Theory of Mind.* Cambridge, MA: MIT Press

Barrett, J. L. (2000). "Exploring the Natural Foundations of Religion," *Trends in Cognitive Sciences* 4, 29–34
    (forthcoming). "Dumb Gods Versus Smart Gods: The Role of Social Cognition in Structuring Ritual Intuitions." In *Current Approaches in the Cognitive Study of Religion.* I. Pyysiainen and V. Anttonen (eds). London: Cassell/Continuum

Barrett, J. and Keil, F. (1996). "Conceptualizing a Non-natural Entity: Anthropomorphism in God Concepts," *Cognitive Psychology* 31, 219–247

Barrett, J. L. and Lawson, E. T. (2001). "Ritual Intuitions: Cognitive Contributions to Judgments of Ritual Efficacy," *Journal of Cognition and Culture* 1, 183–201

Barsalou, L. (1992). *Cognitive Psychology: An Overview for Cognitive Scientists.* Hillsdale, NJ: Erlbaum

Barth, F. (1975). *Ritual and Knowledge Among the Baktaman of New Guinea.* New Haven: Yale University Press
    (1987). *Cosmologies in the Making: A Generative Approach to Cultural Variation in Inner New Guinea.* Cambridge: Cambridge University Press

Bloch, M. (1992). *Prey into Hunter.* Cambridge: Cambridge University Press

Bohannon, J. N. and Symons, V. L. (1992). "Flashbulb Memories: Confidence, Consistency, and Quantity." In *Affect and Accuracy in Recall: Studies of "Flashbulb" Memories.* E. Winograd and U. Neisser (eds.). New York: Cambridge University Press, 65–91

Boyd, R. and Richerson, P. J. (1985). *Culture and the Evolutionary Process.* Chicago: University of Chicago Press

Boyer, P. (1994). *The Naturalness of Religious Ideas.* Berkeley: University of California Press

(1996). "Cognitive Limits to Conceptual Relativity: The Limiting Case of Religious Categories." In *Rethinking Linguistic Relativity*. J. Gumperz and S. Levinson (eds.). Cambridge: Cambridge University Press, 203–231

(2001). *Religion Explained: The Evolutionary Origins of Religious Thought*. New York: Basic Books

Boyer, P. and Ramble, C. (2001). "Cognitive Templates for Religious Concepts: Cross-Cultural Evidence for Recall of Counter-Intuitive Representations," *Cognitive Science* 25, 535–564

Brewer, W. F. (1992). "The Theoretical and Empirical Status of the Flashbulb Memory Hypothesis." In *Affect and Accuracy in Recall: Studies of "Flashbulb" Memories*. E. Winograd and U. Neisser (eds.). New York: Cambridge University Press, 274–305

Brown, R. and Kulik, J. (1982). "Flashbulb Memories." In *Memory Observed*. U. Neisser (ed.). San Francisco: W. H. Freeman, 23–40

Christianson, S.-A. (1989). "Flashbulb Memories: Special, But Not So Special," *Memory & Cognition* 17, 435–443

Clark, A. (1993). *Associative Engines: Connectionism, Concepts, and Representational Change*. Cambridge, MA: MIT Press

(1997). *Being There: Putting Brain, Body, and World Together Again*. Cambridge, MA: MIT Press

Cohn, N. (1970.) *The Pursuit of the Millennium*. New York: Oxford University Press

Colegrove, F. W. (1899/1982). "The Day They Heard about Lincoln." In *Memory Observed*. U. Neisser (ed.). San Francisco: W. H. Freeman, 41–42

Damasio, A. R. (1994). *Descartes' Error: Emotion, Reason and the Human Brain*. New York: Avon Books

(1999). *The Feeling of What Happens: Body and Emotion in the Making of Consciousness*. New York: Harcourt Brace

Dawkins, R. (1982). *The Extended Phenotype*. Oxford: Oxford University Press

Dennett, D. C. (1995). *Darwin's Dangerous Idea: Evolution and the Meaning of Life*. New York: Simon & Schuster

Diamond, J. (1998). *Guns, Germs, and Steel: The Fate of Human Societies*. New York: Norton

Donald, M. (1991). *Origins of the Modern Mind: Three Stages in the Evolution of Culture and Cognition*. Cambridge, MA: Harvard University Press

Eldredge, N. and Gould, S. J. (1972). "Punctuated Evolution: An Alternative to Phyletic Gradualism." In *Models in Paleobiology*. T. J. M. Schopf (ed.). San Francisco: Freeman

Evans-Pritchard, E. (1956). *Nuer Religion*. Oxford: Clarendon Press

Fernandez, J. W. (1982). *Bwiti: An Ethnography of the Religious Imagination in Africa*. Princeton: Princeton University Press

Firth, R. (1963). "Offering and Sacrifice: Problems of Organization," *Journal of the Royal Anthropological Institute* 93, 12–24

Fodor, J. A. and Pylyshyn, Z. W. (1988). "Connectionism and Cognitive Architecture: A Critical Analysis," *Cognition* 28, 3–71

Gardner, D. S. (1983). "Performativity and Ritual: The Mianmin Case," *Man* (n.s.) 18, 346–360

Gellner, E. (1969). "A Pendulum Swing Theory of Islam." In *Sociology of Religion: Selected Readings*. R. Robertson (ed.). Harmondsworth: Penguin

Goodall, J. (1992). *In the Shadow of Man*. Boston: Houghton Mifflin

Goody, J. (1987). *The Interface Between the Written and the Oral*. Cambridge: Cambridge University Press

Gopnik, A., Meltzoff, A. N., and Kuhl, P. (1999). *The Scientist in the Crib*. New York: William Morrow

Guthrie, S. (1993). *Faces in the Clouds*. Oxford: Oxford University Press

Hertz, R. (1960). *A Contribution to the Study of the Collective Representation of Death*. London: Cohen & West

Heuer, F. and Reisberg, D. (1990). "Vivid Memories of Emotional Events: The Accuracy of Remembered Minutiae," *Memory and Cognition* 18, 496–506

(1997). "What Do We Know about Emotion's Effects on Memory?" Address at Emory University, Atlanta, Georgia

Hirschfeld, L. A. and Gelman, S. A. (1994). *Mapping the Mind: Domain Specificity in Cognition and Culture*. New York: Cambridge University Press

Humphrey, C. and Laidlaw, J. (1994). *The Archetypal Actions of Ritual*. Oxford: Oxford University Press

Hunter, I. M. L. (1985). "Lengthy Verbatim Recall: The Role of Text." In *Progress in the Psychology of Language*. A. Ellis (ed.). Hillsdale, NJ: Erlbaum, 207–235

Lanternari, V. (1963). *The Religions of the Oppressed: A Study of Modern Messianic Cults*. New York: New American Library

Larsen, S. F. (1988). "Remembering Without Experiencing: Memory for Reported Events." In *Remembering Reconsidered: Ecological and Traditional Approaches to the Study of Memory*. U. Neisser and E. Winograd (eds.). New York: Cambridge University Press, 326–355

Lawson, E. T. (1985). *Religions of Africa: Traditions in Transformation*. San Francisco: Harper Collins

Lawson, E. T. and McCauley, R. N. (1990). *Rethinking Religion: Connecting Cognition and Culture*. Cambridge: Cambridge University Press

(1993). "Crisis of Conscience, Riddle of Identity: Making Space for a Cognitive Approach to Religious Phenomena," *Journal of the American Academy of Religion* 61, 201–223

(forthcoming). "The Cognitive Representation of Religious Ritual Form: A Theory of Participants' Competence with their Religious Ritual Systems." In *Current Approaches to the Cognitive Study of Religion*. I. Pyysiainen and V. Anttonen (eds.). London: Continuum

Leslie, A. (1995). "A Theory of Agency." In *Causal Cognition: A Multidisciplinary Debate*. D. Sperber, D. Premack, and A. J. Premack (eds.). New York: Oxford University Press, 121–147

Livingston, R. B. (1967a). "Brain Circuitry Relating to Complex Behavior." In *The Neurosciences: A Study Program*. G. C. Quarton, T. Melnechuck, and F. O. Schmitt (eds.). New York: Rockefeller University Press, 499–514

(1967b). "Reinforcement." In *The Neurosciences: A Study Program*. G. C. Quarton, T. Melnechuck, and F. O. Schmitt (eds.). New York: Rockefeller University Press, 568–576

Lord, A. B. (1991). *Epic Singers and Oral Tradition*. Ithaca, NY: Cornell University Press

Lumsden, C. J. and Wilson, E. O. (1981). *Genes, Minds, and Culture*. Cambridge, MA: Harvard University Press

McCauley, R. N. (1996). "Explanatory Pluralism and the Co-evolution of Theories in Science." In *The Churchlands and Their Critics*. R. N. McCauley (ed.). Oxford: Blackwell Publishers, 17–47

(1998). "Levels of Explanation and Cognitive Architectures." In *Blackwell Companion to Cognitive Science*. W. Bechtel and G. Graham (eds.). Oxford: Blackwell Publishers, 611–624

(1999). "Bringing Ritual to Mind." In *Ecological Approaches to Cognition: Essays in Honor of Ulric Neisser*. E. Winograd, R. Fivush, and W. Hirst (eds.). Hillsdale, NJ: Erlbaum, 285–312

(2000). "The Naturalness of Religion and the Unnaturalness of Science." In *Explanation and Cognition*. F. Keil and R. Wilson (eds.). Cambridge, MA: MIT Press, 61–86

(2001). "Ritual, Memory, and Emotion: Comparing Two Cognitive Hypotheses." In *Religion in Mind: Cognitive Perspectives on Religions Experience*. J. Anavesen (ed.). Cambridge: Cambridge University Press, 115–140

Metcalf, P. and Huntington, R. (1991). *Celebrations of Death: The Anthropology of Mortuary Ritual* (second edition). Cambridge: Cambridge University Press

Michotte, A. (1963). *The Perception of Causality*. London: Methuen

Mithen, S. (1996). *The Prehistory of the Mind*. London: Thames & Hudson

Neisser, U. (1982). "Snapshots or benchmarks?" In *Memory Observed*. U. Neisser (ed.). San Francisco: W. H. Freeman, 43–48

(1986). "Remembering Pearl Harbor: Reply to Thomson and Cowan," *Cognition* 23, 285–286

Neisser, U. and Harsch, N. (1992). "Phantom Flashbulbs: False Recollections of Hearing the News about *Challenger*." In *Affect and Accuracy in Recall: Studies of "Flashbulb" Memories*. E. Winograd and U. Neisser (eds.). New York: Cambridge University Press, 9–31

Neisser, U., Winograd, E., Bergman, E., Schreiber, C., Palmer, S., and Weldon, M. S. (1996). "Remembering the Earthquake: Direct Experience vs. Hearing the News," *Memory* 4, 337–357

Paivio, A. (1986). *Mental Representations: A Dual Coding Approach*. New York: Oxford University Press

Parry, M. (1971). *The Making of Homeric Verse: The Collected Papers of Milman Parry*. A. Parry (ed. and trans.). Oxford: Oxford University Press

Penner, H. H. (1975). "Creating a Brahman: A Structural Approach to Religion." In *Methodological Issues in Religious Studies*. R. D. Baird (ed.). Chico, CA: New Horizons Press, 49–66

Perner, J., Leekam, S. R., and Wimmer, H. (1987). "Three-Year-Olds' Difficulty with False Belief," *British Journal of Developmental Psychology* 5, 125–137

Pfeiffer, J. (1982). *The Creative Explosion: An Inquiry into the Origins of Art and Religion*. New York: Harper & Row

Plotkin, H. (1998). *Evolution in Mind: An Introduction to Evolutionary Psychology.* Cambridge, MA: Harvard University Press

Ray, B. (1973). "'Performative Utterances' in African Rituals," *History of Religions* 13, 16–35

Reber, A. S. (1993). *Implicit Learning and Tacit Knowledge: An Essay on the Cognitive Unconscious.* New York: Oxford University Press

Reisberg, D. (1995). "Emotion's Multiple Effects on Memory." In *Brain and Memory: Modulation and Mediation of Neuroplasticity.* J. L. McGaugh, N. Weinberger, and G. Lynch (eds.). New York: Oxford University Press, 84–92

Rochat, P., Morgan, R., and Carpenter, M. (1997). "Young Infants' Sensitivity to Movement Information Specifying Social Causality," *Cognitive Development* 12, 441–465

Rochat, P. and Striano, T. (1999). "Social Cognitive Development in the First Year." In *Early Social Cognition.* P. Rochat (ed.). Mahway, NJ: Erlbaum, 3–34

Roediger, H. L. (1990). "Implicit Memory: Retention Without Remembering," *American Psychologist* 45, 1043–1056

Ross, L. and Nisbett, R. E. (1991). *The Person and the Situation: Perspectives of Social Psychology.* New York: McGraw Hill

Rubin, D. (1992). "Constraints on Memory." In *Affect and Accuracy in Recall: Studies of "Flashbulb" Memories.* E. Winograd and U. Neisser (eds.). New York: Cambridge University Press, 265–273
(1995). *Memory in Oral Tradition: The Cognitive Psychology of Epic, Ballads, and Counting-out Rhymes.* New York: Oxford University Press

Rundus, D. (1971). "Analysis of Rehearsal Processes in Free Recall," *Journal of Experimental Psychology* 89, 63–77

Schank, R. C. and Abelson, R. P. (1977). *Scripts, Plans, Goals, and Understanding: An Inquiry into Human Knowledge Structures.* Hillsdale, NJ: Erlbaum

Schwartz, T. (1962). "The Paliau Movement in the Admiralty Islands, 1946–1954," *Anthropological Papers of the American Museum of Natural History* 49, 210–421

Scribner, S. and Cole, M. (1981). *The Psychology of Literacy.* Cambridge, MA: Harvard University Press

Severi, C. (1987). "The Invisible Path: Ritual Representation of Suffering in Cuna Traditional Thought," *Res Anthropology and Aesthetics* 14, 66–85
(1993). "Talking about Souls." In *Cognitive Aspects of Religious Symbolism.* P. Boyer (ed.). Cambridge: Cambridge University Press, 165–181

Sherzer, J. (1983). *Kuna Ways of Speaking: An Ethnographic Perspective.* Austin: University of Texas Press
(1990). *Verbal Art in San Blas: Kuna Culture through its Discourse.* New York: Cambridge University Press

Shore, B. (1995). *Culture in Mind: Cognitive Dimensions of Cultural Knowledge.* Oxford: Oxford University Press

Somayajipad, C. V., Nambudiri, M. I. R., and Nambudiri, E. R. (1983). "Recent Nambudiri Performances of Agnistoma and Agnicayana." In *Agni: The Vedic Ritual of the Fire Altars: volume II.* F. Staal (ed.). Berkeley: Asian Humanities Press, 252–255

Sperber, D. (1975). *Rethinking Symbolism*. Cambridge: Cambridge University Press

(1996). *Explaining Culture: A Naturalistic Approach*. Oxford: Blackwell

Sperber, D. and Wilson, D. (1986). *Relevance: Communication and Cognition*. Cambridge, MA: Harvard University Press

Staal, F. (1979). "The Meaningless of Ritual," *Numen* 26, 2–22

(ed.). (1983). *Agni: The Vedic Ritual of the Fire Altars: volume II*. Berkeley: Asian Humanities Press

(1990). *Rules Without Meaning: Ritual, Mantras, and the Human Sciences*. New York: Peter Lang

Thompson, C. P. and Cowan, T. (1986). "Flashbulb Memories: A Nicer Interpretation of a Neisser Recollection," *Cognition* 22, 199–200

Tooby, J. and Cosmides, L. (1989). "Evolutionary Psychology and the Generation of Culture, Part I: Theoretical Considerations," *Ethnology and Sociobiology* 10, 29–49

Tovalele, P. (1977). "The Pomio Cargo Cult – East New Britain." In *Socio-Economic Change – Papua New Guinea*. R. Adams (ed.). Lae: University of Technology, 123–139

Tucker, D. M., Vannatta, K., and Rothlind, J. (1990). "Arousal and Activation Systems and Primitive Adaptive Controls on Cognitive Priming." In *Psychological and Biological Approaches to Emotion*. N. L. Stein, B. Leventhal, and T. Trabasso (eds.). Hillsdale, NJ: Erlbaum, 145–166

Tulving, E. (1962). "Subjective Organization in Free Recall of 'Unrelated' Words," *Psychological Review* 69, 344–354

(1983). *Elements of Episodic Memory*. Oxford: Clarendon Press

Van Gennep, A. (1960). *The Rites of Passage*. Chicago: University of Chicago Press

Weber, M. (1947). *The Theory of Social and Economic Organization*. Oxford: Oxford University Press

Wellman, H. M. (1990). *The Child's Theory of Mind*. Cambridge, MA: MIT Press

Wells, G. L. and Murray, D. (1984). "Eyewitness Confidence." In *Eyewitness Testimony*. G. L. Wells and E. F. Loftus (eds.). New York: Cambridge University Press, 155–170

Whitehouse, H. (1989). "The Oscillating Equilibrium of Production among the Mali Baining." *Research in Melanesia* 13, 62–67

(1992). "Memorable Religions: Transmission, Codification and Change in Divergent Melanesian Contexts." *Man* (n.s.) 27, 777–797

(1995). *Inside the Cult: Religious Innovation and Transmission in Papua New Guinea*. Oxford: Clarendon Press

(1996a). "Apparitions, Orations, and Rings." In *Spirits in Culture, History, and Mind*. A. Howard and J. Mageo (eds.). London: Routledge, 173–194

(1996b). "Rites of Terror: Emotion, Metaphor, and Memory in Melanesian Initiation Cults," *Journal of the Royal Anthropological Institute*, 2, 703–715

(2000). *Arguments and Icons: Divergent Modes of Religiosity*. Oxford: Oxford University Press

Wiebe, D. (1991). *The Irony of Theology and the Nature of Religious Thought*. Montreal: McGill-Queen's University Press

Wimmer, H. and Perner, J. (1983). "Beliefs about Beliefs: Representations and Constraining Function of Wrong Beliefs in Young Children's Understanding of Deception," *Cognition* 13, 103–128

Wimsatt, W. (1999). "Genes, Memes, and Cultural Heredity," *Biology and Philosophy* 14, 279–302

Winograd, E. and Killinger, W. A. (1983). "Relating Age at Encoding in Early Childhood to Adult Recall: Development of Flashbulb Memories," *Journal of Experimental Psychology: General* 117, 413–422

Wright, D. and Gaskell, G. D. (1992). "The Construction and Function of Vivid Memories." In *Theoretical Perspectives on Autobiographical Memory*. M. A. Conway, D. C. Rubin., H. Spinnler, and W. A. Wagenaar (eds.). Boston: Kluwer, 275–292

Index

absolution, 90–1, 93, 96, 175, 184, 192
act, 1, 12–13, 16, 38, 41, 69
action, ix, 1, 8–14, 18–26, 29–30, 46,
   49–51, 55–56, 58, 62, 80, 86,
   114–115, 126, 131, 143, 160, 178,
   190, 193, 209, 214
   enabling, 18–19, 25, 29, 33–34, 116,
      144, 213
   representation, x, 11–13, 17, 24, 26,
      29–30, 32, 115, 126, 143
   structural description of, 115–116, 191
Africa, x–xi
agency, 11–12, 18, 23–25, 30, 122, 213
   ascription of, 20, 22, 3
agent, x, 8–13, 16–17, 20–26, 30–32, 83,
   115, 142–3, 189, 191, 220
   causality, 21–22
   representation of, x, 8, 11, 17, 24, 26
   superhuman: see CPS-agents
   recognition/identification of, 8, 10–11,
      21, 23, 34, 115, 124, 218
Agni, 152
Alois Koki, 91
altar, 116, 152–153
America, United States of, 30, 47, 56–57,
   64, 77, 102, 145, 203–204, 206, 209
analogical coding, 65–69, 72–73, 82, 106
ancestor, 9, 20, 24, 30, 36, 51, 67, 71,
   89–92, 94–99, 101, 115, 120, 136,
   158–160, 163–170, 178, 180,
   192–194, 196–198, 200, 212,
   218–219
anthropology/anthropologist, x, 6, 64, 67,
   71, 94, 216
   cognitive, 39
   cultural, 40, 64, 108, 213
apotheosize, 91, 95, 164, 168, 218
Asia, 207
attention, 1–3, 10, 22, 26, 40–41, 45, 50,
   58, 64, 72, 77–79, 82, 87, 97, 100,
   122, 163, 173, 179, 198, 212,
   217–218

attractor, 41–48, 55–56, 73, 86–87, 93,
   100, 103–104, 111–114, 118,
   141–142, 153–154, 158, 160–162,
   184–185, 190, 199–200, 206, 208–211
Augobmin, 54
Australia, 38, 89
awan, 95–96, 159–160
awanga, 96, 98, 111, 122, 159, 193

Baining: see Mali Baining
Baktaman, 47–48, 54–55, 64–69, 71–77,
   79–84, 86–89, 93, 101–102, 106–107,
   110, 119, 128–132, 144, 146–147,
   152–153, 159, 183, 211–212, 214–215
Baninge, 94–99, 102, 158–159, 163–164,
   166–169, 176, 180, 183, 186–187,
   190, 193, 194, 196, 218–219
Baron-Cohen, S., 124, 216
Barrett, Justin, xi, 32
Barth, Fredrick, x, 45, 47, 54–55, 64–74,
   76, 79, 81–84, 86–87, 106, 128, 152,
   211–212, 215
Bernard, 90
Bernard's Temple, 92, 97, 136, 160, 173,
   176, 184, 192
biological, 39, 133
bishop, 3, 116
Bolovip, 74
Book of Common Prayer, 1
Boyer, Pascal, ix–xi, 20–22, 30, 211–213
Brahman, 15–16, 135
Brown, Roger, 57–59, 63, 75–77
Buddha, 86
Buddhism, 109, 140, 147, 203
   Pure Land, 144
   Theravada, 8, 17
   Zen, 145

California/Californians, 61–64, 75, 77,
   215
cardinal, 3–4
cargo cult, 88, 90, 93

ceiling-level effects, 56, 62, 64
Challenger, 59–60, 62, 215
Christ, Jesus, 23, 32–34, 86, 118, 120,
    145, 206, 213, 216, 218
Christianity, x, 27, 31, 74, 86, 89, 120,
    128–130, 145–147, 156, 201–202,
    204–206, 216–217, 219
  Baptist/Southern Baptist, 203, 205,
    210
  Catholic Church, 23, 33–34, 97, 118,
    129, 203
  Church of England, 1–2, 203
  Methodist, 90
  Protestants, 119, 201, 203, 209–210
  Shakers, 39
Christianson, Sven-Åke, 58–59
Church, 2, 29, 86, 90, 118, 124, 145,
    157, 210, 216
Church of Latter Day Saints, 127,
    204–205, 209
clergy, 127, 132
codification, style of, 84, 99, 104–107,
    109–110, 126, 140–141, 201, 203,
    219
cognition, 35, 42, 114, 182, 212
cognitive, 4–5, 8, 10, 21, 26, 34, 40, 42,
    44–45, 50, 52, 54, 73, 77–78, 100,
    104, 107–109, 112–114, 126, 143,
    178, 213–214
  apparatus, x, 8, 10–12, 23–24, 78, 113
  appeal, x, 8, 10–12, 23–24, 78, 113
  development, 11, 115
  dispositions, 67, 214
  dynamics, 45, 54, 73, 108, 110
  factors, 42, 45
  fluidity, 213
  foundations, 184
    of cultural transmission, 38, 42
    of memory, 49
    of religion, x, 7, 112, 140
  micro-processes, 41, 43, 104, 216
  processes, 5, 8, 49, 76, 104–105, 110,
    112, 141, 219
  relevance, 50, 85
  systems, 4, 10, 12, 40, 77, 115
cognitive science, ix, 6, 11–12, 36, 179
communication, 39, 41, 44–45, 50, 52,
    68, 72, 80, 94, 98, 104, 216
competence, x, 4–6, 30, 37
compositionality, 66, 74, 153, 212, 215
constraints
  cognitive, 7, 42
  psychological, 7, 72, 184
  social, 82
Copernicus, 16

cosmology, 82, 93, 108, 159, 215
counter-intuitive properties, 9, 20, 22–23,
    25
CPS-agents, x, 8, 10, 12–15, 17–18,
    20, 22–34, 43–44, 50, 114–118,
    120–123, 133–135, 138, 142–145,
    159, 161, 164–166, 170, 187, 189,
    191, 193, 199–200, 206, 213, 216,
    218
cult leader, 66, 75, 82–83, 129–131, 215
cultural knowledge, 38, 46–47, 66, 69,
    84–85, 107
  transmission of, 38–39, 46, 54
culture, x–xi, 7–8, 10, 16–17, 36, 39–41,
    45–46, 48, 52–53, 57, 63, 67–70, 72,
    75–76, 81–82, 84–85, 87, 90, 104,
    108, 119, 123, 182, 185, 191, 193,
    208, 210, 212–214, 216
  change, 40–41, 84
  form, 40, 42, 49, 51, 54, 70, 85,
    213–214
  innovation, 71–72
  mechanisms, 75, 153, 186, 190
  practices, 87

Dadul, 88–90, 93–94, 96–97, 99, 103,
    111, 123, 158, 172–173, 180,
    195–196, 198, 201. See also: splinter
    groups
Dalai Lama, 203
Damasio, Antonio, 77–78
Dawkins, Richard, 39
Decalogue, 90
deity, 135
Diamond, Jared, 211–212
digital coding, 66
divining, 3, 17, 29
divinity, 90
divorce, 133, 157
Donald, Merlin, 211, 216
dynamical systems, 7

ecstatic movements, 7, 185, 200, 206
Egypt, 2
emotion, x, 1–2, 43, 60, 76, 78–79, 87,
    100–101, 103, 105, 108, 110–112,
    114–115, 119, 123, 141, 174, 185,
    208, 211
  charged, 58, 60, 88, 97, 101–103, 108,
    112–113, 123, 140, 199
  excitement, 6, 87, 101–103, 108,
    113–114, 119, 126
  elevated, 80, 112–113, 122–123
  low intensity, 2, 109
  markers, 79

emotional arousal, 1–2, 6–7, 36, 38, 42,
    44, 47, 57, 60, 63–64, 72, 77–81, 87,
    93, 100, 102–103, 107, 112–113,
    118–119, 123, 138–141, 152, 155,
    164, 187, 191, 201, 217
    response, 2, 79, 102, 110
    stimulation, 7, 61, 78–80, 87–89, 100,
    106–107, 110, 113, 128, 147, 149,
    198–199, 208, 218
empirical
    adequacy, 9, 34, 37, 46, 132, 139, 173
    detectability, 182, 199, 206, 209
    matters, ix, 4–5, 77, 103–104, 124,
    130
    See also: evidence; theory, testing of
Enkaiakmin, 74
Enlightenment, 86, 203
epidemiology, 40–41, 45, 69, 142–143
eschatology, 91
ethnography, x–xi, 5–7, 9, 32, 36–37, 48,
    89, 165, 177–179, 195
Europe, xi, 30, 89, 204, 208, 210, 213,
    219
evidence, x–xi, 5, 21, 35–36, 52, 54, 56,
    58, 60–61, 64–65, 71, 73–74,
    124–126, 133, 151–152, 155, 164,
    166, 177–179, 195, 198, 213,
    215–216, 218
    empirical, x, 5, 7, 21, 139, 146, 155, 171
    experimental, 5, 22, 49, 80
    psychological, 5, 10, 126
evolution, 7–8, 20, 38–40, 42, 44–46, 75,
    82, 85–86, 109, 112, 141, 154,
    157–158, 162–163, 172–175, 177,
    179–180, 186, 190, 197, 208–209,
    213
    biological, 39–41
    cultural, 38–41, 51
excommunication, 3, 31, 133
experiment, x–xi, 6, 23, 34, 47–49, 59,
    61–62, 73, 75, 77–79, 190, 193
explanation, ix, 1–3, 5–10, 16, 20, 22–23,
    29–32, 34–36, 39–41, 44, 46–47, 50,
    55, 58, 64, 69, 72–74, 76, 81–82,
    84–85, 87, 94, 99–100, 105, 112,
    114–115, 120, 123–126, 137,
    139–140, 142, 145–146, 150, 167,
    169, 174, 176, 180, 183–184, 186,
    200, 204, 213–214, 216–218
Eye-Direction-Detector, 217

frequency effects, 48, 56, 68, 107, 142,
    211

Gaskell, G.D., 76–77
Gazelle Peninsula, 89

Gellner, Ernest, 104
Georgia/Georgians, 61–62
Germany, 89
God, 27–28, 86, 90, 97, 116
gods, 3, 12, 18, 20, 22–24, 26, 30–31,
    33, 44, 50, 84, 86, 115–117,
    120–123, 134, 138–139, 143, 155,
    179, 189, 190–191, 199–200, 202,
    205, 209, 212, 217
Guthrie, Stewart, 216

habit, 3, 49, 103, 107, 180, 185–190,
    193–195, 199, 206, 209
Hajar-al-Aswad, 150
Harsch, Nicole, 59–61, 214–215
Heaven's Gate, 204
Hinduism, 35, 109, 140, 146–147,
    150–151
holy water, 18, 116, 120
humanities, ix–x, 8, 22
Humphry, C., 32
Hunter, Ian, 52
hyperactive agent detection device
    (HADD), 21–22
hypothesis, 6–7, 12, 48, 63–64, 70, 79,
    89, 100–101, 104, 124, 126, 208
    cognitive alarm, 48, 77, 87, 113, 115,
    122, 180, 188
    Easterbrook, 58
    emotional strengthening, 60
    Now Print, 76
    ritual form, 6–7, 113–115, 117–119,
    123–127, 132–139, 141–144, 146–149,
    153, 155, 158, 162, 166, 171–180,
    183–184, 187–188, 217, 219
    ritual frequency, 6–7, 99–100, 109–113,
    119, 123–132, 134–142, 144–149,
    153, 155, 157–158, 161, 172–177,
    179–180, 183–184, 187, 216,
    219–220
    testing of, 132, 137, 139, 155, 162

icon, 38, 106–107, 122
ilotka, 96, 98, 111, 122, 159–160, 193
imagery, 60, 106–108, 114, 122, 170,
    180, 184, 192, 219
India, x–xi, 150–151
instruments, 143, 213
intentionality, 11, 20, 24
interpretive, interpretation, ix, 9, 21,
    36, 50, 67, 92, 94, 163, 181–182,
    200, 203–204, 218
intuition, 4–5, 13, 20, 24, 30, 67, 101–102,
    114, 119
Islam, x, 109, 140, 144, 203. See also:
    Muslim

Jain, 86, 146–147
Japan, 89, 121
Jones, Jim, 205
Jonestown, 204
Judaism, x, 10, 16, 35, 146–147
judgment, 4–5, 12, 17, 22, 27, 29, 32, 34,
    36, 78–79, 83, 101–102, 119, 136
    intuitive, 36–37, 101–102

Ka'bah, 3, 9, 150
Keil, Frank, xi
Kennedy, Jacqueline, 57
Kennedy, John, 47, 56, 61
Kerala, 151–152
Killinger, William, 58
knowledge, xi, 4–5, 16, 20, 24, 30, 34–36,
    38, 49, 52, 57, 64–65, 67–70, 77–78,
    80–81, 102
    intuitive, 4–5, 34–36, 67, 100, 113, 119
Kolman, 90–91, 96, 166
Koriam, 90–91, 93–94
Kulik, James, 57–59, 63, 75–77

Lagawop, 98, 99, 107, 169–170, 176, 211
Larsen, Steen, 56
Lawson, E. Thomas, 32, 120
linguistic, ix, 4–5, 52, 73, 107–109, 214
literacy, 38, 46, 52–56, 75, 85, 91,
    108–109, 141, 150–151, 208, 216
Loma Prieta earthquake, 61–62, 64, 75,
    79, 128

Mali Baining, 84, 88, 89–90, 94–96, 98,
    120, 158–161, 171, 192–193
Maranagi, 94–95, 97–99, 103, 111, 123,
    158, 162, 166–173, 176, 187, 196,
    201, 204, 218–219
Marxism, 8
mass, 10, 203
May Day, 9
Mecca, 9
Melanesia, x, 93, 104, 109, 180–182, 198,
    200–205, 207, 212
meme, 39–41
memory, x, 6–7, 29, 38, 41, 44, 46–50, 52,
    55–57, 59, 61–64, 66, 72–73, 77–78,
    80, 82, 84–87, 93, 100, 105–108, 110,
    112–113, 115, 122–123, 126, 128,
    141–142, 144, 150–151, 153–154,
    157, 164, 189, 191, 214, 216
    accuracy of, 44–45, 50, 55, 75,
        81–82, 84, 87
    autobiographical, 36
    episodic, 76–77, 87, 105, 107, 110,
        211, 216

flashbulb, 56–57, 59–60, 62, 64,
    72–73, 77, 80, 87, 142
long-term, 48–49, 87
semantic, 76–77, 86, 105, 108, 110,
    160, 211, 216
mendas, 96
mental
    imagery, 73
    state, 11
Middle Ages, 201–202, 204
millenarian movement, 196, 206
mind, 1–2, 6, 11, 22, 24, 39, 41, 68–69,
    76–77, 122, 128, 216
    state of, 15, 20, 25, 141, 144, 160
    theory of, 24, 30, 115, 143, 216
mnemonic, 43, 53, 62, 73–81, 84,
    86–87, 93, 100, 104, 112, 126, 128,
    149–150, 153, 179, 187, 190, 214,
    216
    accuracy of, 45, 48, 84, 128
mode of religiosity
    doctrinal, 104, 107–109, 111–112,
        124, 141–142, 151, 184, 202, 219
    imagistic, 104, 106–109, 111–112, 124,
        140–142, 172, 184–185
    mixed-mode phenomena, 109, 140,
        144, 146, 148, 155
    stability of, 109, 124, 139–140
    theory of, 100, 104, 106, 110–111,
        114, 124, 126, 130, 139–145, 150,
        172–173, 179, 184, 192, 202, 219
    uniformity of, 93, 109, 124, 139–140,
        143, 151, 184
monk, 17
motivation, 7, 23, 36, 38, 42, 90, 103,
    112–115, 133, 139–140, 143, 148,
    178–179, 181, 187–191, 193, 199,
    202, 205, 208–209, 211, 217
Mountain Ok, 47, 54, 65, 67, 69–72,
    74, 146, 215
Mt. Marwah, 150
Mt. Safā, 150
Muhammad, 86
Muslim, 3, 32, 141, 144, 150, See also
    Islam
myth, 67, 82, 85

Nambudiri, 151–154
narrative, 47, 58–59, 61, 63–64, 81–82,
    215
    consolidation, 47, 59, 63–64, 72, 81
    structure, 47, 58
natural selection, 39, 41
Neisser, Ulric, 56, 58–64, 81, 214–215
New Britain Island, 84, 88–89, 198

New Guinea, Papua New Guinea, 47, 54,
    64–65, 74, 89, 109
Nixon, Richard, 214
non-linguistic, 38, 46, 66–67, 73, 214
non-literate cultures, 6, 38, 46–48, 52–54,
    56, 65, 84–85, 91, 109, 150–151, 153,
    214
North America, xi, 208, 210, 213
North Carolina, 53, 102
Now Print Mechanism, 57, 62, 76, 113.
    See also: hypothesis, Now Print.
Nuer, 32

orators, 92–97, 99, 163
Oswald, Lee Harvey, 57

Paliau Movement, 106, 198, 200–201,
    205, 219
Palme, Olof, 58–59
patient, 13, 16–17, 24, 131, 189, 213
Pearl Harbor, 56, 59
Period of Companies, 90–91, 95, 97–98,
    163, 166, 168, 170, 194, 196, 212
Period of Government, 91
pilgrimage, 9, 13, 150–151
    hajj, 150–152, 155
    Kumbha Mela, 150–152, 155
Pomio Kivung, Kivung, 88, 91–102, 106,
    109–111, 120, 125, 136, 146–147,
    149, 151, 158–164, 168, 172–173,
    175–181, 183–184, 187, 192–193,
    196–198, 200–202, 205, 218–219
pope, 1, 4, 23, 102, 145
possession, 94, 96, 98–99, 107, 169–170,
    176, 190
pray, prayer, 13, 15–16
prayer beads, 3
predict, predictive, prediction, xi, 6–7,
    9–10, 12, 29–30, 32–37, 58–60, 81,
    87, 98, 100, 111–112, 118–119,
    124–125, 127–129, 132, 135, 137,
    139, 141, 146–149, 153–155,
    157–158, 161–162, 171–175, 177,
    179, 183–184, 187, 196, 201,
    216–217
priest, 1–3, 10, 13–19, 27–28, 31, 33–34,
    36, 48, 97, 116, 118, 120–121, 129,
    132, 154, 156, 211
Principle of Superhuman Agency (PSA),
    7, 26–30, 33, 100, 116–118
Principle of Superhuman Immediacy
    (PSI), x, 27–29, 33, 100, 116
proselytize, proselytization, 39, 91,
    108–109, 192
prototype, prototypical, 49, 56

psychology, psychological, psychologist,
    6, 11–12, 20–21, 24, 32, 34, 39,
    46–49, 70–73, 87, 111, 113, 122, 133,
    164, 182–183, 185, 188, 190–191,
    193–195, 200
    cognitive, x–xi, 6, 11, 41–43, 48, 107,
    111
    developmental, x–xi, 10, 21, 23–24, 115,
    126
    evolutionary, 38
    experimental, xi, 5, 45, 48, 64, 86, 114
    foundations, 38, 42
    mechanisms, 85
    micro-processes, 8, 40, 43, 70, 180
    processes, 6, 46, 84
    response, 1
    social, x–xi, 21
Puja, 32, 121–122
punctuated equilibrium, 40
Puranas, 150

rabbi, 10, 15–16, 35, 121
Rapture, 206
recall, 41, 47–49, 52–64, 69–70, 76–77,
    80, 85–87, 110, 114, 128, 215
    accuracy of, 47, 59, 61, 83–84
    long-term, 48, 56
    reception events, 56, 58–59, 61–62, 76
recollect, recollection, 35, 40, 47–50, 55,
    57, 59–61, 66, 71–72, 76–80, 83–84,
    86, 93, 95, 107–108, 110, 151, 153,
    155, 210–211
Reformation, 201, 204
religious
    act, 13–15, 163
    activities, xiii, 13–15, 35, 39, 66, 95,
    97–98, 140–141, 144–147, 150, 155,
    160, 196, 201, 215, 218
    behavior, 8
    conceptual scheme, 15, 22, 25, 121, 190
    knowledge, 38, 46, 48, 95, 114, 212,
    217
    transmission of, 38, 48, 217
    practice, ix, 74, 91–93, 95, 101,
    108–109, 111–112, 114, 140–141,
    144–145, 159–160, 163–164, 172–173,
    183–184, 192, 196–197, 201, 204,
    208–209, 211, 217
    breathing exercises, 140–141, 143, 145
    meditation, 140–141, 143–145
    yoga, 15, 140–141, 143–145
religious ritual competence, theory of, ix,
    4–6, 8, 38, 43–44, 100, 113–115, 124,
    126, 136–138, 141–143, 145, 155,
    183, 189, 217

religious ritual system, ix–x, 2, 4–5, 8, 15,
    17, 19, 22, 30, 34–37, 44, 47–49, 51,
    54–55, 72, 75–76, 82–83, 85–86,
    88–89, 93, 99, 102–104, 106, 109,
    111–112, 118, 123
  balanced, 143, 181–182, 201–212
  dynamical profiles, 179–181, 208
  evolution of, 7–8, 75, 82, 85, 109, 112,
    151, 157–158, 179–180, 208–209
  excess conceptual control, 207–208
  fitness of, 8, 182, 210
  motivation to transmit, 44, 54, 103, 113,
    122, 142, 179, 181, 185, 189–190,
    199, 211–212, 217
  participant of, 15, 103, 132, 134, 155,
    181–182, 185, 188, 194, 199,
    201–202, 206, 208, 210–213, 218
  stability of, 8, 109, 139, 181–182,
    185–186, 192–193, 198, 200, 207
  transmission of, 54, 66, 75, 103, 107,
    112
  unbalanced, 181–185, 187, 192,
    198–202, 207–208, 210–211
representation, x, 4, 6, 8, 11–12, 17,
    19–32, 34–35, 39–40, 43–45, 49–53,
    69–70, 85–86, 113, 115–116, 146,
    159, 163, 188–189
  cognitive, 4, 8, 13, 17, 35, 49, 100, 105,
    115, 126
  cultural, 38–42, 44–45, 50–51, 53,
    64, 69–70, 112–113, 158, 179–181,
    190, 193
  mental, 11, 24, 39–42, 44–46, 214
  public, 38–39, 41, 46, 66–67
  religious, 6, 50–51, 103, 126, 185, 187
  ritual, 6, 8, 10–11, 13, 17, 19–20, 23,
    25–30, 35, 103, 113, 115, 126, 143
retention, 52, 55, 82, 85, 88
revelation, 79, 94, 96, 107, 160, 174, 192,
    197–198, 212, 219
revelatory potential, 104–108, 110, 126,
    140–141, 219
Ṛgveda, 154
ritual
  act, 1, 2, 13–14, 16–18, 22, 25–26,
    29–30, 36, 66, 88, 115–117, 121,
    124, 216
  action, 1, 2, 13–14, 16–18, 22, 25–26,
    29–30, 36, 66, 88, 115–117, 121,
    124, 216
  activity, 2, 50, 70, 92, 103, 125, 143,
    146, 152, 186, 197
  agent, x, 12–13, 15, 16–18, 23, 26–34,
    44, 116–118, 120–122, 131, 134,
    143–144, 164, 166, 168, 189, 191

behavior, 5, 8, 145
bringing about of change, 13–14, 33,
    50, 123, 135, 161, 170, 181–182,
    193, 206, 209
change, 2, 7, 42, 44–45, 48, 71,
    82–83, 85–87, 95–6, 101, 111, 141,
    154, 158–160, 162–164, 167, 169,
    172–177, 179–180, 183–184,
    186–187, 189–191, 193–200, 203,
    205–206, 209, 212, 219
  comparative centrality to religious
    system, 33–35
  criterion of relevance, 127–129, 132,
    217
  depth, 25, 28, 33–34, 116–118, 120,
    216
  efficacy, 5, 17–18, 29–30, 32
  eligibility to participate, 10, 15–17,
    19, 29, 121, 133–135, 144, 179, 21
  embedded, 16, 19, 28–29, 134
  enabling, 18–19, 23, 27–28, 116,
    213
  even-numbered, 28, 30–33, 42, 44,
    117–122, 125–126, 132, 135,
    142–144, 146–153, 155, 162,
    164–167, 171–172, 175–178,
    180–181, 216–219
  experts, 70–72
  failure, 17, 29, 84, 97–98, 167,
    169–170, 176, 178, 194–196,
    199–200, 205–207, 209
  form, x, 6, 7–8, 9, 10, 12, 26, 28,
    38, 42, 100, 112, 114, 119–120,
    137–138, 140, 142, 160, 175
    hypothesis: see hypothesis, ritual
      form structural description of,
    12–13, 18–19, 25–29, 32–35,
    115–118, 124, 134, 153, 159–160,
    217
  frequency
    hypothesis: see hypothesis, ritual
      frequency
    of exposure, 107–108
    of reproduction, 106, 110
    of transmission, 104, 106–108, 110,
      141, 219
  hypothetical, 23, 25, 86
  instrument, 12–13, 17–18, 26–27, 29,
    31–33, 117, 120, 122, 131, 213
  justified repetition of, 166–167, 195
  knowledge, 36, 67–69, 74–75, 82–83,
    86, 88, 90, 116, 215
  least direct connections criterion
    (LDC), 134–139, 147, 149–150,
    155–157, 166, 179, 218

ritual (*cont.*)
  motivation to re-perform and/or
    transmit, 122, 187, 189, 191, 205,
    208, 217
  observation of, 3–4, 9, 15, 35, 55,
    65–66, 74–75, 95, 127–128, 156–157,
    188, 194, 217
  odd-numbered, 28, 30, 32–33, 42, 47,
    55, 117–118, 120–121, 123, 125–127,
    129, 133, 135, 138, 142–143,
    146–147, 155, 157, 159–160, 162,
    164, 166, 170–172, 180–181, 216,
    218
  participant of, ix–x, 1–3, 5, 9–10, 12–13,
    16–18, 23, 25–26, 29, 31–32, 34–38,
    42–43, 49–50, 53, 55, 75–6, 83–84,
    85–88, 93, 99, 102–103, 107, 113,
    116, 119–123, 127, 129–130,
    132–135, 138, 141, 143, 147, 149,
    151–153, 157, 163–166, 169, 177,
    181, 185, 187–193, 199–202, 205,
    209–211, 213–215, 217–218
  patient, 12–13, 16–17, 26, 29, 31–33,
    42, 116–118, 120–122, 129–135, 138,
    143, 146–147, 157–158, 162–167,
    187–188, 191, 193, 199, 206, 213
  performance frequency, 2–3, 6–7, 32,
    34, 38, 42–44, 47–50, 55–56, 65, 68,
    70, 73–74, 86–88, 90, 93, 99–100,
    103–105, 107–113, 119–120, 124–132,
    135–138, 140–142, 144, 146–153,
    155–159, 161–163, 167, 171–173,
    176, 184, 186–188, 190, 198, 206,
    210, 214, 217–220
  performance of, 2, 5–6, 15, 18, 31–32,
    38, 46, 48–51, 53, 64–65, 69, 71,
    82–83, 86, 88, 93, 97, 100, 125–129,
    132–136, 140, 142, 147–159,
    161–179, 181–184, 186–187, 190,
    194–197, 199, 202–203, 205, 209,
    211–212, 214–215, 218–219
  rate, 126, 136, 152, 168, 173–176
  raw count, 135–136, 168, 173–175
  permanent/super-permanent effects or
    changes, 14, 31–33, 120, 122–123,
    133, 155, 187, 191, 194
  practice, x, 1, 8, 14, 23, 35–37, 74–75,
    83, 99, 109, 125, 150, 161, 163, 173,
    200
  practitioner, 18, 48, 53, 86, 116, 121,
    127, 129, 132–133, 154, 167, 188,
    190
  profile, 26, 28, 30, 42, 116–117, 119,
    121, 170, 177, 188, 191–192, 196,
    217

  relevant performance of, 127, 129,
    133–136, 157
  repeatability of, 27, 30–32, 42–43,
    47–49, 55–56, 65, 68–69, 74, 109,
    120–122, 129, 132–135, 138, 147,
    149–150, 152, 155–156, 159–160,
    162–163, 165–167, 171–172, 177,
    187–188, 193, 195–196, 197, 205,
    207–208, 211, 214–215, 217–218
  repetition of, 2, 30, 50, 88, 93, 101,
    107–108, 110, 138, 158, 163,
    166–167, 176, 193, 196, 198–199,
    206, 209
  reversibility of consequences, 3, 27,
    31, 132–134, 150, 152, 157, 218
  role, 8, 10, 12–13, 17, 21, 23–24, 26,
    28–29, 31–33, 42, 61, 63–64, 72,
    74, 86, 114, 116–117, 121,
    129–132, 134, 139, 146, 189, 213,
    218
  sense of continuity, 74, 83, 85, 142,
    215
  special agent, 26–33, 42, 44, 47, 55–56,
    68, 74, 116–118, 120–123, 125–127,
    129–130, 132–135, 137–138, 142–144,
    147–148, 150, 155–164, 166–178,
    180–184, 187–202, 205–212,
    216–220
    conceptual control of, 181–182, 200,
      202, 205–207, 209–210, 212
  special instrument, 26–28, 30–32, 42,
    44, 68, 116–120, 122, 125–127, 132,
    135, 137, 142–143, 146–151, 153,
    180–183, 188, 200, 202, 206–207,
    210, 211–213, 218, 220
  special patient, 24, 26, 30–33, 42, 44,
    116–120, 122, 125–127, 132, 135,
    137–138, 142–143, 146, 148–150,
    152–153, 159, 162, 165–166, 175,
    179–183, 187–188, 190–193, 198,
    200, 202, 206, 210–212, 218, 220
  substitution of elements, 3, 27, 30–33,
    213
  temporary effects, 14, 31–32, 120
  transmission of, 38, 42–43, 46–47,
    54–56, 64–65, 72–73, 81, 85, 87–88,
    108, 151, 153, 189, 211, 216
  type
    Agnicayana, 151–155
    Agnyadhana, 35
    baptism, 18, 27–28, 33–34, 116,
      121–122, 128–129, 147, 156,
      191–192, 196
    bar mitzvah, 16, 35, 121, 127, 132,
      147

berit milas, 127
blessing, 1, 3, 18, 25–26, 116, 120–121, 147, 150
Cemetery Temple, 92, 94–95, 136, 158–161, 163, 168, 171, 178, 184, 192–194, 219
circumcision, 10, 15, 17, 26, 136, 144
communion, Holy Communion, 15, 18, 26, 31, 33–34, 74, 122, 133
confession, 97, 165, 198
confirmation, 27, 129
consecration, 17–18, 25, 28, 134, 157–161, 168, 171, 178, 193–194
coronation, 2
dedication, 95–6, 159, 193
divination, 3, 26
earpiercing, *qhumbaza*, 19, 146
enthronement, 1
Eucharist, 118, 132, 147
excommunication, 3, 31, 133
exorcism, 98, 169
Family Temple, 93
feast, 95, 97–99, 101–102, 130, 158–159, 162, 168–169, 188, 193–194, 212, 219
funeral, 26, 89, 121
garden, 176, 184, 192
grouping-up, 19
Gryha, 152
inauguration, 1, 90, 97, 122, 166, 177, 187, 198, 206
initiation, 13, 18–19, 30–31, 47, 55, 64–76, 79–82, 86–88, 90, 96, 101–102, 107, 116, 120–122, 128–132, 143–144, 148, 152–153, 158–161, 164, 166, 168, 179, 188, 192–194, 214–215, 218
investiture, 102, 116
marriage, 1–2, 19, 26, 29, 31, 33, 36, 40, 98, 102, 116, 118, 121, 128–130, 132–134, 147–148, 157–158, 160–162, 169, 178, 194, 209, 214, 217
    mass, 98, 148, 158, 160–162, 169, 178, 194
    multiple, 209
mass murder, 204
mass suicide, 204–205
membership, 98, 158, 160–161, 167, 169, 178, 194
naming, 19
Oban dance for the dead, 121
offering, 13, 30–31, 91–92, 94, 97, 120, 136, 147, 150, 152, 160, 164–166, 175–177, 192

ordination, 3, 17, 19, 36, 116, 121, 147
penance, 26
preparation, 98, 158, 194
puberty, *thomba*, 19, 146
Puja, 86
purification, 3, 91, 95, 101
ring ceremony, 97–98, 111, 158, 160, 162–178, 187, 194, 198, 218–219
    vigil complex, 168–170, 174–177
rites of passage, 3, 19, 55
sacred thread, 15–16, 135, 144
sacrifice, 3, 9, 13, 25–26, 30, 32, 51, 74, 116, 120–121, 147, 150, 152, 188, 190
scarification, 133
transfiguration of Christ, 86
upanayana, 133
vigil, 94, 98–99, 101–102, 158, 162, 167, 169–170, 174, 176, 180, 194, 196–197, 219
washing, 32
well-formedness, 29–30
roundhouse, 98–99, 101, 111, 158, 160–161, 167–171, 178, 194
Rubin, David, 52–54, 59, 80, 214–215
Rundus, Dewey, 49

St. Michael's church, Cambridge, 133, 157
St. Peter, 23, 216
Satan, 98–99, 169–170, 176–178, 187
Scandinavia, 119
schema theory, 76–77, 108
science, ix, xi, 5, 9, 48, 91, 133, 179, 196, 208, 213–214
script, 49, 55
sensory overload ceiling, 199–200
sensory pageantry, 1–2, 6–7, 38, 43, 47, 55, 73, 79, 98, 101–104, 107, 110–115, 118–119, 122–123, 125, 128–131, 134–135, 138–141, 144, 147–151, 153–155, 157, 159–165, 167, 169–190, 193–199, 202, 205–210, 212–213, 216–219
sensory stimulation, 2, 6, 36, 42, 44, 80, 101–102, 106–107, 113, 119, 130–131, 144, 152, 172, 175, 178, 180–181, 183, 186, 190, 197
sermon, 92, 160
Shaka, 136
Shembe, Isaiah, 110
Shintoism, 127
shrine, 3, 13

social, 20–23, 31, 34, 45, 48, 50, 54, 56,
61, 64, 70–73, 75–76, 84, 100,
104–105, 107–108, 114–115, 119,
131, 133, 143, 200, 212–213, 216
sciences, 8, 22
sociobiology, 38–39
Soma, 152
sorcery, 65, 81
Sperber, Dan, 39–42, 44–45, 50, 53,
69–70, 72, 163, 185, 213–214,
216
spirit, 12, 90–91, 95, 215
splinter groups, 180–182, 184–185,
187–188, 191, 194, 200–207,
209–210, 220
crash of, 181, 194, 196–198, 200–201,
204–206
Dadul-Maranagi, 94–5, 97–103, 106,
110–112, 125, 146, 148, 157–159,
161–188, 191, 194–198, 200–207,
218–219
Dissenters, 191
Ghost, 106, 198, 204–206
Noise, 106, 219
Śrauta Sūtras, 152–153
Staal, Fritz, 151, 216
state of mind
ecstatic, 40, 188
mystical, 109, 140
Sunam, 90, 97, 196
symbol, 2, 5, 54, 66–69, 71, 73, 85, 97,
212, 215
symbolic cultural systems, 4–5, 37, 54

Tanotka, 94–99, 111, 158–160, 163–164,
166, 169, 175, 183, 187, 193–194,
218–219
Taosim, 109, 140
tedium, 50, 179–180, 184–188, 190, 193,
196, 198–200, 202, 204, 206–208,
210–211, 220
temple, 17, 68, 81, 89, 92, 94–96, 98, 102,
120, 147, 159, 161
Ten Laws, 90–92, 95
test, 6, 12, 32, 34–35, 37, 46, 54, 56,
59–61, 65, 155, 178
empirical, 12, 178
theology, 8, 22, 36, 120, 141, 151, 190,
207–208, 210, 212
theory, ix–xi, 4–9, 12–13, 15–16, 20–21,
23–26, 29, 31–35, 37–38, 40–42, 44,
46, 56, 64, 84, 87–89, 95, 98, 102,

104–105, 108, 110, 112, 115, 119,
124, 126, 131, 140, 142–146, 148,
154, 165, 173, 178–179, 181–184,
195–196, 202, 213, 216, 219
cognitive, ix, 88, 108
testing of, ix–xi, 5, 16, 37, 46
Tolai, 89–90
Tovalele, P., 198
transubstantiation, 33
Tulving, Endel, 49, 77, 105

umuzi, 15
United Kingdom, x, 2

Van Gennep, A., 3
variable, x, 7, 21, 26, 34, 41, 47–48, 56,
58, 60, 63–64, 69, 71–75, 82, 85–87,
93, 100, 104–105, 108–110, 112–113,
119, 124–126, 137, 140–141, 148,
180, 196, 202, 205, 208, 216,
218–219
cognitive, 6–7, 100, 124, 142, 179, 184,
218
cultural, 105
independent, 113, 124, 126, 137, 139,
145, 148
psychological, 46–72, 179, 199
social, 105, 196
Vatican, 4
Veda, 152–154
Vedic, x, 151–154
Village Government, 90, 94–95, 97

Weber, Max, 104, 180
Whitehouse, Harvey, x–xi, 7, 50, 52, 73,
76, 83–84, 87, 89–90, 92–94, 96–97,
99–111, 114, 123–126, 128, 130,
139–144, 146–147, 149–151, 159,
163–168, 170, 172, 174–176,
178–185, 192–198, 201–202, 205,
211–212, 215–219
Winograd, Eugene, 58
witch, 12, 116
witness, 92, 94–96, 159–160, 163, 168
worship, 1, 20
Wright, D., 76–77
Wutka, 94–96

yajamāna, 152
Yoruba, 3, 147

Zulu, 92, 94–96, 159–160, 163, 168